Postslavery Literatures in the Americas

Postslavery Literatures in the Americas

FAMILY PORTRAITS IN
BLACK AND WHITE

George B. Handley

New World Studies

A. James Arnold, Editor

University Press of Virginia

Charlottesville & London

The University Press of Virginia
© 2000 by the Rector and Visitors of the University of Virginia
All rights reserved
Printed in the United States of America

First published in 2000

∞ The paper used in this publication meets the minimum requirements of the American
National Standard for Information Sciences—Permanence of Paper for Printed Library
Materials, ANSI Z39.48-1984.

Library of Congress Cataloging-in-Publication Data
Handley, George B., 1964–
    Postslavery literatures in the Americas : family portraits in black and white / George B. Handley.
        p. cm. — (New World studies)
    Includes bibliographical references (p.) and index.
    ISBN 0-8139-1976-2 (alk. paper) — ISBN 0-8139-1977-0 (pbk. : alk. paper)
    1. Domestic fiction, American—History and criticism. 2. Slavery in literature. 3.
Literature, Comparative—American and Caribbean (Spanish) 4. Literature,
Comparative—Caribbean (Spanish) and American. 5. Caribbean fiction
(Spanish)—History and criticism. 6. Afro-American families in literature. 7. Plantation
life in literature. 8. Cuba—In literature. 9. Blacks in literature. 10. Whites in literature.
11. Race in literature. I. Title. II. Series.

PS374.S58 H36 2000
813.009'358—dc21   00-031921

For all of my family, of course

Contents

Acknowledgments

I AM INDEBTED to several individuals and institutions who have shaped this project, supported my research, and offered their critical skills at various stages. In my initial research at the University of California at Berkeley, I was aided by Mellon dissertation funding, the Chancellor's Dissertation Fellowship, and the Provost Research Fund (which funded trips to Puerto Rico and Cuba). In Puerto Rico, Juan Gelpí gave important guidance through the resources at the University of Puerto Rico at Río Piedras. Rosario Ferré was kind enough to allow me to interview her. In La Habana, Cuba, I benefited from the expertise of Ana Cairo, Luisa Campuzano, and the staff at the Sala Cubana in the Biblioteca Nacional "José Martí." Interlibrary Loan services at UC Berkeley, Northern Arizona University, and Brigham Young University have been consistent and reliable. Without the generous research funding I received for two summers at Northern Arizona University, with the help of Suzanne Shipley, Henry Hooper, Tom Cleman, Karl Webb, and Sandra Lubarsky, I would not have been able to complete this book when I did. My thanks go also to Van Gessel and George Tate, who arranged for release time and research assistance upon my arrival at Brigham Young University. My research assistant, Heather Helton, has been a lifesaver.

I can hardly measure adequately the impact of the teaching of Julio Ramos, Francine Masiello, Anthony Cascardi, Josefina Ludmer (who, despite my initial reluctance, taught me structuralism at its best), and VèVè Clark, all of whom inspired the ideas and framework for this comparative study. I was fortunate to have the invaluable and careful guidance of Francine and Julio in getting this project off the ground. I pay tribute to Jenny Franchot, whose exceptional intellectual talents will be sorely missed. The following individuals were kind enough to read portions of the project at different stages and have provided invaluable encouragement: Lois Parkinson Zamora, Lillian Guerra, Elizabeth Matthews, Marvin Lewis, Nancy Ruttenburg, Allison Brown, Deborah Cohn, Nara Araujo, Silvia Spitta, Walter Mignolo, Donald Pease, Reynolds Smith, Don Norton, and the anonymous readers at University Press of Virginia. I am also indebted to James Arnold, Cathie Brettschneider, and Hannah Borgeson for their editorial expertise. I express my appreciation to Marvin Lewis at *Publication of the Afro-Latin/ American Research Association,* who granted permission to reprint portions of my article "Rereading the Nation as Family: Corrective Revisions of Racial Discourse in Martín Morúa Delgado and Charles W. Chesnutt," *PALARA* 1 (fall 1997): 66–79. Portions of the introduction and of chapter 5 first appeared in the chapter "'It's an unbelievable story': Testimony and Truth in the Work of Rosario Ferré and Rigoberta Menchú," published in the collection *Violence, Silence and Anger: Women's Writing as Transgression* (ed. Deirdre Lashgari; Charlottesville: University Press of Virginia, 1995). Thanks to Deirdre Lashgari for aiding me so carefully in the early drafts of that essay at a crucial stage in my thinking about this book.

John Torres listened for hours on end—over lunch and in the great Utah outdoors—to my ideas, frustrations, and aspirations, and as a true friend he still had the courage to believe in me. My study of genealogy inevitably has brought me to appreciate my own legacies of kinship. I am, as always, indebted to my brother, Bill Handley, who read and critiqued various versions of this study and whose intellectual companionship, profound love, and unwavering support of my goals have inspired every aspect of my life. My parents, Ken and Kate Handley, are my models of optimism, trust, love, and intellectual curiosity. And finally, my gratitude is for Amy, to borrow from the words of the Poet,

> in whom our children
> . . . settle
> simply, like rhymes,
> in whose side, in the grim times
> when I cannot see light for the deep leaves,
> sharing her depth, the whole lee ocean grieves.

I have consulted available English translations of several of the texts used in this study, but for the most part I used my own translations of the original Spanish. Therefore, unless otherwise noted, all translations from the Spanish are mine.

Postslavery Literatures in the Americas

Introduction

THIS BOOK is a response to a series of intellectual impasses I experienced starting when I first sat down with the two advisers of my undergraduate honors thesis. I was intent on comparing the journals of Christopher Columbus and the magical hold of books on his imagination with Shakespeare's Prospero and his similarly maniacal reliance on the written word. It was my first in-depth introduction to the problems of colonialism and the challenges of those who emerge in the wake of such magic and attempt to create and name their own worlds. It was also my first introduction to what would become all too familiar as a comparatist: the challenges of comparative dialogue. As I watched my advisers—one a Shakespearean scholar, the other a Latin American and Chicano literary critic—struggle to understand each other's idioms (since they recognized that I needed a comparative model that singly they could not provide), and as I struggled to make sense of what confusion this juxtaposition had caused, I was moved by their determination to establish dialogue for my sake. I was struck by the power of comparative work, despite my rather rudimentary understanding of its potential, to forge new and rare partnerships and to create discomforting yet necessary conversations.

My graduate training in comparative literature led me to similar impasses. Though I had the advantage of most comparative literature programs in being given the freedom and, indeed, the official sanction to take courses in different departments, no one course or professor could provide the needed comparative models. Although we students were no longer held to the Eurocentric integrative standard of what comparative literature should be, the different language departments remained relatively loyal to rather territorial conceptions of their fields. So in a sense, we were free to do comparative literature beyond the bounds of European cultures, and yet the discipline of literary criticism—manifested in the organization and rationale of different language and literature departments—still reflected the impulses of colonialism on a singular, national scale. Like the majority of my graduate colleagues in comparative literature, then, I felt torn by the push of yet-to-be-delineated configurations for postnational comparative study and the pull of a still-kicking nostalgia for nationalistic and European models. It wasn't until the fall of 1992, when I began reading novels about slavery simultaneously in classes on the U.S. Civil War (through the English department), on Caribbean women writers (through African American studies), and on Cuban literature (through the Spanish department), that I began to see a profound coincidence of postslavery, postcolonial anxieties among various writers; even more striking was the writers' keen awareness that they were participating in a discussion that implicated various nations and histories in the Americas. The diasporic approach of African American studies, in particular, helped my various sallies into different departments to gain coherence.

Though the structures of the academy have not always proved adequate to the challenge of postnational readings—a challenge posed by many writers in the Americas—we can fortunately benefit from groundbreaking scholars who in different ways have pointed to various models for understanding literatures of the Americas. In my case, those critics have included Eric Sundquist, Vera Kutzinski, Lois Parkinson Zamora, Doris Sommer, Werner Sollors, José David Saldívar, Edouard Glissant, and Antonio Benítez-Rojo. Each has moved beyond simply theorizing about the Americas or about a criticism of postnationality and has engaged in comparative work in the Americas and provided the needed historical justifications for it. Even more important, I am indebted to novelists for the way their fictional and historical imaginations have carved out a new hemispheric geography of postslavery America.

Because slavery was abolished at different times in different places, the term *postslavery,* like many *post*s, inevitably runs the risk of awkward, anachronistic applications. Throughout the Americas, slavery was typically abolished in stages, beginning with the trade itself and then moving toward varying methods of enacting full emancipation. Legal slavery ended as early as 1794 in Haiti (1848 in other French territories), 1834 in the English territories, and 1865 in the United States, and as late as 1873 in Puerto Rico, 1886 in Cuba, and 1888 in Brazil. In most cases, though, the slave system persisted in different forms after formal abolition. Thus, the question of exactly when a nation obtains postslavery status, if ever, is deeply complicated.

In my use of the term *postslavery*, I primarily want to emphasize the ideological thrust of those works of literature that, although written after the demise of slavery, return to slavery's past in a genealogical exploration of its deep, historical roots in order to understand its relationship to the present. Postslavery literature moves us away from a fixation on the more formal manifestations of slavery and into the more complex social relations before and after its legal abolition. Antislavery literature was primarily aimed at moralizing, with the use of black speech, about the humanity of the slave and the inhumanity of slavery, and it pointed primarily to a future where such speech would find legitimacy and where the black subject could reconstruct a family community (Schulman; Davis and Gates; Fleischner). In the case of Cuban antislavery literature, such moralizing was also wedded to a critique of Spanish colonialism. Postslavery literature, on the other hand, makes a more careful distinction between colonialism and slavery in its investigation of the past, and it represents the dynamics of black speech within the larger interfamilial and sociological context of the plantation system. In other words, although postslavery literature borrows from the traditions of the slave narrative and antislavery novels in its exploration of black speech and the reconstitution of family in slavery's wake, it more self-consciously argues that the amnesia caused by slavery has yet to be answered by authors' respective national cultures and even by their own attempts to resurrect slavery's enigmatic past. These texts are haunted by their own shortcomings in attempting recovery of repressed histories and in finding meaning in such failures.

To this end, family history is the thematic and structural sine qua non of postslavery narrative. Writing about family history allows the authors to revise the metaphorical meanings of genealogy that have been assumed by the plantocracy and by emergent nationalists and that have contributed to a consolidation of their landowning social power. That is, by following biological links across races, sexes, and generations, family history exposes the genealogical ideologies that have concealed evidence of sexual contact across racial and class lines in order to protect a white elite patrimony and to evade the widely syncretic and contestatory nature of plantation cultures. Genealogy also enables the reconstruction of family ties (the very antithesis of slavery, according to Orlando Patterson) that were ravaged by the whims of slave owners.

In my thinking and writing I certainly exclude such "postslavery" works as the white supremacist plantation novels written after the U.S. Civil War because of their explicit defense of slavery, but I do not contend that postslavery novels are immune to degrees of nostalgia, if not for slavery, at least for origins. This is because genealogy, as an intergenerational and frequently oedipal drama, functions as a way of working through the complex struggle with origins and with historical process. But to the extent that the oedipal drama represents an overdetermined relationship to the past, in many cases it tells the story of failure in finding freedom from slavery's legacies. The postslavery writer must respond to a past of tremendous rupture, trauma, and amnesia without falling into Hegelian notions of historical process that have contributed to and justified those losses in the first place. In postslavery writing, these challenges of slavery's history frequently become the writer's greatest opportunities precisely because the imagination is no longer bound by a fixed and singular origin. It is for this reason that we sometimes see that genealogy escapes its own oedipal entrapment by organizing, even founding, a new collective identity within the particular range of contradictions and tensions exposed. Genealogy involves, then, a measure of ambivalence about identifying the moment when we have broken free or when we will finally break free from slavery's past.

The best postslavery writing—of which I believe the novels examined here are a sampling—wrestles with the contradictions of depending on a reprehensible history for establishing new postslavery life and identity and warns against any simple or hasty solutions, for men and women, blacks and whites, and people from different nations, to the persistence of slavery's legacies. This literature by implication teaches that because of the persistence of slavery's legacies in our economies, our modes of thinking about race, and our discourses of nationalism, we need to be reminded of the importance of identifying and weeding out, with determination, those legacies wherever we may find them. For this reason, to put slavery behind us, we must not make simplistic assumptions about the inviolability of literature or of certain social and racial positions, because, as Toni Morrison has put it, "the master narrative could make any number of adjustments to keep itself intact" (*Playing* 51).

Although most of the novels examined in this book deal directly with the history of slavery, not all of them are obvious choices to represent a postslavery corpus. William Faulkner's *Absalom, Absalom!*, George Washington Cable's *The Grandissimes*, Frances Harper's *Iola Leroy*, Martín Morúa Delgado's *La familia Unzúazu* and *Sofía*, and Alejo Carpentier's *Explosion in a Cathedral* (trans. of *El siglo de las luces*) all clearly reach back from a postslavery vantage point to a previous era under slavery, and through their representations of family history the authors are able to expose the historical roots of social contradictions that have yet to be transcended. But what of Cirilo Villaverde's *Cecilia Valdés,* a novel begun in 1839 at the inception of Cuba's antislavery movement but not published in its final form until 1882, still four years prior to full emancipation in Cuba? What distinguishes it from Villaverde's earlier writings and from other Cuban antislavery literature is its rich historical and genealogical density (its plot extends back to the early decades of the nineteenth century), qualities it shares with other novels published after abolition. Because it is a novel that appeared in two forms more than forty years apart, years that saw the demise of slavery in all of the Americas with the exception of Cuba and Brazil, its final form provides us with a chance to see the impact of the end of slavery on literary and national imagination. It is exemplary, then, of the continuity of antislavery traditions in the founding of a national identity, and it demonstrates, along with such postslavery novels as *Wide Sargasso Sea, Sweet Diamond Dust,* and others examined here, the complicated crossovers among cultures produced by various forms of New World colonialisms and by slavery. The fact that novels written about nations under direct colonial rule (all of which were also written by authors in exile) share so many parallels with other postslavery literatures of independent nations is particularly helpful in rethinking the national departmentalization of New World literatures.

Finally, although Charles Chesnutt's *The Marrow of Tradition,* Toni Morrison's *Song of Solomon,* Rosario Ferré's *Sweet Diamond Dust,* and Jean Rhys's *Wide Sargasso Sea* do not directly represent the era of slavery, they clearly engage in an important and broad genealogical investigation into how slavery's legacies have been refashioned and given new life since abolition. In form and content, they argue that slavery's persistent legacies are as much a result of how we choose to remember historical events as are the events themselves.

These novels, which I discuss two or three at a time in the chapters that follow, gravitate toward one another, begging for comparison, because of what I consider to be their uncannily similar postslavery cultural quandaries. That is, they reveal parallel narrative anxieties about genealogy, narrative authority, and racial difference. Plantation discourse, always dependent on structures of colonialism, wedded itself to the growth of U.S. imperialism after emancipation, and therefore the stark distinctions between Caribbean and U.S. cultures that emerged in the twentieth century are, in fact, alienated cousins, as it were, of the same plantation family. U.S. culture tried to shed its own miscegenated, Caribbean image of itself during its period of greatest expansion into the Caribbean, and this allowed the United States to pretend to its own whiteness and civilization against the background of a new, extranational "barbaric" miscegenation. At the same time, in response to the encroachment of the United States, different Caribbean islands invoked divergent discourses on race, miscegenation, and the legacies of slavery to imagine their own national autonomy. My study, then, responds to the call of Sundquist, Morrison, and others to examine the interdependency of black and white in the constructions of U.S. national identity, but it goes further, to demonstrate the interdependency of plantation cultures in the Americas in the construction of divergent national identities.

Organizing our knowledge of literature according to such new trans- and postnational paradigms provides us with numerous advantages that are also our greatest challenges. Postslavery literary criticism, for example, does not allow for an easy separation of disciplinary or theoretical tools, an indication of our current academic microscopy. Because slavery's history implicates the full range of the Americas' constituents, postslavery criticism encourages the juxtaposition of authors of different languages, political status, race, and sex, and while insisting on the difference such identities can make, it also problematizes our assumptions about those differences. We come to see an interdependence of the distinctions commonly made between black and white, male and female, United States and Caribbean. The cross-fertilization of theories of diaspora, race, gender, and postcoloniality no doubt comes with inherent risks of oversimplification and anachronistic misapplication, and I do not pretend to be invulnerable to such problems. To the extent that I err, I hope that future studies might correct the course.

I also do not intend to provide a paradigmatic frame, but rather a provisional one, for comparisons of postslavery literatures. I certainly do not exhaust the possibilities of linguistic comparisons (my study neglects Portuguese, French, and Creole languages and is limited by the absence of analysis of orality, music, visual art, poetry, and dance—all vital forms of expression that could establish other comparative understandings of slavery). Nor do I argue that whatever parallels I discover will be consistently found in all literatures of former slave societies. Nevertheless, I suspect that the specific comparisons I make will find applications in other contexts.

The first three chapters focus exclusively on Cuban and U.S. literature from 1880 to 1962. The U.S.-Cuba relationship is a key example of how slavery diverged into distinct national cultures north and south. As far back as the early 1800s, Cuba was of particular political interest to the United States because of its location—close to the United States and at the gateway to the Caribbean and to Central and South America (Pérez xiii). Beginning when discussions of abolition first surfaced in the region, Cuba and the United States engaged in a kind of rhythmic dance of mutual attraction and fear. Consequently, as my comparisons show, their national identities in the wake of slavery have been codependently forged. The comparisons are particularly helpful precisely because of the countries' differences in language, racial makeup, and religious sensibility; they provide insights into the larger distinctions among the various American nations affected by similar histories of enslavement and violent transplantation. Moreover, Cuba's relationship to the United States from the late nineteenth century to the present has many features that exemplify the dynamics of the region. For one, Cuba was, like many islands of the Caribbean, a site of U.S. hegemonic control, if not the most heightened case of annexionist desire. U.S. imperialism, when read in the context of the extended Caribbean, reveals itself as a result of the United States' own failed struggle to heal slavery's wounds. Consequently, even before the Revolution of 1959, Cuba exhibited a persistent caution concerning the encroachment of its northern neighbor and therefore provides a helpful point of reference for other forms of anti-imperialist resistance in the Caribbean and its influence on Caribbean nationalisms.

Such comparisons also bear the weight of their own potentially overdetermining paradigms, however. I do not intend to ignore J. Michael Dash's warning that the complexity of the Americas cannot be reduced to Cuba as a metaphor for "the quintessential American crossroads—the ultimate New World paradigm" (*Other America* 5). Cuba's experience with slavery, U.S. imperialism, racial difference, syncretism, and miscegenation is distinct to that of the other islands, even other former Spanish colonies. Cuba does not share the intensity of the Dominican Republic's conflicted struggle with its own racial identity, which has been exacerbated by its proximity to Haiti, or Puerto Rico's marked ambivalence regarding its continued colonial status under the United States. Nor can the Cuban experience adequately substitute for Francophone or Anglophone Caribbean experiences, which are marked by their own religious and political distinctions and unique plantation and slave economies. Not only is there much more work to be done in comparative postslavery Caribbean literatures, but the connections between the Caribbean and other former slave societies in Central and South America (which, in addition to Brazil, would involve the Guianas, Surinam, Venezuela, Colombia, Peru, Ecuador, and other areas) have largely remained unexamined, except among small academic circles where truly hemispheric work in the African Diaspora is undertaken. And yet work that limits itself to a particular racial lens does not provide us with the broadest picture of the impact of slavery on New World societies. My work is an attempt to begin the comparative discussions of postslavery literatures, which when undertaken aggressively throughout the Americas will undoubtedly yield new and illuminating theses. I include in my final chapter a discussion of novels from other areas of the Caribbean in order to test the strength of some of my conclusions based on U.S. and Cuban comparisons and to highlight possible directions for further study. My conclusion explores some of the ramifications of this study in terms of contemporary cultural politics in the region.

The introductory chapter, "Narrative and Genealogy: Toward a Postnational Study of Postslavery Literatures," explores the historical and theoretical bases for such an enterprise. I begin with an examination of the uses and abuses of genealogy in plantation cultures in order to establish an understanding of why genealogy figures so prominently in postslavery writing and how we might read the ideological underpinnings of representations of family history. Important to this understanding are various theoretical analyses of the plantation system that I review in order to elucidate how genealogy in the hands of the plantocracy inadvertently contributed to greater genealogical confusion and cultural diversification than plantocratic ideology intended. What the plantation has left in its wake is a series of mutually concealed parallels of experience and of history throughout Plantation America. Consequently, the task of the comparative critic, which I argue is also that of the postslavery writer, is to unveil those parallels across the geographical and political landscape of slavery. Thus, while genealogy moves us back through time diachronically, the juxtaposition of texts from distinct languages and nations helps to bring to the fore synchronic parallels.

The cross of diachronic and synchronic is familiar to traditional models of comparative literature that assume the independent existence of given national entities; once delineated diachronically, they are then compared synchronically. However, I am urging for a postnational comparatism that breaks down the more facile pairing of synchronic with international and diachronic with intranational contexts. In so doing, I take to task in chapter 1 recent developments in American studies that, in my view, have dangerously replicated the imperialist extension of the United States into Latin American territories. As an attempt at a kind of exemplary criticism that searches for theoretical consensus in the extended Caribbean, I engage Americanists, Latin Americanists, and Caribbeanists in a rare but necessary dialogue.

Finally, the last section of chapter 1 explores common narrative strategies employed by the novelists in this study. Because narrative structure is crucial to the construction of race and to communicating to the reader genealogical ties, it is also the most advantageous framework to expose the ideological dimensions of the fictional worlds created by these writers. Deconstructing narrative voice in these novels enables us to see the dual tension between greater openness toward racial difference and further enclosures that simultaneously exclude new categories of difference.

Chapter 2, "Reading in the Dark: Cirilo Villaverde and George Washington Cable," begins in the 1880s, a crucial period of national consolidation for both the United States and Cuba. The latter was reeling from its failed attempt to establish independence from Spain in the Ten Years' War of 1868-1878 and was looking to completing the final stages of full emancipation of the slaves. During the same period, the United States was initiating a more earnest discussion of annexing Cuba while also confronting the failures of Reconstruction. For both nations, it was essentially a period of anxiety concerning the possibility that slavery's legacies would persist after formal emancipation. In response, both Cable's *The Grandissimes* and Villaverde's *Cecilia Valdés* offer a call to greater national consolidation that unfortunately enacts forms of exclusion that contradict their pointed criticisms of slavery. The authors' narrators decipher the new categories of racial difference created by the legacies of slavery and colonialism in order to ensure that the new nations they project as possibilities in their fiction will not become infected by an undesired racial presence. Each resolves this crisis with a similar narrative strategy aimed at "training" the reader's gaze. This enables each author to celebrate "local color" while also containing it, a characteristic strategy of the New World Creole.

Chapter 3, "Reading behind the Face: Martín Morúa Delgado, Charles W. Chesnutt, and Frances E. W. Harper," which examines Morúa's *La familia Unzúazu* and *Sofía,* Chesnutt's *The Marrow of Tradition,* and Harper's *Iola Leroy,* is a study of the narrative strategies of three mulatto writers who in the years following the Spanish-American

War attempt to loosen white culture's grip over the categories of racial difference. These novels' explicit responses to the narrative dilemmas of Cable and Villaverde help to establish an intertextual postslavery corpus. They also offer intriguing comparative insights precisely because they exhibit uncanny parallels and therefore speak more powerfully of the deep and hidden forces across postslavery American nations, even though they ignore the more hemispheric interests in the African Diaspora we find in, for example, Martin Delaney's *Blake*. All three attempt, with varying success, to expose the political and racial personality of the seeing eye of regionalist fiction, such as that employed by Villaverde and Cable, in order to criticize the genealogical claims of the white family on the national patrimony. I argue that in their revisions of the terms that identify racial and moral difference, these authors open a greater space in the nation for the black family. I also point out some of the enclosures that result from their narrative strategies, which are indicative, particularly in the cases of Morúa Delgado and Chesnutt, of their profound ambivalence toward the more "Africanized" sectors of their societies.

Chapter 4, "Between the Insular Self and the Exotic Other: Alejo Carpentier and William Faulkner," is a study of *Explosion in a Cathedral* and *Absalom, Absalom!,* both of which add to the postslavery discussion. Faulkner and Carpentier stand as two of the most significant literary figures of this century in the Americas because of the depth and breadth of the transnational postslavery dialogue implicit in their novels. I explore various narrative strategies that these writers use to explain their cultures' insularity, a characteristic that represents the continuing legacy of a history that has scattered identities in the Americas and left us largely ignorant of our parallel experiences. Each author utilizes the history of the plantation in his respective nation in an attempt to criticize the growing U.S. presence in the Caribbean in the twentieth century and to outline those sites most threatened by a menacing imperialism. Their struggle is to delineate them without arguing for a postcolonial cultural identity founded on impermeable boundaries, doomed to the very insularity imperialism has exacerbated. My readings expose the contradictions of such an enterprise as well as explore the larger, hemispheric context implied in the authors' readings of their own nation's cultural heritage. Faulkner and Carpentier have both been seen as crucial influences on the "boom" generation of Latin American literature, and these parallels provide reason to believe that their dual impact has much to do with their hemispheric approach to slavery in the Americas. Because of a U.S. readership largely ignorant of Carpentier's considerable literary stature, I also hope this chapter decenters and contextualizes our understanding of Faulkner's contributions to the postslavery dialogue.

I chose the writers for the fifth and final chapter, "The Emancipation of/from History: Jean Rhys, Rosario Ferré, and Toni Morrison," because their work continues treatment of the issues raised in the previous chapters but does so in other regional contexts in Plantation America. As such, they demonstrate the possible applicability of this postslavery discussion to other novels and regions beyond Cuba and the U.S. South. These writers attempt to emancipate histories from the ideological grip of postslavery narratives that have neglected the voice of women and the sounds of music and orality in their account of history. In their novels *Wide Sargasso Sea, Maldito amor,* and *Song of Solomon,* the legacies of slavery are as much the ways in which slavery has been remembered (or not) as the historical events of slavery themselves. That is to say, the yearning for a postslavery autonomy becomes in their accounts its own burden. These writers suggest that it is thus our contemporary responsibility to "unread" history, to read for what has been buried by ideology, what Rhys calls "the other side" of truth. I argue that the apocalyptic closures in these novels serve to expose the very driving forces of the historical imagination and suggest the possibility of new histories beyond the memory of slavery. These novelists point to new directions in relating to our literary past and in constructing national literary histories, directions this comparative study of postslavery "American" literature opens.

1 Narrative and Genealogy

Toward a Postnational Study of Postslavery Literatures

Narratives of Genealogy

A ghost steps from you, my grandfather's ghost!
Uprooted from some rainy English shire,
you sought your Roman
End in suicide by fire.
Your mixed son gathered your charred blackened bones
in a child's coffin.

And buried them himself on a strange coast.
Sire,
why do I raise you up? Because

Your house has voices, your burnt house
shrills with unguessed, lovely inheritors,
your genealogical roof tree, fallen, survives,
like seasoned timber through green, little lives.

I ripen towards your twilight, sir, that dream
where I am singed in that sea-crossing, steam
towards that vaporous world, whose souls,

Like pressured trees, brought diamonds out of coals.
The sparks pitched from your burning house are stars.
I am the man my father loved and was.

—from "Verandah" by Derek Walcott, 1965

Derek Walcott writes of the continuing legacies of slavery in a postapo-
calyptic New World in which the plantation has been burned, the slave
owner buried, and yet new ghosts emerge from the old, sparks of death
turn to stars of life, and "unguessed, lovely inheritors" emerge from the
decay of the plantation. His message, and that of each postslavery writer
in this study, is that slavery is never finally behind us, not only because
similar conditions may exist in the present, but because it provides the
strangely fertile soil from which a wide array of unpredictable, beautiful
cultural forms emerge. The postslavery writer is compelled to write of
the slave owner's legacy because, as Walcott implies, our very opportunities for expression of our postslavery contemporary life ripen in pro-
portion to their vital connection to the plantation's twilight. The struggle is to resurrect slavery's past without paying it obeisance. Walcott
suggests that we can avoid the pitfalls of an unintended nostalgia for
slavery by paying heed to the many voices in our contemporary cultures,
the "green, little lives" of the "unguessed, lovely inheritors" that have
emerged in the postslavery world and that have fed off the dead genealogical dream of the slave owner.

Genealogy in the hands of postslavery writers serves to tell the story
of the slave owner's aspiration to a clear and exclusionary line of descent
and of inheritance from white father to white son, but also of the rich
and beautiful ironies of that dream's failure; it describes how transcultu-
rations on the plantation gave rise to an ultimately victorious and more
persistent, even if unanticipated, inheritance. Slavery's legacy is the violence and injustices of its practices, but just as important is the cultural
life its passing has sustained. Genealogy, though traditionally understood to reach back through time, becomes a means of unveiling the la-
tent heritage of the present. It is this turn from a diachronic search into
slavery's past to synchronic connections across the cultural landscape of
the nations of Plantation America that forms the crux of this study.

If slavery and its plantation structures constitute the diachronic origins of these writers' cultures, their struggle is how to revisit that past so
as to then move beyond it; in other words, how to sustain the paradox
of Toni Morrison's *Beloved* and affirm, "this is not a story to pass on"
(275). Comparative historians have identified a triad of common origins
that define Plantation America: European colonizers, displaced indigenous populations, and imported African slave labor.[1] And yet, even as a
common past brings various American nations together, the writers
from this region emphasize a new, contemporary identity made possible
by the past. They nourish their art and the newness of their aesthetic on

the demise of a reprehensible system of exploitation, and if individually they do not entirely escape nationalistic yearnings for slavery, their synchronic parallels with one another across languages and national borders become the principal means of producing postslavery, and ultimately postnational, meanings.

Diachronic Readings

This postslavery challenge begins with the writers' preoccupation with genealogy. Genealogy is, on one hand, an ideological and metaphorical tool of exclusion, one that aided the plantocracy in publicly denying blacks a rightful place within the national family. On the other hand, it is a biological tool for the writers to identify the ellipses of the planter's scheme, the moments of contact with those who have been excluded. As the central theme of postslavery novels, it potentially cuts both ways in that it can become a metaphorical privileging of patriarchy even if its intent is to dismantle the symbolic order of plantation society.[2]

Plantation owners clung to their monopoly on property and to their claim of being the progenitors of New World nations by insisting on their own aristocratic family and blood lines, which divided their societies according to caste and color. The landed classes of Europe provided for the plantocracy in the Americas a model of resistance to the autonomy and the legitimate participation of the masses in political life (Genovese, "Slavery" 29). Often in denial of biological kinship with the colored classes, the plantocracy insisted on its own genealogical and racial purity in order to ensure that property could change hands over generations without a loss of economic control.[3] That slavery outlasted its economic usefulness well into the nineteenth century and that plantation systems have had an even more persistent impact on nationalism in the New World illustrate the tenacity with which the plantocracy and its descendents have held on to the power generated by the dynastic and antidemocratic authority of the family line.

New World slave owners maintained a keen interest in controlling the representations of their origins so that they might negotiate with their colonial overseers for greater cultural and economic autonomy. Jamaica's Edward Long and Cuba's Francisco Arango y Parreño are two examples of planters who also became historians in order to inscribe their protonationalist authority. Planter historians played a key role in the consolidation of an emerging Creole consciousness and in overseeing the formation of independent national identities. Historiography, of course, is itself a kind of genealogy that relies upon an interdependence of events, where events are seen as giving birth to new events, and where, as Patricia Drechsel Tobin has argued, "ontological priority is conferred upon mere temporal anteriority . . . and time is understood as a linear manifestation of the genealogical destiny of events" (7). The exclusivity of this kind of historical consciousness, duly apparent in those early histories of the Caribbean, results from a diachronic approach; it sees events as they move down through time from some origin, perhaps obscured but nevertheless real, that has given birth to history.

However, the excessive preoccupation of planters with establishing legitimacy by means of historiography and genealogy often betrayed their interests because they found themselves led into more complex nets of synchronic cross-racial identities and to a discovery of their own questionable racial origins. Long's *History of Jamaica* (1774) provides an excellent example of how the plantocracy's attempt to mitigate the cultural effects of miscegenation paradoxically contributed to a growing sense of "unguessed, lovely inheritors" of a Caribbean multiracial identity. His sometimes tedious explications of racial origins, although ostensibly used to denigrate miscegenation, leave inscribed an anxious fascination with racial mixing. The innumerable legal codes regarding racial identity and social rights were intended to segregate and thereby mitigate cultural development rather than create cultural syncretism, as they often inadvertently did.[4]

The intent of genealogy, in the hands of writers of postslavery novels, is to contribute to this seemingly unavoidable symbolic collapse of the plantocracy's power and thereby complete the unfinished business of decolonization throughout Plantation America. Genealogy enables these writers to point to the miscegenated roots of their nations and thereby expose the unnatural marriage between slave owning and nationalism. To the extent that it does not collapse into an expression of nostalgia for the past, this strategy is akin to Michel Foucault's advocacy of a kind of genealogical investigation that paradoxically "opposes itself to the search for origins" (*Language* 140). Foucault explains: "to follow the complex course of descent is to maintain passing events in their proper dispersion; it is to identify the accidents, the minute deviations—or conversely, the complete reversals—the errors, the false appraisals, and the faulty calculations that gave birth to those things that continue to exist and have value for us" (146). This method becomes imperative when we consider, as Orlando Patterson argues, that slave societies have procured "the slave's natal alienation," which is the slave's "loss of ties of birth in both ascending and descending generations, . . . a loss of native status, or deracination" (7). The symbolic instruments of the master class stripped the slave of genealogy and defined him "as a socially dead person. Alienated from all 'right' or claims of birth, he ceased to belong in his own right to any legitimate social order" (5). The New World's manifestation of slavery deepened this natal alienation by introducing to world history "permanent and hereditary slavery of the most onerous sort, breaking with any geographical restraint and displaying an unquenchable thirst for slave labour and slave lives" (Blackburn 585). Genealogical inquiry, in the novels of postslavery, attempts to follow biology rather than ideology, to follow the traces of transgression, of human errancy, of breaks or ruptures that have generated new cultures and that expose planter authority as illegitimate.

The use of genealogy does not guarantee that the writer will avoid playing a duplicitous role vis-à-vis the history of slavery. Simply to kill off the slave owner in our literary imagination is to risk ignoring the vitality of those ordinary people whose cultures have survived the contempt of the slave owner; demands for historical justice risk what Walcott in 1974 called "the malaria of nostalgia and [even] the delirium of revenge" ("Muse" 7). As other postnegritude writers in the Caribbean have concluded, Walcott believes that nostalgia and revenge pay equal obeisance to the authority of history. He prefers a New World aesthetic that "neither explains nor forgives history" and that gives a "strange thanks" to acknowledge the originality that history's violence has made possible (2, 26). He argues that "by openly fighting tradition we perpetuate it, that revolutionary literature is a filial impulse, and that maturity is the assimilation of the features of every ancestor" (1).

This is a tension that appears inherent to genealogical inquiry, since it is both a way of forefronting the biological acts of history and of looking forward to future offspring. In other words, genealogy expresses a deep sense of historicity as well as points to a path of liberation from the past. Genealogy is tenuously balanced, then, between an impulse to found the dimensions of a more inclusive community and an apparent need to perform new acts of exclusion. Eric Sundquist's first book (1979) explored the foundational aims of early nineteenth-century U.S. literature and concluded that home is both found in genealogy and founded by future offspring.[5] This tension between the generative and genealogical taps a deep vein that, given common anxieties of influence, runs across New World cultures and has also been explored in Doris Sommer's important 1991 study of nineteenth-century Latin American literature, *Foundational Fictions*. Sommer suggests that contemporary

Latin American writers are weighed down perhaps by a greater sense of their own historicity than their nineteenth-century counterparts, but history-related anxieties and fears plagued many families throughout Plantation America in the nineteenth century. Within the context of slavery, families of all classes were concerned about the genealogy—the racial and cultural ancestors—of their children's potential spouses, since that heritage would become the property of the child who was married off.[6]

Conversely, the weight of the past for many twentieth-century, postslavery writers is not always a burden. Lois Parkinson Zamora explains in her groundbreaking work on the historical imagination in literatures of the Americas that "the knowledge that legitimate sources of communal identity have been destroyed or are unevenly available" preempts any anxiety about origins since it liberates the writer's representational agency (*Usable Past* 7). This also means that if Harold Bloom's articulation of writers' anxiety about previous literary or historical influence has any application here, we must "effectively differentiate between writers in *colonized* cultures, whose relation to their cultural fathers is radically different from that of writers working from *colonizing* cultures" (Zamora, *Usable Past* 7). This difference is particularly acute in the case of postslavery cultures whose historical memory must recover from immeasurable amnesia. If the community forged in postslavery fictions is under perpetual revision, we should avoid the temptation to see in any given work what the nation already is; rather, we can see in the text evidence of resistance to a textual discourse that has come before and a projected image into the future of what a revised version might look like.[7] This allows us to see the full range of dynamics at work in the text, and, most important, removes literature's hold on the privileged place of the Adamic origin of national formation.[8]

Synchronic Readings

Literary criticism's romance with national origins and identity has done little to broaden our hemispheric understanding of slavery's legacies. What have been taken as signs of national consciousness and exceptionality frequently have been plucked out of a much broader history. Literary studies remain locked within national languages, deriving conclusions concerning slavery's legacies in given nations and all but neglecting the tremendous literary production throughout the Americas during slavery and the impressive body of literature that has examined slavery's legacies since abolition. Amazingly, this is despite the fact that slavery "played a major role in the discovery and economic exploitation" of the

Americas (Solow 717); despite nearly four hundred years of slavery in the region stretching from the Caribbean islands to Brazil and to the Caribbean coasts of South, Central, and North America; despite the capture and scattering of an estimated 12 million Africans from West African shores, the death of another estimated 9 to 10 million in the Middle Passage, the death of countless others shortly after arrival in the New World, and a total slave population that reached 6 million in the 1850s; despite the centrality of slavery in international trade, the growth of industrialization and the struggle for empire involving six European nations; despite the obvious impact of the plantation system on the diaspora of European, African, and Asian peoples; despite the fact that the slave trade "determined the living and dying patterns of the black communities that developed in the New World . . . and their ultimate cultural adaptation to the new American environment" (Klein, *Middle Passage* xix); despite the impact of the slave trade on central features of modernity, including nationalism and the emergence of racialist conceptions of identity, of consumer culture, market economies, and others.[9]

The "reciprocal isolation," in the words of Antonio Benítez-Rojo, of historical memory among nations of Plantation America is symptomatic of the very history that brings them together ("Repeating Island" 85). Initially, the plantation united on a mass scale economic, political, and social power in the hands of an oligarchy that then passed on its power from father to son. Although a formidable acculturating force because of its social power, its exploitation of land, and its attraction of foreign investment, this power discourse has also resulted in sharp and contrasting diversification of cultural and political development, particularly at its margins. As Benítez-Rojo's 1992 study of the postmodernity of the plantation system argues, the "acculturating impact [of the Plantation] will make itself known asymmetrically" (29).

The plantation is hardly a phenomenon that can be properly understood within a single nation's borders, especially since it was defined by large-scale, foreign capital investment, international trade and commerce, and external political control.[10] So the plantation, a "tomb" but also a "forge" according to the Cuban historian Manuel Moreno Fraginals, transplants and brings together under its expansive and brutal reach various races, lands, and moneys, and yet it distances itself from the cultures produced under such circumstances (126). Those cultures, the "unguessed inheritors" of slavery's legacies, were "new social subjects—Patriot planters, rebellious creoles, coloured slaveholders, Black Jacobins, African Methodist preachers, and many more—who were difficult to reconcile to the official protocols of colonial slavery" (Blackburn 589). In essence, these new cultural syncretisms were created and then pushed away from the plantation's centers of power while their parallels with one another remained largely unseen. And since the plantation's power has had so many manifestations throughout Plantation America—including the stark geographical and economic differences among tobacco, cotton, sugar, and coffee plantations under various colonial governments—a mutual isolation of cultural development and production has resulted.[11]

In his analysis of the Cuban sugar industry at the height of its reinforcement under U.S. rule in 1940, Fernando Ortiz notes the plantation's adaptability in the wake of national consolidation and independence. Ortiz explains that the sugar industry, the raison d'être of slavery in Cuba, "was not established for individual, nor domestic, nor local consumption but for mercantile production on a grand scale and for overseas exportation" (41). Consequently, the industry has always required cheap, mass labor—hence, slavery—and heavy, foreign capitalist investment. That investment is largely the reason sugar contributed so much to the growth of European imperialism, to England's thirteen colonies (particularly in the industrial North), and eventually to U.S. imperial growth after the Civil War (Moreno Fraginals 22; Solow 733). By the time of Ortiz's writing in the 1940s, Cuba's sugar plantation system had survived the abolition of slavery and the antislavery rhetoric of Cuba's war of independence because it never depended on clear definitions of national boundaries or interest; it was not subsumed under the rubric of Cuban nationalism because the absentee owner had become the "yanqui" from the north. Ortiz writes that the United States behaved in the twentieth century "as if all of the territory of our native land were an immense sugar cane field; and Cuba, merely the symbolic name for a great sugar mill dominated by a foreign corporation of anonymous agents" (54).

As I will explore further in chapter 2, despite its domestic attempt to move beyond the legacies of slavery after the Civil War, the United States manifested the symptoms of the plantation discourse by exploiting land and slave labor beyond U.S. boundaries while attempting to keep at bay the Africanized Creole cultures that it had helped to forge. The South essentially was the first colony of U.S. imperial expansion.[12] The Union's attempt to integrate the New South after the Civil War fortified on an international scale the very plantation structures the North had decried, structures it had depended on for its economic growth.

If the plantation offers a model for a Pan-American approach to literary criticism, it does so with rich complications, since it represents an early form of capitalist globalization at the same time that it spreads and diversifies its own sites of resistance. Additionally, according to the Caribbean historian Gordon Lewis, the plantation has a history characterized by "violent and sudden upheavals, widespread social and cultural shock." He points to three main "moral earthquakes that have shaped the area": discovery and slavery, emancipation and postplantation society, and independence and postcolonial national sovereignty (*Main Currents* 15). These ruptures in the history of Plantation America have led to an often oxymoronic vocabulary; the region is defined by its indefinability; it is unified by its incapacity to be so. If the historical origins of this region are riddled with ruptures, its historical memory in fiction is both responsive to and liberated by them.

Thus, even though I am following the lead of comparative historians in delineating a territory marked by plantation discourse, that history is varied and has produced different cultural identities. It is, however, a territory marked by a decided antithetical impulse to the imperatives of European colonialism and also by new cultural expressions that have emerged from the area's historical ruptures. Named "Our America" by the Cuban revolutionary and poet José Martí, this territory seeks an opposition to "European America." Martí's thinking was initially forged in his own paradoxical circumstance as a pro-independence Cuban exile within the United States, a nation poised to annex his former island home in the late nineteenth century before Cuba would have a chance to break from Spain. Perhaps due to the exacerbated tensions between Cuba and the United States since 1959, Martí's late nineteenth-century ideas have been reduced by Roberto Fernández Retamar and others to a kind of Calibanic socialist cursing of European and Yankee colonialism, and this has occluded our understanding of the complexity of his views. As useful as his ideas have been in rethinking American studies, evidenced by José David Saldívar's provocative examination in 1991 of the "tensions between 'Nuestra América' and 'El Occidente'" within the context of U.S. cultural discourse, such dichotomies potentially elide the particularly Western forms of Martí's democratic and racial vision (12).

I will explore Martí's views in more detail in chapter 3, but it is worth noting here that he was a great admirer of aspects of U.S. society, expressed sympathies for the U.S. South, and was greatly influenced by Walt Whitman's conception of New World democratic possibility despite Whitman's own troubling romance with Manifest Destiny.[13] Whitman wrote in 1871 that "we see the sons and daughters of the New World, ignorant of its genius, not yet inaugurating the native, the universal, and the near, still importing the distant, the partial, and the dead" (52). Similarly for Martí, the struggle for a New World consciousness that potentially included the United States was between "false erudition and nature" (*Nuestra América* 12). The "natural man," whom he imagines as a kind of Whitmanesque homegrown intellectual, "topples the authority derived from books" and governs according to an organic understanding of the local reality. If Martí's conception of "Our America" escapes the rhetoric of reified differences, it is because he stresses that this process does not lead to the discovery of some autochthonous essence but involves the active engagement of the imagination: to be a "governor, in a new country, is to be a creator" (13). "Our America" is a kind of transnational political geography of the Americas where obscured or even obliterated realities—the local histories of the folk that were without representation in colonial memory—can only be made known through creative acts of representation.

This is not a one-time task, however. As Martí explains, to some degree in all American nations "the colony lives on in the republic" and manifests itself in the republican governments' disregard for a "local reality" (13). Recovery from the dizzying contradictions of the colony within the republic is understood by the longtime Cuban exile as a perpetual process of refurbishing one's language and readjusting one's perceptions according to that local reality but not through recourse to fixed notions of oppositional difference. The polarization of Martí's views notwithstanding, they resonate with more recent thinking about the territory by the Martinican writer Edouard Glissant. Glissant's postnegritude philosophies have been forged during his life outside the island, in France and in the United States, in a similarly ambiguous moment of Martinique's as yet unrealized political and cultural independence from France (it remains a Department of the French government since 1946, a status supported by the champion of negritude, Aimé Césaire). Working through the contradictions of the colony within the republic means living "the relative after having suffered the absolute." He explains: "When I say *relative,* I mean the Diverse, the obscure need to accept the other's difference; and when I say absolute I refer to the dramatic endeavor to impose a truth on the Other" (*Caribbean Discourse* 147-48). Dash contends that Glissant never saw return to Martinique as a refuge from contradiction or as a return to a homeland. "Martinique," he explains, "became . . . his point of insertion in the world," an "impulse to

move outwards and not back" (*Glissant* 21). Novelists of this postslavery territory, Glissant contends, create their world from both historical
denial and reconstruction, forgetting as well as remembering, and do not
pretend to present a dichotomous opposition to Europe of disinterred
truths or essentialized difference.

One important example of this return to the relative and local of a
postslavery region is theorized by the Cuban Alejo Carpentier in his famous prologue to his novel *El reino de este mundo* (trans. *The Kingdom
of This World*). Carpentier, another wandering exile who awaited his
own nation's postcolonial, postslavery liberation, celebrates America's
marvelous reality, which liberates the New World from the hold of European cognitive and political grasp. Unlike Europe's rather fabricated
notions of the surreal, a New World aesthetic simply "is reaffirmed
throughout our history" ("Marvelous Real" 83). Carpentier argues that
this reality is found in the "virginity of the land, our upbringing, our on-
tology, the Faustian presence of the Indian and the black man, . . . its fe-
cund racial mixing" (88). But if Carpentier's return to the local, explored in so many of his writings, demonstrates anything, it is that the
return involves carrying some excess baggage, so to speak, from trips
abroad. We cannot capture the marvelous reality that has escaped our
perception and see it as marvelous without collapsing back into the "absolute" ontological position of a European outsider. So the process ends
in failure and must in turn begin again.

It is my contention that the shifting identities in New World literatures can be correlated, in part, to the degree of self-consciousness with
which the New World writer reflects on the ironies involved in this return to the local and the relative. I see here an insightful connection to
Octavio Paz's salient argument of 1985 concerning the differences between the United States and Mexico. His essay explores the varying degrees of irony in the construction of a New World Creole subjectivity
and thus has important implications for understanding literatures of the
Americas. According to Paz, both sides of the north-south divide have
struggled to reconcile equality with difference, and the distinctions
across the border are constituted by the contradictory ways in which a
pretended solution has been offered. Mexico, and much of Latin America by implication, has emphatically fashioned itself as a culture that celebrates and includes difference, particularly that which is marked by the
presence of the Indian and the African. The problem is that it has done
so within a hierarchical, centrist system, which is a legacy of Spanish interaction with Arabs and of the Counter-Reformation. On the other

hand, "the historical memory of Americans is European" (*Labyrinth* 362). The United States inherited the English Reformation, which did not perceive the hypocritical discrepancy between its modern notion of democracy and its rather aggressive exclusion of difference. The United States pretended to independence by means of an explicit adoption of European ways, excluding Indians and blacks from their definitions of citizenry.

Paz's thesis appears to agree with the more recent argument of the Americanist Sacvan Bercovitch in *The Rites of Assent,* that "'America' . . . relocated the seat of empire from the Old World to the New; it reversed the very meaning of 'newness' from its colonial status of dependency to a declaration not just of independence but of superiority" (7). The United States has managed to disguise its imitation of European imperialism through its claims to exceptionality and in particular through the ways it has co-opted images of revolution from within, a process that Bercovitch insists means to "incorporate by exclusion" in order to protect an image of its "open-ended inclusiveness" (14).

This rhetorical openness of the United States was the threat Martí perceived to Cuba and Latin America. It is also the reason why the United States continues to ignore its historical parallels with other former slave nations. The United States nakedly manifested on an expansive scale "the colony within the republic" in its blatant disregard for difference; its aspirations to imitate its imperial forebears; its unabashed willingness to impose itself on others of whom it was patently ignorant; and yet it maintained a pretense to revolution and independence by celebrating the differences that distinguished it from Europe, differences that it in reality were little understood. Glissant explains that the United States has been divided by two desires, "that of wanting to continue politely a European tradition to which the United States felt itself to be the ultimate heir; and that of wanting to dominate the world savagely in the name of this ultimate legacy" (*Caribbean Discourse* 149–50). If postcolonial status involves not just political independence but a nation's decisive cultural and epistemological break with its forebears, then Anne McClintock is correct in arguing that the United States belongs in the category of *"break-away settler colonies,"* which are "distinguished by their formal independence from the founding metropolitan country, along with continued control over the appropriated colony (thus displacing colonial control from the metropolis to the colony itself. . . . [Such colonies] have not undergone decolonization, nor . . . are they likely to in the future" (89). To the extent that Latin America and the

Caribbean repeatedly emphasize the contradictory behavior of the United States in their deliberations about self-identity, however, they will delay a confrontation with the racial hierarchies inherent in their own advocacy of *mestizaje* as a political and cultural alternative.

The celebration of the multicultural "melting pots" of U.S. society has been matched only by a repulsion of the new cultural entities U.S. imperialism has facilitated. Because U.S. imperialism imitates the very ideological structures of a colonial plantation discourse, one wonders if the South didn't win the Civil War. Crucial to the process of decolonizing U.S. culture appears to be an investigation of alternative "American" geographies beyond the reach of such an overdetermined discourse. Bercovitch's argument warns us of the problems in yearning for such alternatives, however, since the erosion of differences in the name of preserving U.S. exceptionality has been the ironic and perhaps unwitting result of invoking difference. The problem with Bercovitch's provocative thesis is that he would posit it for all U.S. literary expression, which elides the ideological accountability of the reader as critic. If we are always reading U.S. texts to tell us something about U.S. national culture, our readings will undoubtedly select interpretations that ultimately reaffirm the boundaries of U.S. nationality. Even though Bercovitch searches for "the other America hidden from view by [his] interpretation," he remains trapped within his own overdetermined paradigm of American exceptionalism (27).

Nevertheless, his sense that this "other America" will reveal itself when we "illuminate the conflicts implicit in border-crossing" is to the point (27). If we cross the border in American studies only to bring back knowledge intended to illuminate "America," we will not successfully reexamine "America." If we cross the border in order to examine the contradictions of doing so, we perform in our criticism the same reflexes of writers in Glissant's "Other America." Such writers come together in a kind of Pan-American task of sustaining what Glissant calls a "matured 'modernity'" by breaking down the borders of national differentiation that have led to historical ironies (150). This approach emphasizes the neglected spaces among Africa, the Americas, and Europe that Paul Gilroy highlights in his study of the Black Atlantic and moves us away from the model of U.S. or even African American or other ethnic exceptionality (itself a borrowing from mainstream U.S. culture, according to Gilroy). When looked at in a contextual setting, U.S. and Caribbean literatures become representations of what Gilroy sees as competing countercultural narratives against modernity and nationalism, of transcultural spaces that are legacies of hemispheric slavery and plantation ideologies.

To read across borders is to read against the notion of national cultures born in some "monolithic cradle," as the Caribbean novelist and critic Wilson Harris has noted (*Womb of Space* 56). If we can avoid the temptation to allow our understanding of literary imagination to be overdetermined by obsessions with nationalism or originality, we can begin to "assess a kind of seismic quality in a changing culture [of transplanted peoples], an epicentre that releases a suddenly fissured crack" on the global surface of human culture. That is, a given work of cultural imagination within one nation becomes an expression, or a "fissured crack," in a larger landscape shaped by subterranean, submarine cross-cultural forces. Harris envisions that literature, sometimes more radical and cross-cultural than even its own authors envision, is constantly drawn in and "conscripted by collective 'imperatives.'" Literature is "subtly enriched within and against other apparently alien imaginations," and by reading cross-culturally, "each work complexly and peculiarly revises another and is inwardly revised in turn in profound context" (127).

A postnational study of Plantation America will not simply cross the various languages of the region in order to unveil a new paradigm of the plantation's transnationality that simply duplicates the same function of nationalism over a larger geographical territory. Comparative studies no doubt run this risk, but just as the plantation system spread its control across the region and unwittingly multiplied the possibilities for resistance, so too does the transnational reach of comparisons consistently open the possibility of other imagined communities that are not bound by imperial or nationalistic discourses. This openness toward a series of submerged transnational histories, which burst forth in fragments as momentary reorganizations or countermemories, directly opposes the imperialist thrust of the plantation system, which has restricted our readings of postslavery literature to reciprocal national isolation.

Colonialisms of various kinds have relied heavily on a conception of identity as a fixed essence rather than as a process of negotiation and, in the words of another Caribbean exile, Stuart Hall, as a "positioning, which makes meaning possible" (216). The boundaries of identity, in other words, are as contingent and arbitrary as the boundaries of the nation-state, whose meaning is also produced by arbitrary "breaks" disguised as "natural" and "permanent." We cannot adequately do postnational work if we do not aggressively contextualize what comes before and after such "breaks." This is particularly important in the context of Plantation America, a region shaped by transplantation and migration. Hall argues that "the diasporic experience is defined, not by essence or purity, but by the recognition of a necessary heterogeneity, diversity. . . . Diaspora identities are those which are constantly producing and reproducing themselves anew, through transformation and difference" (220).

A diasporic poetics becomes essential to any postnational discourse in the Americas because it can address overlapping, transnational ethnic formations and can therefore bring to bear a comparative cultural knowledge. This makes it possible, for example, to understand the complex negotiations of identity for Afro-Caribbean immigrants in the United States (such as a Marcus Garvey or a Claude McKay) in their relationship to African American and Caribbean enclaves, something most studies of African American culture have ignored.[14] As Werner Sollors has argued, a comparative approach to studies of ethnicity means that "what is praised as the accomplishment . . . of a single text may be more fairly viewed as the nuanced refiguring of themes that are familiar from many other texts; what is regarded as the defining motif of a certain ethnic group may really be a shared feature of many other ethnic and national literatures" (*Neither Black nor White* 26).

U.S. imperial and academic expansion into Latin America has often, paradoxically, exacerbated the difficulty of assessing ethnicity comparatively. This is because U.S. expansion frequently provides the illusion of racial essences beyond fixed national boundaries and an escape valve for avoiding internal racial and social contradictions at home. It is no coincidence that the ideology of Pan-Americanism, articulated by U.S. Secretary of State James G. Blaine in 1889, arose just as the United States began to confront the failure of its domestic racial policies.[15] Even before emancipation, the question of what to do with the slaves after they were freed caused Thomas Jefferson and later Abraham Lincoln to propose sending them to Haiti, a country where U.S. interventions seem to be continually erased from U.S. national memory. As we will see in a number of examples, exercising hegemony in Latin America has allowed the United States to imagine its own "civilization" in contradistinction to some kind of Latin American "barbarism." For this reason, not only has U.S. culture ignored its historical and cultural affinities with Latin America, but Latin Americanists as well have been reluctant to engage in comparative studies of Latin American and U.S. cultures in their effort to protect the autonomy and exceptionality of their literatures.[16] Both sides have canonized books, interpretations, and vocabularies that confirm this dichotomy while impoverishing our understanding.

The recent awakening in U.S. English departments and American studies programs to the limitations of a study of "American" culture and literature that is restricted to U.S. national borders has been long overdue. This reassessment of the meaning of "America" has come largely in response to a growing interest in immigrant literature, in particular Chicano and Latino literatures, and studies of the African Diaspora.[17] Carolyn Porter reminds us that departments, like Benedict Anderson's conception of nation-states, are "imagined communities" demarcated in part by the books they choose to read. A reading of multicultural literature in the United States could clearly reinvigorate American studies. But what is going to guarantee that Bercovitch's overdetermined paradigm of incorporation by exclusion won't rear its ugly head? This enterprise of rethinking American studies has yet to demonstrate how it will avoid a neoimperialist expansion into the field of Latin American studies; indeed, one wonders if the impulse behind such rethinking is not to create yet another exotic frontier that, once crossed, might redeem "America."[18] Sundquist has urged that "our thought . . . requires more than another repetition of the various pieties about crossing boundaries that have been the central topic—or at least the most frequent trope—at virtually every conference devoted to American culture studies in the past decade" ("Introduction" 793). Martí, often the only Latin American invoked in Americanist circles as the figurehead for this new hemispheric understanding, warned prophetically in his 1891 essay "Nuestra América" that ignorance and expansion went hand in hand in U.S. imperialism.

The insistence of Amy Kaplan and others in the 1993 collection *Cultures of U.S. Imperialism* that we examine the cultures of U.S. imperialism through the lens of postcolonial criticism is well warranted. Otherwise the radical heterogeneity of American cultures will be subsumed under the umbrella of a multicultural America, and therefore America as "an infinitely expansive and absorptive entity" will exercise its muscle, as noted by Bercovitch, perpetually appropriating internal signs of resistance and revolution (Cheyfitz 848). The problem is that until Latin America and the Caribbean are understood as protagonists and not simply as sites of U.S. imperialistic aspiration and exploitation, they will function as fixed identities of exotic difference and will further reify the imperialistic tradition within American studies. In light of the absence of a truly rigorous comparative examination of the Americas, we can only conclude that "expanding borders" may very well lead to expanding the realm of U.S. ignorance regarding Latin America.[19]

A view of U.S. borders as dynamic and unsettled can only produce postcolonial knowledge in the field of American studies if the otherness of Latin America and the Caribbean is equally understood as unbounded on its own terms, free from the containments of U.S. self-obsessions. To understand Stuart Hall's notion of diasporic identities, we must first have a solid grounding in the differences through which they operate. Otherwise, "contingent" and "arbitrary" end up as a vocabulary that disguises ignorance of real and different lived experience. The language that has helped to demarcate national and racial identities in the Americas is itself a series of signs contested in a hemispheric context. And if "the sign . . . is an arena of struggle and a construct between socially organized persons in the process of their interaction," according to Hazel Carby, then "we must be historically specific and aware of the differently oriented social interests within one and the same community" (17). If we extend and specify our historical knowledge of the "differently oriented [and, I would add, contestatory] social interests" of areas of the United States, the Caribbean, and Latin America, we gain a much richer knowledge of normally narrowly understood ideas such as miscegenation, hybridity, mestizo, mulatto, Creole, incest, insularity, black and white, feminine and masculine, and so on (17).

Clearly I do not mean to argue for a simple formula of comparative literature that presupposes prior existence of separate and distinct national literary traditions that have followed their own internal genealogies. A multilingual approach to Plantation America is not inherently protected against the kind of covert, even unwitting, colonialism I am describing, since it too can lend itself to an expansion of the scope of a nationalistically centered practice. If colonialism is, as Walter Mignolo has defined it, essentially an "expansion of the place of enunciation," then the sites of knowledge production must be plural and varied in their geocultural locations so as to avoid an expanding and subsuming appropriation of difference ("Occidentalización" 39). This necessarily involves uncomfortable geographical displacement, north and south, of academic practices and cultural imagination: new reading lists, new research, new dialogues among disciplines and among places of scholarship. This no doubt implies the possible dissolution of "American studies" per se into a variety of fields. It also entails a broader conceptualization of language practice as radically contextualized by other nonliterary forms of communication that, together with literature, express the quality of particular, situated identities.

How then might we go about a comparative study of postslavery literatures? The comparative critic needs to act much like Foucault's genealogist (and much like postslavery writers themselves), which means to follow accidents of biology rather than the rules of ideology. Our role is to insist rigorously on criticism that is not bound by national or linguistic boundaries, by ideologies, or by what Foucault calls "any monotonous finality" (*Language* 140). Otherwise we will miss accidents, lost events, or even, just as important, "those instances where [events] are absent, the moment when they remain unrealized" (140). The fact that racial relations, for example, have been imagined in Plantation America in a variety of ways raises questions about why some representations of race are chosen over others. Within the works of individual authors, we can look for and identify within the text the writer's own consciousness of the historical erasures that have made a pretended knowledge of origins possible. But this kind of reading impels us to go beyond the study of single texts or of single national traditions; if we are to understand how any nation in the wake of slavery has imagined its origins, we must also consider the historical erasures that have resulted when individual texts have been incorporated into a national literary history. My readings of these novels show how they share common roots, like a crop in the fictional landscape that has been reaped, and its individual fruits placed, somewhat arbitrarily, in separate national baskets.

The aim of insisting on textual juxtaposition is to allow parallels to emerge from the texts themselves, parallels that speak to the synchronic realities, as opposed to the diachronic origins, of postslavery cultures. In this way, textual parallels serve as a check against the temptation of nostalgia because what is more important in my readings than evidence of intertextuality is what I call textual simultaneity. It is important to acknowledge the genealogies of literary influence, such as William Faulkner's influence on Carpentier, Morrison, and Rosario Ferré, and to identify the lines of descent from *Uncle Tom's Cabin* to both *Cecilia Valdés* and *Iola Leroy*, which then influenced later writers within their given traditions. However, such genealogies can fall victim to a nostalgia for a sure knowledge of literary, diachronic origin. What is more indicative of cultural identity in the hemisphere are moments when texts resonate synchronically with one another and thereby provide telling evidence of divergent authorial and discursive agency within common sets of representational choices.

If historical discourse traces a diachronic origin of events and peoples, what then is the history of slavery and its attendant colonialisms if not what Glissant has called Plantation America's "nonhistory," the displacement and transplantation of events and peoples (*Caribbean Discourse* 62)? And if, as Walcott observes, "amnesia is the true history of the New World" ("Muse" 4), Glissant insists our task is to unveil the region's "concealed parallel in histories" (*Caribbean Discourse* 60). Saldívar has made a similar call for "finding historical, ideological, and cultural simultaneity in the imaginative writing of the Americas" (22). Our criticism need not trace cause and effect in an attempt to lead us back to a common origin, since that will only lead to dead ends, but it should trace present commonalties and hidden parallels. Comparative north-south criticism should not be a nostalgic search for the remote or lost paternal culture but must learn to seek alternative forms of legitimacy and authority; we must look horizontally across national lines at cultural expressions in order to unveil, if possible, evidence of shared origins that may also be nothing more than common points of divergence. This amounts to tracing evidence of Walcott's "green, little lives" that have emerged from the plantation's demise. After such analysis, we may be less confident of a nation's origins or of the past's relationship to the present but perhaps more confident that we are safeguarded against narrow nationalistic assessments of contemporary voices in a postslavery world.

Because plantation discourse expels from its center the creolized cultures it helps to create, it perpetually lends itself to a doomed insularity and solitude, as I will explore further in chapter 4. Hence my study is, in one sense, an extension of the recent call by Morrison and others to read for the interrelated construction of whiteness and blackness in American literature so as to "spring the whole literature of an entire nation from the solitude into which it has been locked" ("Unspeakable" 16). Specifically, she and others have recommended a study of American literature that is attentive to "a mutually constitutive relationship between African and European cultures in America" (Wonham 14). Not only should we examine critically the use of blackness in the construction of whiteness and vice versa, but we should also consider the ways in which those categories of identity have been shaped according to other "American" presences in the extended Caribbean. I would suggest a dual problematization of the "America" of which these critics speak: How does the meaning of "America" shift when we understand not simply the interdependency of black and white cultures in the United States, but also black and white cultures in the Americas?

Genealogies of Narrative

My study deals with thematic questions but simultaneously considers how the political duplicity of the writers is apparent in the very structure of the narratives. The narratives all have a double movement of resistance and complicity because they all contain an oscillation between an omniscient narrative control, which I see as symptomatic of a foundational, generative impulse, and disruptive testimonial languages, which I will show are symptomatic of the genealogical impulse to wrestle with the questions of historicity and contingency. The fictional narratives of Plantation America in this study bring forth new national subjects, represented by means of slave dialects, Creole languages, accents, and testimonies, in order to broaden the definition of the national family. Theirs is a struggle against the legal authority of the plantocracy in order to assure that, institutionally, the rights to citizenship and to property are extended to greater numbers.[20]

However, we also find evidence of a narrative anxiety to control and mitigate the disruptive effect of these new voices. That is to say, in many cases we see that the narrative, which is itself the power of organizing and dispersing knowledge, orchestrates access to the telling of the story with authorial control similar to that exercised by the plantocracy. This seemingly impossible tension consequently pulls narrative in multiple ideological directions and "obligates us to read . . . the constitution of the subaltern not simply as an empty space that passively receives and is filled, as it constructs itself through speech with the signs of power, but as an agent whose silences, gesticulations, inflections and secret languages, reveal strategies of flight and resistance" (Ramos, *Paradojas* 7). In their incorporation of speaking and witnessing subjects, these novels are "speakerly" texts, as Henry Louis Gates defines them, because they exhibit this tension between the authority of written language and the elusiveness of orality (*Signifying*). I read the aesthetics of narration as the politics of narration, since how the history of slavery is told plays an important role in establishing an understanding of both the implied reader and the implied author's ideological position vis-à-vis slavery's legacies. Reading this way, we can trace in the narrative itself the boundaries of the national project as it is forged out of the vestiges of slavery and against any signs of resistance.

In each of the novels I examine, a narrator or a group of narrators undertakes the oedipal responsibility to investigate a crime that has resulted in a plague in the polity. They seek evidence of some event in the dark past of slavery, some breech of civil or natural law that is ostensibly constitutive of the present. In this sense, as Hayden White has argued, the narratives "presuppose the existence of a legal system against or on behalf of which the typical agents of a narrative account militate. And this raises the suspicion that narrative in general, from the folktale to the novel, . . . has to do with the topics of law, legality, legitimacy, or, more generally, *authority*" (13). Specifically, these writers understand, as Jenny Franchot has argued, that "the story of America . . . is at base a crime story: . . . How did the nation become "white" in the face of all this nonwhiteness, innocent in the face of all this terror, and empty in the face of all these material traces?" (515).

But just as Oedipus's investigation incriminates the investigator, the narrative fails to remain above complicity because the act of narration cannot be separated from the forms of power that have given shape to the history narrated. In each of the novels, I find evidence of the narrative's complicity by virtue of the markers of the narrator's locality in the time and place of the story he or she is relating. By identifying these markers, I hope to demonstrate that no legitimate authority can pretend to be entirely independent of the history of slavery. Knowledge cannot be separated from power any more easily than narrative truth can be separated from narrative authority. That is to say, there is no way to investigate that history, to speak of its origins or legacies, without implicating oneself in the process; our historicity is also our complicity in the crimes of the past. But to the degree that the authors' narrators consciously expose their historicity in their historical investigations, they create an authority that more effectively questions the legality of slavery and its legacies.[21] Moreover, as this study moves into the twentieth century, we find that the master narrative becomes more self-conscious, more threatened on the outside by the challenges of testimony and orality. Consequently, the fabric of law and authority in slave cultures is more nakedly exposed, and the narrative becomes more self-conscious.

I am indebted here to Foucault's reading of Sophocles' play *Oedipus Rex*, which demonstrates the inseparability of knowledge of the truth from the power to represent truth. Foucault interprets the story of the Theban King as "representative . . . of a particular type of relationship between . . . political power and knowledge" (*La verdad* 39).[22] Political power is characterized, according to Foucault, by its ability to divide a truth in two parts repeatedly, a process he calls "the law of halves," and to conceal those parts from each other. Thus a coherent whole becomes fragmented and incoherent, unintelligible in any of its individual parts.

The investigation and ultimately the discovery of the truth, then, is a process of unifying or matching up these halves until the coherent whole is again found. The truth of Oedipus, that he is the son of Jocasta and Laius and is exiled because of the prophecy concerning his fate, does not return to its whole and intelligible form until all of its fragmented pieces come together in the form of various testimonies. The most significant testimonies come from the slaves and herdsmen, who bring Oedipus to a knowledge of his true identity and confirm the prophecies of the gods, thereby establishing a correspondence "in which the memory and discourse of men are something like an empirical image of the great prophecies of the gods" (48). Oedipus the detective discovers that he is the criminal he seeks, a circularity that symbolizes the self-implication that is inevitable in the process of reconstructing a knowledge of the truth from testimonies.

In the novels analyzed here, the investigation into the truth is also an investigation into the past. This helps us to understand how Foucault's law of halves operates: The passage of time, as a kind of paternal authority and power, disperses the links that could bring the various pieces of the puzzle back together again. The oedipal repudiation of the father, as John Irwin has shown in his study of William Faulkner, is an attempted repudiation of Father Time because the basis of patriarchal authority "is priority in time" (103).[23] Because of their secondary place in time, the writers' struggle is against historical consciousness itself. In order to resist the authority of the past, which is the authority of the father, they must somehow move backward in time in order to conquer or change that past at the risk of discovering their own dependence on that past.

Nevertheless, the narrators' success in repudiating the father is potentially no less ambiguous than Oedipus's own. John Irwin demonstrates that Faulkner's Quentin Compson, for example, attempts to remember the past in an effort to free himself from its entrapments, "to reverse the will of time within whose grip man is helpless," only to discover that he is a living repetition of the story he narrates; his is a memory of the future (77). In Foucault's scheme, human memory and testimony serve as the means to bring the fragments of divine prophecy back together and to recollect the fate of the future. Remembering and retelling are narrative acts that fail both to reverse the will of time and to provide an organized causal chain because narration is subject to its own historicity, to the external flow of time to which the reader is also subject. According to John Irwin, Quentin's tragic discovery is that there is no "virgin space" from which one can obtain authority of originality. This ambiguity of independence from the father must be tolerated if the community is going to advance; otherwise the result will be perpetual violence and rebellion that will never achieve its desired end of original authority.

John Irwin explains that Quentin's flaw, like Sutpen himself, is that he cannot tolerate his own evils and therefore divorces his idea of himself from them, a separation that "involves a kind of narrative bipolarity typical of both compulsion neurosis and schizophrenia. The split is the result of the self's inability to handle ambivalence. . . . The solution is primitive and effective: one simply splits the good-bad self into two separate people" (29). The two parts of the same whole split off from each other and face off as oppositions. Quentin cannot and will not reconcile his hatred and love for the South, or his obsession and fear of his past fathers, for example, and the result is self-destruction. It would appear, then, that contrary to Foucault's argument, intolerance of ambiguity and the violence that results from it, rather than political power, effectively break the truth in halves that then get dispersed into the possession of various individuals as they move through time. This moves us towards an ethical or moral critique of knowledge.

These writers struggle with the indeterminacy of their own narrative authority because the inclusion of testimonial language, ostensibly the narrator's means of breaking down the paternal authority that has impeded knowledge of the past, paradoxically contributes to the breakdown of authorial control. The narrator interpolates a plurality of witnesses to the past in order to uphold a more democratic model of the truth and of society, for the sake of bringing down patriarchal authority. However, testimonial language at the same time reveals the impersonal and omniscient authority of narrative control to be the particular personality of the narrator. That is to say, as Julio Ramos contends, the "same liberal elite" who turn to the margins of society as a tool of political liberalization also expose themselves as the paternal engineers of the new democratic polity since they "never manage to dominate their own anxiety before the unavoidable ethnic heterogeneity" around them. Consequently, the process of formulating a new "national imagining is undermined from within by the stimulus of its own negation, by the vestige of that heterogeneity that never ceases to reemerge . . . as an unassimilable remainder" (*Paradojas* 24–25).

This tension between narrative control and testimonial language is characteristic of the "double bind" of historical narratives.[24] They pretend to "speak in the name of the 'real,'" according to Michel de Certeau, by attempting to eradicate "any memory of the conditions under which [the narratives] were produced" (135). Those conditions could be anything from institutional and economic conditions to the discursive and authoritative practices of a field at a particular time. The specific time and place of the speaker of history was not deemed important until the emergence of fields that "put the subject/producer of history into question," such as ethnic studies or women's history. Previously, historiography was an "epistemology that constructed the 'truth' of the work on the foundation of the speaker's irrelevance" (146).[25] The effect is that the events represented seem to speak for themselves. An impersonal historical narrative, analogous to fiction's omniscient narrator, might not explicitly ever say "we," but the implication that such narratives speak in the place of a larger whole in order to construct "our" history is a fallacious use of metaphor.

Testimonial truth poses as a counterdiscourse to historical truth because of the unique vantage point provided by the particular personality of the witness, but for that same reason it does not have power to forge collective memory. Gordon Lewis has remarked that in the case of Haiti, private narrative acts, such as the political pamphlet and essay, did not have the metaphorical power to contribute to the growth of national thought and ideology. Such thought prospered when the pamphlet and the essay were "replaced by the extensive tomes of written history, using the accumulated archival material to present the great drama and development of the nation" (*Main Currents* 257). We are led to ask, By what authority can we meaningfully include under one collective "story" of what happened to "us" the particular and marginalized accounts of events? Can sufficient attention be paid to the particularity of circumstances out of which various testimonies emerge? Without sufficient mediation, will not a truly democratic history, which includes contradictory and varied testimonies, verge on being an incoherent one?

Critical examinations of the Holocaust and other forms of violent trauma have provided some of the most provocative theories of testimony, and although they do not derive from plantation experience, these theories explore relevant epistemological concerns.[26] Shoshana Felman and Dori Laub, in their study *Testimony*, explain that the excessive trauma of the Holocaust has caused a "crisis of truth" because "as a relation to events, . . . [the victim's testimony] seems to be composed of bits and pieces of a memory that has been overwhelmed by . . . events in excess of our frames of reference" (5). Jean-François Lyotard has argued that this crisis of truth is typically the result of an exercise of power, like that of the Nazis, which attempts to eliminate the possibility of any witness to its consequences. The question of truth is then phrased according to certain rules to which reality cannot possibly correspond; hence Lyotard's term *differend,* in which there is an irreconcilable incongruity in the rules of judgment, an incongruity that potentially silences the victim of terror. In response to the differend, testimonial language becomes figural or, as Elaine Scarry has remarked, it resorts to an "'as if' construction," which is a "work of projection into metaphor" (172).

Testimony may employ metaphorical language, but that does not mean that we should read one account as a metaphor for all others. If we were to read an account of one Auschwitz survivor as a representation of other possible accounts of fellow victims, we might appear to be denying the need for further witnesses. A generous metaphorical reading, then, can have its own kind of silencing effect on other needed voices and can make the reconstruction of history too easy and unproblematic. Reading testimony this way makes us vulnerable to the claim that one varying account is sufficient to prove that the event did not occur. Metonymically, then, is perhaps how we might best read the metaphorical language of testimony. Sommer explains that a metaphor provides "an identity through substitution of one (superior) signifier for another, . . . [whereas] metonymy, a lateral movement of identification through relation, . . . recognizes the possible difference between 'us' as components of a decentralized whole. It is here that we can enter as readers, invited to be with the speaker and not to be her" ("Sin secretos" 135–54). One account points only to the possibility of—indeed, the need for—further accounts, rather than seeking to stand in their stead. The reconstruction of historical events, particularly those resulting in full or partial erasure of their own witnessing, can take place only in a slow and continual accumulation of witnesses that must be teased out of the cultural fabric. A metonymical reading helps us to maintain an appropriate distance from the event so that we don't assume that simply by reading a testimony we can somehow become the eyewitness ourselves.

Certainly the trauma of the Middle Passage, of slavery, and of other historical ruptures in Plantation America has created a similar crisis of truth that postslavery authors must confront. The confrontation is evident in their increasing recourse to an imagined re-creation of testimonial language to counter the metaphorical reach of traditional narratives that have justified plantocratic authority. I say *imagined* because in most cases little or no historical documentation is available, and so fiction steps in not merely as an imitation of historical memory but as its substitute. Walcott, for example, has insisted that "History is irrelevant, not because it is not being created, or because it was sordid, but because it has never mattered, what has mattered is the loss of History, the amnesia of the races; what had become necessary is imagination, imagination as necessity, as invention" ("Muse" 6). Morrison has similarly suggested that language's incapacity to capture the entirety of slavery's history is not cause for lamentation but is its greatest opportunity. In her appraisal of Abraham Lincoln's Gettysburg address, she observes that "language can never 'pin down' slavery, genocide, war. Nor should it yearn for the arrogance to be able to do so. Its force, its felicity is in its reach toward the ineffable" ("Nobel Lecture" 321). This places an important obligation to read such fictions cross-culturally, as Wilson Harris urges, which in this case means to imagine the silence they share with those voices that remain without representation. One act of testimonial representation is like a metonym in that, in the words of Elizabeth Fox-Genovese, it "captures dimensions of the experience of innumerable [others] who, remaining in slavery and being unlettered, could not easily tell their own stories" (31). A more complete image of plantation history emerges when we read each testimony as incomplete, as always dependent for its meaning on the possibility, or indeed the impossibility, of other witnesses.

The historical and social conditions of plantation society make necessary this metonymical reading of testimony. The term *master narrative* takes on a very real historical sense when used in the context of slave societies, since it correlates to the ideology of the slave owners. These "master's tropes," as Gates calls them, stand in tension with the orality of the slaves, or the "vernacular," a term that literally means "slave born in his master's house" (*Signifying* 52). Fox-Genovese suggests that the master's language acquires its metaphorical power from labor relations over which he is lord and from the absence of black speech in the narratives about that labor. She explains that a master's claim to have "ploughed [his] field" is really "a man with twenty or so slaves resort[ing] to metaphor in claiming to perform his own labor" (128). Slaveholding women often resorted to the same metaphors when referring to work done in the household. In the West Indies, where absentee ownership was very common, the plantation owner's metaphorical power was limited because it was filtered through other agents at the plantation who acted on his behalf. Conversely, in the United States, the plantation owners came to the New World "determined to put down roots and make the land and plantations their own" (Mullin 484). The West Indies style of authority was "managerial, impersonal, and more highly ration-alized," whereas on the mainland it was "patriarchal, personal and in-formal" (485). I will discuss later the narrative implications of an absen-tee father figure, but suffice it to say here that the slave owners' genealogical discourse became a silencing metaphor to the extent that they referred to their slaves as "my people," or as "the black members of my family" (487). Trauma certainly played a role in shaping language in the aftermath of slavery, as it did in the case of the Holocaust, but rela-tions of production and of gender in slave society also helped to produce profit as well as the metaphorical power of the master's language; it placed the testimonies of those on the margin in a metonymical relation to one another and to the history of Plantation America.[27]

The limits of metaphor that have often been noted by critics of the modern novel are, in the context of slave society, the literal limits of the slave owner's project and of the socioeconomic positions of the various narrators.[28] The plantation dream is a metaphorical projection of the master's self that depends on the subjugation of an underclass of slaves and the maintenance of the family line. When either fails, so does the metaphor, making it imperative that we consider the literal limits of the slave-owning project in any discussion of the theoretical limits of meta-phor. Even if some of the slaves were the biological children of the slave owner, they would rarely, of course, hold the same social and economic status as the master's family. The economic and social power of the slave owner maintained and nurtured the symbolic power of his ostensibly impersonal position, but his power was a lie, a false equation, whose de-ceptiveness can be revealed textually by a juxtaposition of testimonial language from those who are beneath the metaphorical expanse of the slave owner's projected self, from the slaves or from women and chil-dren within the plantation household. Attention to the silences that one testimony shares with other witnesses that are unavailable necessarily brings us across texts from various national and historical contexts within Plantation America; there is always the need to hear someone else tell us how the same story happened differently. Because of the expe-rience of the African Diaspora, Gates has argued, "the fragments that contain the traces of a coherent system of order must be reassembled. . . . To reassemble fragments, of course, is to engage in an act of specu-lation, to attempt to weave a fiction of origins and subgeneration. It is . . . to imagine the whole from the part" (*Signifying* xxiv).

This metonymical approach leads to a more aggressively trans-national approach than Gates may have intended. The metonymical force of literature in the diaspora necessarily points us to parallel regions and experiences beyond the limits of given nationalities. Literary criticism's romance with national origins can potentially have the same silencing effect of an overly generous metaphorical reading of testimonial language precisely because we gain the confidence of having arrived at the origins too soon, too fast. Comparative juxtapositions will bring new voices into the context of our analyses and will thus productively disrupt that confidence. In the study of novels that follows, textual juxtaposition reveals the specific ideological personality of the master that lies behind the universalizing thrust of his metaphors as well as that of national traditions that, in their readings of these works, have pretended their own innocence.

2 Reading in the Dark

Cirilo Villaverde and George Washington Cable

LOST IN THE DRAMA of post-1959 U.S.-Cuba relations is an appreciation of the almost two centuries in which the two countries shared a common fate and acted, as Louis Pérez has persuasively argued, as each other's alter ego. This long history of "mutual and stubborn deceit," to use the words of Octavio Paz, is one important manifestation of the denied affinity between Latin America and the United States that will inform my readings in the following three chapters (*Labyrinth* 358). Although I do not wish to argue that the U.S.-Cuba relationship is paradigmatic, it is clearly symptomatic of the larger contradictions of "two distinct versions of Western civilization" north and south of the border (*Labyrinth* 357).

Cuba's second war of independence, launched in 1895, marked an almost century-long relationship between the United States and Cuba during which U.S. investors had made their formidable presence known in Cuba's sugar industry and off-and-on discussions had taken place in the U.S. Congress and in Cuba regarding the possibility of Cuban annexation. For the United States, Cuba offered the chance to solidify its economic and political presence at the Caribbean gateway to the Americas, but chief reservations had always been the racial makeup of the island and the ever-present fear of a black uprising, which might threaten U.S. interests and property in Cuba and could incite similar uprisings in the United States. Many white Cubans shared the fear of a black uprising and saw annexation as a means to preserving and stabilizing slavery (Pérez 34). Since the conclusion of the Haitian Revolution (1804), the specter of Haiti had loomed large for both countries and was a significant factor in the reluctance of the Cuban white elite to participate in Simón Bolívar's wars of independence in 1810 (Helg 47). It was also one of the factors in the U.S. decision to intervene in Cuba's war of independence in 1898, when it became apparent that a mostly black military force in Cuba was gaining the upper hand against Spain (89). As Robert Paquette contends, "'africanization' of Cuba would add one more link to a chain of territories to the south of the United States populated by free blacks and indebted to Britain for their freedom—a chain that could obstruct United States expansion and also endanger slavery in the South" (184).

Creole fear of Africanization, or the infusion of African culture, brought U.S. and Cuban slave systems together in the nineteenth century, but their divergent colonial histories would shape the twentieth-century outcomes of their seemingly oppositional racial and cultural histories and create the conditions for their mutual attraction and repulsion that figure so centrally in much of their postslavery literatures. In the colonial United States, according to Herbert Klein, slavery was marked by mercantile prevalence over monarchic interests, and this resulted in increasing autonomy for the mercantile classes. In Cuba, on the other hand, the Creoles "were left in undisputed control over the local colonial economy, [but] they were totally excluded from political and social power" (*Slavery* 21). Klein points out that, unlike the active role of the Catholic church in Cuba's colonial government, "no resident bishop would ever be sent to the [North American] colony" (36). As has been well noted, Protestants were less likely to tolerate miscegenation or the practice of African language and religion, and since their slave economies never required the intense manual labor of Cuba's sugar plantations, the U.S. slave population was smaller, more dispersed, and more self-sustaining due to much lower mortality rates; consequently, the slave trade was abandoned earlier and the free colored population never reached high levels in the English colony, nor were they ever given openings for increased social and political power as they were in Cuba. Because of the brutal conditions of sugar-based slavery and the slaves' correspondingly high mortality rate, Cuba imported slaves at extraordinary rates and encouraged miscegenation as a means to mitigate the effects of this influx of African culture.[1] Klein concludes that "Cuba was truly a thoroughly materialistic society in which money, connections and breeding counted for everything; but in [the American South], these factors could never overcome that of the color of the skin" (244).

The first U.S. intervention (1898–1902) saw the formal emergence of the United States as an imperial power in Latin America. In order to wage a measure of control over the outcome of Cuba's socially reformist goals, the United States placed mostly conservative white Cubans in positions of power in the provisional government and encouraged reforms that would facilitate continued social differentiation along racial lines. Despite unusually high rates of Afro-Cuban participation in the war for independence, and their similarly high rate of social organization before and after abolition, they were not proportionately represented either economically or politically in the newly independent Cuban Republic.[2] The Platt Amendment of 1902 allowed Cuba "just enough space to keep the independista vision alive" and thereby also "served to transform the substance of Cuban sovereignty into an extension of the U.S. national system" (Pérez xv, 109). In other words, the Platt Amendment was an extension of the plantation discourse within the United States since it kept at bay the cultures of difference with which its own imperialism came into contact. It was also the perfect middle ground in Cuba between the extremes of separatism and total annexation, both of which had failed to dominate the Cuban political scene. The Platt Amendment ironically allowed Cubans to continue their pursuit of independence through acquiescence to U.S. rule (Pérez 114).

The question in the late nineteenth century in Cuba and in the United States was increasingly, as Benigno Sánchez-Eppler keenly puts it, "how to shuffle—how to both mix in and thrust aside—the black body of the slave with/in the body politic" (78). Despite the benefits they enjoyed from the slave trade, some Cuban Creoles favored abolition because they felt it might help to whiten the population. Others hoped they could be integrated into the U.S. slave system and thereby continue simultaneously their white identification and slave ownership. Their hopes were defeated with the end of the U.S. Civil War in 1865, which also brought increased British pressure to abolish slavery in Cuba. Still other Creoles believed that interracial marriage, as well as continued white immigration, would sufficiently whiten the population. The Creole José Antonio Saco, for example, believed that racial mixing was essential to the overall economic, technological, and political development of the island.

At the same time that Creole *independista* politics leaned toward a practice of whitening the island's population, it also appropriated the symbolic signs of cultural blackness without embracing de facto racial difference in order to stand apart from Spain. Cuban *independistas* celebrated Cuba's ethnolinguistic diversity as a national trademark that opposed Spanish colonial rule, which was frequently portrayed as the propagator of racial and social division within Cuba. And once independence became a possibility, a threatening new presence found its way into the Cuban psyche: an aggressive U.S. imperialism. A significant number of white elite Cubans greeted this intervention warmly and eagerly became imperialist collaborators because they shared similar economic and social visions of North Americans; for those opposed to intervention, it served to prolong the symbolic celebrations of Cuba's racial and cultural difference. It would be overzealous and historically inaccurate to argue that U.S. imperialism created Cuba's racism, but it did allow Cuban patriots to exploit the myth of racial democracy and cast responsibility for racial conflicts within Cuba to its colonial past and its neocolonial present. In 1893, José Martí insisted that for Cuba to become an independent nation, it was necessary to eradicate slavery and to become "one people." In the interest of overcoming the numerous gradations of racial differences and the social and cultural differences they implied, Martí believed that "everything that divides men, everything that differentiates or herds men together in categories is a sin against humanity"; therefore, in a new Cuban nation, "there can be no racial animosity because there are no races" (*Obras* 486). Racial democracy became, in essence, the idea of a raceless society where talk of difference was silenced. This fear of Africanization inherent in Martí's racial democracy was, then, a fear that integration was impossible, that slavery and colonialism had produced a separate, unassimilable black cultural tradition that in its radical difference was a vivid threat to the survival of Creole culture and to the hope of a coherent national identity. What Cuba established was not racial democracy, but rather a system by which racial and social status could be negotiated by means of "legal colorization," a process that was helpful in protecting against the socially chaotic tendencies of racial diversity (Martínez-Alier 71–81).

Racial mixing in the United States led to a disappearance of a clearly identifiable color line after abolition and Reconstruction, which in turn led to increasing white anxiety and violence projected toward the black population. Jim Crow laws and the one-drop rule sought to maintain control over the lines of difference. Jim Crowism "conceded the central conservative argument that social discrimination was unavoidable. . . . Black and white racial difference appeared to be the most sensible way to bring order to an unruly social scene" (Warren 108). The-one drop rule, however, "only raised another and more subtle range of difficulties around the central problem of 'invisible blackness.' Well before one was down to the single drop of African blood, that heritage was lost to sight" (Williamson, *People* 98). That anxiety was calmed when the United States found its new imperialist destiny, and with it, a unique opportunity to extend its profound ambivalence toward its own history of miscegenation outward toward George Washington Cable's proposed idea of the "New South": the lands of "barbarous" racial hybridity in Latin America. As the United States came into neocolonial relations with other races and cultures abroad in 1898, paternalistic plantation ideologies found new life in an international context. C. Vann Woodward explains that the South, by pointing out the exotic races of which the Union had assumed custody, used 1898 as an opportunity to advance Jim Crow legislation. Externally, white America saw itself as the benevolent father, while internally it was the estranged neighbor of the darker races; both imagined relations were part of the same paradigm that refused to incorporate otherness within the nation as both equal and different.

Cubans and North Americans found their destinies intertwined at the turn of the twentieth century, but perhaps in ways they did not fully comprehend. Certainly, they understood the dimensions of their economic and political relationship, especially after the U.S. imposition of the Platt Amendment in the Cuban Constitution of 1902, but their own contradictory desires for postslavery democracy, nurtured over decades in the context of an extended Caribbean, blinded them to their dependence on the other as backdrop, or point of contrast, against which to placate their own consciences. By the early twentieth century, Cuba failed to recognize how race relations on the island were fast resembling those in the land of their northern neighbor, while the United States refused to acknowledge its own racial hybridity.

Transculturation and the Plantation

In the rush to construct consolidated national identities in the latter decades of the nineteenth century, both countries witnessed the emergence of a literary tradition of realism that was critical of slavery, but the signs of racial injustice in this fiction were frequently used to criticize the legacies of colonialism, and not to legitimate black cultural difference. Although I believe William Luis is correct in observing that "the tension that resulted from the struggle between the black slaves seeking their freedom and the colonial forces prolonging their enslavement contributed to the creation of a new culture," the conspiracy between colonialism and slavery nevertheless at times occluded a needed treatment of their distinct evils ("History" 18). The cultures that emerged against this conspiracy often neglected to listen to the voice of black protagonism under slavery on its own terms, free of subordination to the primary concern for political and national independence. Despite the desire in both nations to move beyond the history of slavery in order to preserve, or found, a national identity, the criticisms of that history frequently collapsed, perhaps from the pressure of a conflicted future, into nostalgic discourses that longed for a return to an increasingly remote past.

Nineteenth-century postslavery novels, such as Cirilo Villaverde's *Cecilia Valdés* and George Washington Cable's *The Grandissimes,* typically launch their criticisms of colonialism by identifying the unintended results of the plantation's acculturating impact. Writing in 1940, Fernando Ortiz argued for the neologism "transculturation" because it more accurately describes this unpredictability: It "implies necessarily a loss or uprooting of a preceding culture as well, what we might call a partial *deculturation,* and what's more, it means that a creation of new cultural phenomena will take place that could be denominated *neoculturation*" (90). Transculturation, for Ortiz, means that the violent amalgamation of cultures and races in the plantation system, its irrefutable *mestizaje,* ultimately renders the planter unable to maintain an unbroken line of cultural continuity. Although the planter's power makes adjustments to this chaos of transculturation by occasionally adopting signs of African culture, Cable and Villaverde attempt to identify traces of unassimilated difference that remain behind to haunt the master's newly adjusted claims of sovereignty.

Despite some theorizations that would like to see the chaos of transculturation as preideological, Angel Rama reminds us that signs of *mestizaje* never signify prior to their mediation into metropolitan discourses. That is, transculturation is itself a process of mediation between dominant and marginalized cultures whereby writers expand the boundaries of the national community by identifying sites of newly miscegenated cultures. When they do so, however, they too leave behind haunting traces of unassimilated difference. The ideological impact of their mediation has varied tremendously depending upon their situation between races, between urban and rural settings, or between colonial or neocolonial powers and their subjects.[3] Ideologically, writers are never evenly situated among all poles in a culturally heterogeneous context, and the instability of the cultures that emerge from transculturation may also indicate, according to Antonio Benítez-Rojo's *The Repeating Island,* that they will at times vacillate between resistance to and compliance with preceding forms of cultural domination.

In *Imperial Eyes,* Mary Louise Pratt identifies this ambivalence as endemic to the position of the New World Creole. The term *creole,* or *criollo* in Spanish, originally was used in the New World slave market to refer to black slaves born in the Americas (as opposed to *bozales,* who were direct from Africa), but it later came to refer to white-identified Europeans born in the New World and suckled by black wet nurses, or *criadas*. This white appropriation of the term was useful for those who sought justification for independence from Spain in the nineteenth century, many of whom were known as *gente de la tierra* (people of the land), as opposed to the slaveholders, who were frequently identified as Spaniards. The ideological bind of the Creole, according to Pratt, is the seemingly impossible task of borrowing from models of oppression and hierarchy that stem from dominant metropolitan, colonial cultures in order to legitimate egalitarian ideals and to facilitate cultural independence. Effectively, this means that as New World writers engaged in the project of national consolidation in the nineteenth century, their projects simultaneously founded a newly identified, resistant cultural independence in which local color was typically given prominence, and yet they often borrowed from colonial ideologies in order to exercise control over the chaotic potential of the new *mestizaje*. This ideological reading of transculturation demonstrates the process by which new forms of exclusion emerge in response to a prior dominant discourse. Homi Bhabha explains that, as in the case of Pratt's Creole, "the colonial presence is always ambivalent, split between its appearance as original and authoritative and its articulation as repetition and difference" ("Dissemi-Nation" 313). Transculturation implies that New World texts that seek to wrest control from imperial powers are perhaps more indebted to colonial ideology than we may have suspected, and that planter texts, if you will, that seek to exercise hegemony over the chaos of New World plantation life may in fact unwittingly allow darker and more subversive presences.

I see Cirilo Villaverde and George Washington Cable as New World Creoles who negotiate between the centers of power (Spain and the U.S. North, respectively) and emergent mestizo cultures. My readings attempt to delineate the transculturation of plantation ideology—its losses, gains, and transmutations—in *Cecilia Valdés* (1882, a significant expansion of an 1839 version of the work), published just prior to Cuba's abolition of slavery in 1886, and in the New Orleans Creole novel *The Grandissimes* (1880). Both Villaverde and Cable criticize the dependence of the plantation system on colonial ideologies. In particular, they criticize both the planter class's fallacious claims to genealogical and racial purity and to economic exclusivity and the neglect of the colored classes that resulted from such claims. However, in their efforts to shed the historical legacy of these paternal abuses of the absentee slave owner, they employ many of the same colonial ideologies by which the plantation system held these nations captive and, ultimately, yearn for the father's return. Their novels perform the dual function of exposing rampant Africanization in Creole cultures while simultaneouslyattempting an exorcism or taming of this influence in order to found a newly imagined polity. This replication of planter ideology, even if unintended, represents a historical paradox of postslavery cultures. Although much critical attention has been given to how these authors provide an opening in national discourse for new voices, my analysis will emphasize the enclosures that their representations make possible. This will also provide us with a context by which to assess and understand how such writers as Charles Chesnutt, Frances Harper, Martín Morúa Delgado, William Faulkner, and Alejo Carpentier respond to these Creole mishaps.

The lives and fictional works of Cable and Villaverde are characteristic of the divergent histories of their nations, which lie so geographically close but remain so culturally and politically distant.[4] Beginning in 1849, Villaverde spent most of his life in the United States in exile for his participation in the Mina de la Rosa uprising against the colonial government, which had earned him a death sentence. He spent the 1850s writing for the newspaper *El Independiente* in New Orleans, where Cable was born in 1844 and wrote for the *Picayune* in the 1870s. Following a brief period in Philadelphia, Villaverde spent the late 1850s until the 1880s in New York. There he joined the exiled Cuban community led by José Martí that was plotting a war against Spanish colonial rule. It is clear that there was the possibility of considerable contact between Cuban and U.S. intellectuals and artists—Cable's close friend Mark Twain had met Villaverde, and José Martí had met Walt Whitman and others—but there is no evidence that Cable and Villaverde ever met. (Unfortunately, Villaverde's journal of his New York years is still at large.) Cable's residence in New York after 1880 had a sense of exile as well, since southern compatriots had accused him of selling out to northern interests; he was labeled a traitor. *Cecilia Valdés* and *The Grandissimes* were published just two years apart, both in New York. From the North, then, both writers composed fiction about events in their native lands during the early nineteenth century, historical representations that have been read as metaphors for the cultural polemics of their time. To this day, Villaverde and Cable enjoy a reputation for their ability to depict the exotic "local color" of their homelands and to revive past eras and customs.

The U.S. Civil War had opposing influences on Cable and Villaverde.

Cable fought for the Confederacy in his youth and witnessed the fall of New Orleans only to become convinced of the moral bankruptcy and colonial backwardness of the South's resistance to the North. The war was for him a shameful example of how the South had clung needlessly and wastefully to an outdated European conception of aristocracy and had therefore perpetuated its own crippling regionalisms. After the war he strongly advocated a full cultural integration of the South into the Union. Villaverde was against Cuban slavery before he came to the United States, yet, curiously, his sympathies seem to have been with the South. The complaints of the South about northern hegemony appeared more analogous to the Cuban situation—by virtue of both areas' subjugation to an outside political and economic foe—than the North's cries for abolition. Before the war ended, Villaverde translated and published the Confederate historian Edward Pollard's history of the first year of the Civil War (1863).[5] Despite his position against slavery, Villaverde was more concerned with the protection of local autonomy.

The comparison that follows provides a crucial example of how the Africanist presence in U.S. literature that Toni Morrison has criticized serves as a shadow to demarcate the outlines of whiteness in the larger hemisphere of Plantation America. The presence of the black marginal subject in *Cecilia Valdés* and *The Grandissimes* both subverts and upholds prevailing ideologies of white supremacy and is essential for the author's task of consolidating a newly imagined national identity. When the white reader allows black language and testimony to shape his/her cognitive understanding of the novel and of the white family's genealogy, this allowance potentially signals that the black character has "passed" within the boundaries of the national imagination. Julio Ramos, moreover, argues that the text of the novel itself can "pass," like a surrogate for the body of the subaltern. Novels about race act as a subaltern subject introduced onto the national stage in that they ask of us a careful reading of differences and a consequent integration into the national culture ("Cuerpo"). In order to monitor the potentially transformative effects of this passing on prevailing cultural norms, both writers employ a narrative technique that performs a Foucaultian function of discipline by fixing the subaltern's body and personality in the specificity of place and time by means of an incorporeal, omnipresent narrative gaze. Ramos explains that any intellectual, scientist, or artist cannot produce representations and knowledge of the subaltern subject without assuming the "incorporeal position of writing, . . . of the distant eye that can only gaze and represent" (*Paradojas* 32). Despite the elaborate representations of the subaltern's speech, in phonetic dialect and vernacular, all information we receive from the narration comes filtered through a position outside the boundaries of the black body, a position that thereby establishes a taxonomical hierarchy of racial difference. The black voice, as it emerges from the body, is entrapped and encoded with signification within the epistemology of the seeing narrator; the black character does not speak beyond the boundaries of his or her own body because the gaze of the narrator constantly limits and qualifies all verbal expression. This means that the narrative framework inoculates represented black speech, rendering it a signification of a racial other rather than a signifying produced by that other. Although strongly prevalent in many late nineteenth-century novels, then, orality is not multivalent.

However, Ramos insists that control over signifying is never complete. He explains that in the case of Cuba "the discourses about ethnolinguistic heterogeneity . . . , as an enigma that needs resolution . . . in the process of configuring a new nationality, speak to us instead of the phobias of that very same liberal elite" (*Paradojas* 24). As Villaverde's narrator says of the protagonist Don Cándido's attempt to hide his responsibility, "the more one washes [stains of guilt] the more clearly visible they become" (158). The narrator leaves seemingly unconscious traces of his anxiety and personality within the text, traces that are indicative of the limitations of the narrator's power to control knowledge of his subjects. Although the gaze of Cable and Villaverde's narratives ostensibly provides a means of critiquing certain social and racial injustices, the seeing eye fails to represent the voice of the subaltern as expressive of the subaltern's own awareness of being subject to that gaze. If the difficult renderings of dialects in written speech produce a nonthreatening, exoticized, subaltern presence, at least the representation of that speech ultimately provides an idea of the anxiety that limits narrative authority. These voices, represented within fictional works, cannot be easily separated from the political framework of the white liberal elite project. This is true even for many slave narratives—to which many of the speeches in these novels have been favorably compared, most notably by Lorna Williams ("Representing" 84). The liberalizing effect of black testimonial language in these novels cannot be denied, but to read them as testimonials is to also forget that slave narratives were for the most part solicited and framed, to begin with, by the white liberal elite. The black voice is destabilizing of white authority to the extent that it points to what cannot be said and exposes the narrator's resistance to ceding control; that is the moment when the author's visibility and profound ambivalence toward racial difference is exposed in the text. Consequently, this ambivalence suggests the need to reconsider the ideological complexity of transculturation, since imagined cultural newness does not always signify a presence purely resistant to colonialist ideologies in the New World.

Looking through a Glass Darkly

In Cuba, the symbolic appropriation of cultural blackness began in the abolitionist Domingo Del Monte's salons of the 1830s where several writers, including Villaverde, met to explore possible ways of criticizing the slave system through fiction. One member of that group, Felix Tanco, claimed that "the only poetry among us is the slaves: poetry that is being spilled like blood everywhere and that is only invisible to the inhumane and ignorant" (qtd. in R. González 137). The constant threat of censorship under which these writers explored a new realm of fiction meant that they would have to cautiously negotiate their representations of the slave. Tanco's short stories, for example, went largely unpublished because he pushed his descriptions of the slave's condition beyond their allowable limits. Villaverde himself felt that Tanco's stories were "very graphic" (Cairo 6). Although influenced by Tanco, particularly his story "Petrona y Rosalia," Villaverde felt that to write truthfully and graphically about slavery would risk censorship and ineffective anonymity.[6] Villaverde's equally unattractive alternative was to "transform the runaway blacks into Indians and remove the scene to a country where such were found, something that completely contradicted my ideas about the novel whose local character I believe is indispensable" (Cairo 6).

It would be a mistake to assume that all textual signs of ambivalence toward blackness and miscegenation are necessarily symptoms of this political environment and not indications of the writers' own Creole ambivalence. A majority of criticism on *Cecilia Valdés,* accepting the subtitle "Novela de costumbres cubanas" ("A novel of Cuban customs"), sees Villaverde's nineteenth-century Cuba as an unambiguous historical representation of the colonial past. This was how he would have it, since he repeatedly and emphatically insisted that he drew his material from the reality of Cuban society and history, that he never read any novels that might have influenced the stylization of the narrative, and that he portrayed his Afro-Cuban characters "speaking the same language that they used in the historical scene in which they played a part and copying to the extent possible, *d'après nature,* their moral and physical physiognomy" (qtd. in Ette 75).[7] What is significant is how this scientific rhetoric underscores his diagnosis of the corruption and contamination caused by Spanish colonial rule, particularly given the correlation between the birth of Cuban antislavery literature in the 1830s and the concurrent emergence of new discourses of physical and public health (Ramos, *Paradojas* 23–36).

The 1882 version of Villaverde's novel anticipates the increasing anxieties of the white liberal elite concerning the possibility of a postslavery and independent Cuba. The novel is set in the years 1812–1832 during a particularly corrupt period of Spanish colonial rule. This historical focus provides a prognosis for Cuba's future after slavery in attempting to identify the impact of that corruption on the origins of Cuban nationality. It tells the story of a Spanish merchant and planter, Don Cándido Gamboa, who fathers an illegitimate daughter, Cecilia, with his mulatto mistress. Don Cándido takes great pains to conceal his paternity even as he clandestinely and anonymously supports his daughter. His hypocrisy catches up with him when his son and only heir, Leonardo Gamboa, unwittingly commits incest with Cecilia.

In the 1839 edition of the novel, published in Cuba, the relationship between Cecilia and Leonardo has little or no incestuous and racial overtones despite the novel's concern with genealogy and identity. Villaverde's 1846 novel, *Comunidad de nombres y apellidos* [The community of names and surnames], plays with a kind of Shakespearean confusion of individuals and how they are identified. The frequent shifting of identities occurs as a result of a genealogical confusion of names and signatures, not because of racial mixing. The central concern of his early fiction appears to be the means of properly identifying the appropriate object of one's affection, a task that moves the lover beyond appearances and into essences and is, according to Doris Sommer, typical of many nineteenth-century authors' foundational aims.

In his 1882 edition of *Cecilia Valdés*, published in New York, a rather dichotomous view of appearances and essences is still apparent in the narrative's yearning for the possibility of uncovering true identities. However, unlike his earlier fiction, this version acknowledges in its conclusion that this dependence leads to a dead end. The 1882 narrative distinguishes between Spanish and Cuban identity on the basis of his representations of deceptive, external appearances (the legacy of Spanish customs) and reliable, internal essences (the site of Cuban identity). The novel's incestuous conclusion takes stock of these assumptions about Cuban essence and posits the possibility that Cuban origins remain "elusive, persistently moving away. Thus [the search for origins] implies a failure, a never-ending story which attempts to legitimize itself by means of its own fiction" (Benítez-Rojo, "Cirilo Villaverde" 262). Villaverde's recourse to historical documentation, literary realism, and essential, knowable identities points to a national identity that has not been historically documented but, as Norman Holland argues, literarily fashioned: "[T]ailoring Cuba into a nation does not require the revelation of 'true identities' as much as a newly stylish incorporation, the amalgamation of various minorities into an encompassing plural voice. Although compelling in its apparent inclusiveness, this national voice serves to police the emerging national body" (152). This fashioning, I believe, is not the novel's aim but is what results from its representation of genealogical horror, that is, from the admission of failure to recover true Cuban origins. For Villaverde, the cause of that failure is the irrevocable consequences of Spanish colonialism.

As in the case of Cable's portrayals of French Creole life, Villaverde clearly demonstrates ambivalence toward his own elaborate descriptions of Cuban fashion, dance, music, vernacular, and racial color. Villaverde tries to shed the burden of Spanish rule as manifested in those customs, since they are, in his mind, the product of unequal race relations perpetuated by colonialism, and to appropriate from them a cultural essence that will serve his foundational aims. Villaverde represents Cuban society's emphasis on the external visibility of social and racial identity as a kind of vulnerability to a corrupt and illegitimate colonial power. His novel's stance appears to be more anticolonial than antislavery; slavery and racial injustice are secondary because they represent the legacy of Spanish rule. On this point, Jackelyne Kaye has argued: "[F]or Villaverde, slavery was not a specific evil, rather it was merely an aspect of the absence of liberty and of the corruption of a society where everyone lacks liberty" (75). Villaverde himself stated in an 1884 letter to his wife that he did not expect his novel to accelerate the emancipation of the slaves because he wrote it primarily as a treatment of the "slavery of white Cubans" under Spanish rule (qtd. in Ette; see also Friol). This confirms Paquette's claim that Cuba's antislavery writers "put [Afro-Cubans] on center stage, but to a great extent to show how the system was corrupting whites" (101).

Villaverde's ambivalence is manifested in the narrative's simultaneous resistance and obeisance to the surveying gaze of a colonialist outsider on the Cuban "body." According to Reynaldo González, many nineteenth-century Cubans molded "a pastoral, picturesque and facile image of the Island and its peoples, for external consumption and as something seen by foreigners and for them . . . in captivating images" (8). González explains that images of Cuba created by the colonizer were often internalized in Cuban culture, and illustrations and engravings from travel literature "formed a vision of Cuba that ended up being appropriated by 'the natives'" (10). In turn, these new visual delineations of Cuban identity "constituted 'local color.' The consumer's eye that wished to enjoy the tropical goods without being contaminated by 'blackness' on an island of black slaves was given its fill" (12). Villaverde's effort to train the reader's eye to look for reality beyond deceptive appearances is the policing force that shapes the reader's view of the new independent polity. This visual training as it pertains to racial identification is meant to clear Cuba's confusion of identity. For example, Cecilia's identity is made clear to us, even if it is not to those around her, or even to herself. The narrator asks: "To what race, then, did the little girl belong? Difficult to say. But what could not escape *the knowing eye* [*a un ojo conocedor* no podía esconderse] was the dark band or border of the red lips and the brightness of the child's face that ended in a sort of shadow at the hairline. Her blood was not pure, and it was certain that back in the third or fourth generation her blood was mixed with the Ethiopian" (7, emphasis added). The narrative trains us to see the shadows and dark traces on the edges of her beauty and whiteness. Ultimately, the narrative eye proves to be the most reliable producer of knowledge concerning identity and origins; in the end we learn that Cecilia has a birthmark on her shoulder that serves as a sign written onto her body (although disguised by her clothes) and that identifies her as the mysterious orphan whom María de Regla nursed and as the mulatto offspring of Don Cándido.

Villaverde creates the reader's dependence upon the narrator's discerning authority by making us aware of the weakness of others' superficial visual apprehension. Repeatedly, characters encounter each other in dark streets or poorly lit corners of rooms, or they are disguised by their clothing, and this visual weakness obstructs their proper genealogical, racial, and social identification. Villaverde's almost Shakespearean pairing of visually similar characters across racial lines additionally increases our dependency on the narrator. Dolores, the daughter of María de Regla, the black servant, imitates Don Cándido's white daughter, Adela, in dress and manners; the mulatto José Dolores and Don Cándido's white son, Leonardo, both competitors for the love of Cecilia, have the same physique and fit into the same clothes tailored by Uribe; and, of course, despite their differences in attire, the half sisters Cecilia and Adela are often mistaken for each other.

As the narrative progresses, we learn how to see beyond appearances and into the darkness of hidden identity. Isabel, Leonardo's fiancée, encounters Cecilia in the street with him. Because of the obvious affection Cecilia displays toward Leonardo, she mistakes Cecilia for his sister, Adela: "[T]his is not a matter of interpretations, Señor Don Leonardo, it's a matter of what I saw with my own eyes . . . no matter how blind love may have made [me]." Her supposed blindness, which we know to be unwitting insight, contrasts with Leonardo's reliance on deceptive appearances. Leonardo insists, "I see clearly [Veo claro], Isabel, that in all this there has been a mistake on your part." Isabel is unshaken in her suspicions: "I imagined that she was your sister. Not only did I take her to be *the living portrait* of Adela [*el vivo retrato* de Adela], but I couldn't . . . imagine that any other woman would be intimate enough with you to play those kinds of tricks" (emphasis added). Leonardo declares, "You have black eyes [ojos negros tienes]" (Gest 335). Villaverde associates lightness with deception and darkness with illumination. Leonardo sees "clearly" while Isabel has "black eyes," yet we know that her dark vision of the world, much like the reader of Villaverde's text, reaches the essence of truth more directly. She may not have been able to recognize the woman properly, but she was able to recognize the improper expression of intimacy. The irony is that we know long before Isabel or Leonardo that Cecilia is Leonardo's sister and that his affections for her are unwittingly incestuous; the similarity of Adela and Cecilia's appearances is merely the surface of the darker truth of miscegenation.

We are likewise trained to see essences in the dark when Rosa recommends the dismissal of the overseer for his mistreatment of the slaves. Despite Cándido's view of a symbiotic, even parasitic, relationship between colonialism and slavery, Rosa rebukes his crassness and suggests the need to do away with Cuba's colonial status altogether. In the 1839 edition of the novel, the respective Spanish and Creole origins of Cándido and Rosa are not identified, and nor does this dialogue between Rosa and Cándido take place, suggesting the possibility that Villaverde advanced his *independista* sentiments in the revision and that he may have been influenced in the interim by the sentimentality of Harriet Beecher Stowe's female characters in *Uncle Tom's Cabin* (1851–1852). Villaverde is believed to have authored a biography of his wife, who was influenced by Stowe and the women's movement while in the United States and intimately involved in the struggle for Cuban independence (Luis, *Literary Bondage*). What is intriguing is that the Spanish edition of the novel describes Rosa's reasoning as "la lógica parda de las mujeres" (214). Sydney Gest's 1962 English translation renders this as "the irrefutable logic of a woman," clearly avoiding the implications of the original Spanish *parda* (402). The term has historically been used to refer to a mulatto shade of the colored population. That we are led to reason with "darkey" logic and to see with dark eyes, the domain of both Afro-Cuban and white women in the novel, demonstrates how Villaverde opposes Don Cándido's Spanish corruption with a symbolically blackened and feminized Cuba.

When the British threaten to impede the arrival of his slave ship *Veloz*, Don Cándido reasons: "One must be blind if he cannot see on such a clear day [Ciego el que no ve en día tan claro]. Rosa, don't you understand that if we dress the cargo in clean, new clothes, they can pass for Hispanicized Negroes [pueden pasar por ladinos] from—from Puerto Rico, from anywhere except Africa?" (Gest 218). The implication is that the contraband slave trade survives by virtue of the deception of appearances. Cándido's deception works, providing further capital for those white classes that might otherwise resent the Spanish merchant. The majority of the whites after 1840 were Creoles, who made up an emerging *independista* bourgeoisie, but there was a small but powerful minority of Spanish merchants who, like Cándido, were often resented because of their power, colonial ties, and patriarchal traditions. Cándido's marriage into Rosa's Creole slave-owning family and Leonardo's marriage to the reformist Isabel, whose family owns slaves on a coffee plantation, signify the tense but symbiotic relationship between the white elite classes. Villaverde suggests that this tension will be eased by repudiation of the Spanish invader and Creole devotion to white Creole women like Isabel and Rosa. Rebecca Scott has shown that to the Cuban reformers, "the contraband slave trade appeared . . . as a weapon of Spanish merchants against Cuban planters, and the influx of Africans seemed a threat to the racial balance of the island. (Ironically though some of these same reformers continued to purchase contraband slaves at the same time they called for an end to the traffic)" (*Slave Emancipation* 39). We see this contaminating hypocrisy when Rosa reminds Leonardo that despite his misgivings about the slave trade, slavery and colonialism sustain the appearance of his well-to-do social status.

Our moments of confusion regarding identities coincide with the covert actions of Don Cándido in his effort to create appearance in order to "break with the past once and for all, to erase from his memory the last traces of certain deeds" (158). From the novel's first pages, Don Cándido walks the dark streets incognito and unidentified, looking after the financial welfare of his mulatto daughter. That Afro-Cuban and white women perceive the essence behind the colonial appearances perpetuated by Don Cándido signifies Villaverde's appropriation of cultural marginality for the purposes of fighting off Spanish domination. The narrative, however, does not fully confront the racial and social implications of such advocacy. In fact, Villaverde's use of shadows, of unseen faces and unrecognized identities, returns us to a reading of the absent father, the absent patrimony of colonial Cuba. For example, Cecilia surmises, "my mother died a long time ago and . . . my father as well. I don't know anything more and don't ask me either" (9). The missing words allude to Cecilia's and our initial ignorance that Cándido himself participates in the burial of his name. As a direct contrast to Cecilia's statement, Don Cándido explains to Josefa, Cecilia's grandmother, that "this cannot have been more painful for the mother, as I well know, than for . . . all of us" (3). Cándido's crime is not miscegenation per se but his effort to disguise his duplicitous "obligations as a lover and as an adulterous father" and "the sacred ones of a husband and an honorable father of a family" (154). The harder he tries to obscure his sin of duplicity, however, the more visible it becomes to those around him and to the reader. The narrator explains: "[F]or guilt is very much like certain stains, in that the more one washes them the more clearly visible they become" (158). Cándido's paternal dishonesty sets off a reaction of frantic destructive energy that breaks up and pushes away both black and white mother-daughter pairs.

Arguably, no one is more negatively affected by Cándido's dishonesty than María de Regla, who plays the role of mother to the white, mulatto, and black family lines that Cándido has attempted to split apart. She once nursed her own black child, Dolores, along with the mulatto Cecilia and the white child Adela, and "made no distinction between them" (124). Adela and Dolores in particular "loved each other like sisters despite their opposite condition and race" (125). Appropriately, her name and appearance represent the Virgen de la Regla, a syncretic figure in Cuban popular culture who represents the confluence between Catholic and Yoruban beliefs. For this reason, she initially offers the most powerful counterforce to Cándido's irresponsibility, especially since, as Williams explains, her nurturing potentially heals the genealogical wounds of slavery: "[M]otherhood is . . . grounded in the act of nurturing, rather than in the biological process of giving birth" ("Representation" 73). By nursing all three races, she has power to forge community in the wake of Cándido's and slavery's genealogical misdeeds. Williams insists that part of this process is her verbal articulation of her own sexuality, since typically "slaveholders attempt to locate the primary site of differentiation in the body of the female slave by equating the signs of sexual desire with the presence of 'mulatas y gente sucia' [mulattoes and lowly folk]" (81). That is, the original sexual desire for the black female slave is displaced onto the mulatto, thereby erasing from memory the primal desire for blackness. Literary representations of the tragic mulatto, she argues, function as a kind of liberal bravado that disguises "the initial problem of how the white founding father overcame his repugnance of the black woman in order to create the primal mulatto" ("From Dusky Venus" 135). Unfortunately, despite Williams's intriguing attempt to rescue María de Regla from the cultural politics of the novel, she acknowledges that "there is a retreat from the disruptive implications embedded in the celebration of black female beauty" (121).

Toward the conclusion of the novel, María gathers evidence among the Afro-Cuban classes of Don Cándido's duplicity. María's testimonial language is invoked, then, to counter her master's narrative by bearing witness to the genealogical secrets that Don Cándido has attempted to bury. She ultimately interprets the meaning of Cecilia's birthmark and unveils to Leonardo the incestuous nature of his relations with Cecilia. María's language undermines the authority of Don Cándido and potentially that of the narrator, since the knowledge she possesses renders the visual control over racial difference useless. Testimonial language is an aural means by which the reader can confirm the genealogical truths that the narrator has represented visually on the body. But in the end, the narrator's mediating authority is further sustained by addressing and containing the representations of oral language (Ette 85). María pretends to the role of a primary narrator by gathering the witnesses and narrating the submerged plot of miscegenation to the white scion, but the implications of black female legitimacy inherent in her narration ultimately prove too threatening. Despite Villaverde's claim to historical verisimilitude, her speech follows "literary stylizations of oral language" and is always italicized, thus marking it visually within the framework of the narrative (Ette 85). In this way, Villaverde preempts orality with the visual training we have already received before we encounter her testimony. Juan Gelpí argues that the language in italics, or *bastardía*, "marks (contains, represses, sets) the character that, not conforming to the law or to Cuban linguistic normality in the nineteenth century, represents his/her condition as a bastard, which in this case would be the person that is not a 'legitimate child' of the homeland" ("El discurso" 51). In the space of a few years, Cecilia is taken from her mother and María de Regla is exiled to the country for attempting to nurse her child along with Adela, removing her from her husband, Dionisio, her children, and her surrogate child, Adela. The maternal bond is broken into smaller and smaller pieces, fragmenting the ties that could have made a national family possible and ostracizing the very members of that alternative polity. Villaverde's pessimism regarding black resistance was premature, however; in the late 1870s, presumably when he was revising the novel in New York, many slaves were buying their way into freedom, and Afro-Cubans were playing a significant role in the Ten Years' War. They were also to play a major role in the war of 1895. Villaverde, in other words, ignores the historical fact that "Cuban slaves were protagonists in their own liberation" (Scott, "La dinámica" 91).

Although maternal genealogical lines temporarily pose as alternatives to Don Cándido's hypocritical need "to secure a title in Spain by constructing a genealogical tree in which not a drop of Jewish or Moorish blood was to be seen," ultimately the incestuous outcome of Don Cándido's actions expresses Villaverde's indecision between a nostalgia for a proper identification of the paternal line and a yearning for the mestizo culture that could replace the old paternal order (62). One indication of Villaverde's hesitancy to let go of this nostalgia is that genealogy remains indicative of legitimacy and ownership in the novel. The narrator identifies Rosa as "the legitimate mistress of the plantation" because "she had inherited it from her father." Don Cándido, in contrast, was not Creole and therefore "even though master in deed was not master by right [aunque señor de hecho, no lo era de derecho]" (208). The Spaniard's presence on the island and in the slave trade is illegitimate; his usurpation "in deed" of what is not his "by right" and his abuse of genealogy have drained Rosa's Creole wealth. She laments that she married a Spaniard, because "a Creole, a fellow countryman, would have treated me with more loyalty and decency." As a result of her mistake, she accuses Don Cándido that the money he has taken to provide for Cecilia "did not come out of your pocket but mine; better yet, you stole from me with one hand only to return it to me with the other" (152).

Don Cándido's confusion of Cuba's genealogy has resulted in financial loss and also the misdirected and destructive, rather than sanctified and procreative, affections among his family subjects; his children are incestuously attracted to apparent likenesses because they are ignorant of essential differences. Leonardo has an incestuous affection for his sister, Adela; has sexual relations with his half sister, Cecilia; and feels only a mild affection for his fiancée, the daughter of another Creole slave-owning family. Cándido's dishonesty tragically crosses Leonardo and Cecilia's erotic passions with familial affections. Unlike Sommer's claim for nineteenth-century national romances, Leonardo is fundamentally incapable of foundational desires; his relationship to Cecilia cannot symbolize the alternative to his father's colonial rule because his passions have no political dimension. Sommer argues that perhaps because of Cuba's prolonged colonial status its writers could not participate in the same romance between fictional affections and national aspirations ("Who Can Tell?").[8] While his erotic desire for Cecilia cannot be controlled, he has no passionate love of country because his "patriotism was of a platonic nature" (Villaverde, *Cecilia* 53). In fact, the novel suggests that it is precisely his ability to disavow political ambition in the interest of pursuing mulatto sexuality that is the foundation of Spanish colonial slave-owning power. Because Leonardo never occupied himself "with politics, and as much as it may have occurred to him that Cuba suffered like a slave, it never crossed his mind that he or some other Cuban should make an effort to make her free" (55). As Sánchez-Eppler contends, Villaverde represents "the inseparability of the exercise of power and desire . . . [and] makes available interconnected images of privilege and abuse that are inextricably racial, productive, and reproductive" (85). So even though, as Williams states it, "Leonardo defers the consolidation of his social power to the pursuit of sexual satisfaction with Cecilia," that deferment to satisfaction is, in fact, the very privilege of his white social power ("From Dusky Venus" 135).

By the time María de Regla pieces together the incestuous tale of the two young lovers and Leonardo takes interest in the genealogical basis of his passions, the narrative has already trained us to understand the tragic dimensions of his state. When Leonardo begins an oedipal investigation into his liaisons, he questions where the money to support Cecilia has come from, money we know has been drained from the Creole family line. Leonardo insists that Cecilia knows the money's source: "I read it in your eyes [Lo leo en tus ojos]," he claims. She responds: "Then you are a bad reader [Mal lector es usted entonces]" (272). The tragedy of Leonardo's failure to read the signs of racial and genealogical origins is dual: It is Cándido's tragedy because his preoccupation with a racially pure lineage has resulted in a failure to further the family name beyond Leonardo, and it is Leonardo's because his union with the object of his affections produces only social death. But the oedipal punishment is also Cecilia's, since she "meets her tragic end precisely because of the steps she takes to avoid the fate that was determined for her" (Williams, "From Dusky Venus" 131). Spanish rule produces an expulsion from the national household of Cecilia as well as other colored characters and the difference they represent; beginning in a prostitute jail, Cecilia ends up in a hospital for the mentally ill (Gelpí 57).

If Villaverde does offer the Cuban nation a curative to this moral determinism of colonialism, it is by ensuring that his readers are not bad readers like Leonardo.[9] We are not asked to arrive at the same oedipal confrontation with our own complicity in the crimes we have been investigating. This is because we do not discover anything inherently dangerous about the way we have been taught to read but are in fact confirmed in our suspicions that race and genealogy, despite the interventions of colonialism, are still knowable and controllable. The incestuous ending is intended to be cathartic for Villaverde's reader, but it is only thematically cathartic while cognitively deceiving us further. Race remains a visible category of identity, and therefore we have simply repeated an incestuous tautology: To see race is to see Cuba is to see race. Villaverde's narrative training attempts to convince us of the need to restore a legitimate patrimony that will sanction familial affections and avoid the dangers of racial mixing; the Spaniard is duly condemned, and the mestizo cultures are ostracized. If Villaverde expressed a yearning for the latter as an alternative, it is a desire made safe by the horror we are asked to feel toward the act of incest. The tragic enclosure of genealogy suggests Villaverde's despair that the damage may already be done and that consequently there is an inherent risk of oedipal self-deception if Cuban nationality is to be rooted in the island's colonial and miscegenated past. For Villaverde, Cuba must come to a postslavery awareness of the contradictions of its colonial past—its twisted and deeply rooted genealogical transgressions—but exactly how, or if, it could then redeem itself from the dark corners of its history remained to be seen.

"The Shadow of the Ethiopian"

George Washington Cable once stated that his novel *The Grandissimes* was "a study of the fierce struggle going on around me, regarded in the light of that past history—those beginnings—which had so differentiated Louisiana civilization from the American scheme of public society" (*Negro Question* 15). This struggle was a function of the larger cultural distinctions between Caribbean and U.S. cultures, particularly those due to more frequent racial mixing and greater numbers of middle-class, free colored citizens in the Caribbean.

Long after the Louisiana Purchase of 1803, New Orleans was still the site where U.S. culture wrestled with its own miscegenated legacies, which, according to Barbara Ladd, were often associated with the encroachment of French and Spanish cultures in the New World. Was New Orleans American or a foreign body within? By attempting to establish a cultural zone characterized by a plantation ideology that crosses national borders, my comparison between the novels by Cable and Villaverde suggests that New Orleans was both foreign and American and is a unique location to understand how American culture began attempting to erase its kinship with slavery and with the Caribbean. This erasure, as I have already suggested, is symptomatic of the emergence of new forms of plantation discourse in the United States, particularly in the North's conquest of the South and then its further expansion into Latin America. In this expansion of the Union, the United States consolidated its centers of power and pushed from them the cultures and legacies left in slavery's wake. I will show how Cable participates in this "de-Latinamericanization," as it were, of U.S. culture in his representations of French Creole life in Louisiana. Like Villaverde, Cable gives much attention to the local color of the early decades of the nineteenth century, a time he saw as representative of the South's colonial dependence. His aim is to exorcise that color and thus to liberate a new postcolonial national culture. Unlike Villaverde's historical confrontation with Cuba's tragic past, however, the signs of a consolidated national culture that emerge in Cable's novel, particularly in its romantic conclusion, demonstrate a kind of deus ex machina dismissal of the miscegenated, "Caribbean" history within the United States.

When northerners such as Cable's own family arrived in Louisiana after 1803, their Protestant ways clashed with the freer social interaction between races and the mesh of Catholic and African beliefs in the region. In the antebellum years, political measures that increasingly sought to integrate the region more completely into the Union helped to put the French Creoles on the defensive. In response to a northern perception of their cultural and racial blackness, whites appropriated the term *Creole* to refer only to those of European extraction born in Louisiana, even though the term originally referred to blacks born in the New World (Tregle). This appropriation was, ironically, symptomatic of the process of Americanization that they were intent on resisting. After the Civil

War, the white Creoles further disassociated themselves from the culture of the colored classes because of their African and Caribbean elements (G. M. Hall 98). They feared that "they might be confused with blacks, . . . as half-brother to the black, a sort of mixed breed stripped of blood pride as well as any claim to social or political preferment" (Tregle 172–73). In a Creole newspaper in the 1870s, one editorial proclaimed: "We must prove by our acts that we are not hybrid creatures, that we are a united whole!" (qtd. in Tregle 170).

Their fear of being identified with blackness had less to do with any real or imagined racial mixture in their ancestry than it did with a shift in the way the United States defined race after the emancipation of the slaves and ultimately after Reconstruction failed. In New Orleans, as in the Caribbean islands, birth and skin shade were the main indicators of social status and race. Once emancipation promised freedom to former slaves, it also made possible economic and social ascension for the already freed coloreds of New Orleans, who could lay claim to the same social privileges in the wider spectrum of the nation. However, they soon discovered that Jim Crow laws saw them as black as the former slaves. White-identified French Creoles also discovered that these laws often saw them as black as well, unless they could prove otherwise. This predicament is evidence of Joel Williamson's claim that disciplinary mechanisms in the United States had moved away from the epistemology of the eye to one of cultural behavior (*New People* 108).

Creole fears of a northern perception of their blackness were realized with Cable's literary success. In his hugely successfully 1880s reading tour with Mark Twain, his renditions of Creole songs and speaking style were often the highlight of their performances. One commentator wrote concerning his renditions: "But the singing . . . the go, and the lilt, and the solid, keen, enjoyment he took in it! And the strong pulsing wild melodies! Nigger from the ground up and full of life. The huge house woke up as if you had turned a dynamo on it" (qtd. in Turner 66). The Creoles likewise complained that Cable's representations of their dialect resembled "more the speech of black Virginia or South Carolina field hands than their own, closer to the 'orang-outan' barbarisms made familiar in the pages of the Carillon than to anything heard in their parlors" (qtd. in Tregle 175). Cable intended to expose Africanization of Creole life in two essays he published in 1886 in the *Century Magazine* on Creole folk traditions and speech patterns. Gavin Jones contends that Cable did so to show "how the African-American cultural products of dialect, song, and satire were transmitted to the white community even as they subverted it" (244–45). My reading of the novel insists that the subversion works both ways; French Creoles knew also how to subvert blackness through its appropriation, as is evident in their very appropriation of the term *Creole.*

The paradox of Cable's work is that despite his exploitation and exoticization of Creole "local color" in his fiction, he consistently urged southerners generally to "hasten to be no longer a unique people" (*Negro Question* 17). According to Cable, the southern tendency toward cultural isolation and provincialism, especially in its literary sensibilities, is due to the South's British-colonial mentality. He writes: "Our country was America but the impulses of our thought still found the old highways of English literature" (43–44). Like Villaverde, Cable exhibits desire for cultural emancipation from Old World models, a cultural enslavement he sees linked to slavery, and he also seeks to wrest from the legacies of slavery signs of the South's potential for integration into the "postcolonial" nation the North purported itself to be. Ultimately because of his desire to exorcise Latin influence and presence in American culture by means of its very representation, Cable was more a French Creole than perhaps he or the Creoles imagined.

The worst legacy of slavery for Cable was miscegenation, because it created a divergent and provincial cultural identity in the South. In his mind, if southern whites could understand that the divisions between North and South and between the civil rights of blacks and whites were unnatural, regionalism and miscegenation would dissipate. In his famous essay "The Freedman's Case for Equity," he insists that if a clear line can be drawn between the freedoms of personal choice, which pertain so directly to marriage and family (and hence property), and the civil rights to which every citizen is entitled, the security of those rights will assure that the races do not mix and that family lines remain racially pure. He asserts that "the common enjoyment of equal civil rights never mixed two such races; it has always been some oppressive distinction between them that . . . has done it" (161). That is, the hierarchical legacies of colonialism have simply exacerbated the attractions between the races. Maintaining a "natural" separation of racial genealogies means that our "natural" repulsion toward racial mixing will return and that southern cultural expression will naturally align itself with, rather than provincially diverge from, the Union.

The presence of people of mixed race, so prevalent in the Caribbean and Latin America, signifies for Cable oppression and lack of civilization. For this reason the South's only alternative to accepting its destiny as part of the Union is to be like Latin America. He urges that "when someone comes looking for Southrons [southerners], we can send them on to New Mexico, and say 'That is the New South. And make haste, friend, or they will push you on into South America, where we have re-shipped the separate sort of books printed for the Southern market.'" (48) In Latin America and the Caribbean, "Nationalization *by* fusion of bloods is the maxim of barbarous times and peoples. Nationalization *without* racial confusion is ours to profess and to procure. . . . to make national unity without hybridity—the world has never seen it done as we have got to do it" (130). Cable's "South" is an ideology of difference that seeks to distinguish civilization from barbarism and is shown here to be pliable enough to allow Cable to cast responsibility for the barba-rism of interracial mixing onto the lands beyond U.S. borders. Cable's rhetoric concerning the barbarism of Latin America is, of course, not new to U.S. cultural polemics. However, coming as it does in the last decades of the nineteenth century, when the United States begins to cast its imperialist eye toward the lands to the south, it is symptomatic of the globalization of plantation structures that seek new and wider frontiers between a more consolidated, "civilized" center of power and the many manifestations of barbarism that it must conquer. These symptoms of the plantation's globalization are both a product of U.S. imperialism and the reason why the North, and U.S. culture since the Civil War, has been blind to the truth of itself as the seat of imperial ambition.

The Grandissimes is the story of a long family feud that begins when Epaminandas Fusilier wins the hand of marriage of a Natchez-Tchoupi-toulas princess, Lufki-Hamma, against the competing desires of Demos-thenes de Grapion. The feud's latest offense occurs when Epaminandas's descendent, Agricola Fusilier, kills a de Grapion, the spouse of Aurora Nancanou, in a duel over a card game. Honoré Grandissime, the up-and-coming leader of the Fusilier family, falls in love with Aurora only to discover that his own family has held on to de Grapion plantation land and thus left Aurora and her daughter, Clotilde, in economic de-cline. To add to our confusion, Honoré has a half brother, Honoré, f.m.c. ("free man of color"), who, although ostracized by the white side of the family, is a relatively powerful landlord who happens to control Aurora's living quarters.

The eyes through which we view these frontiers of civilization are those of Joseph Frowenfeld, a northerner who arrives in New Orleans in 1805, the year that the slave trade is declared illegal and that the United States begins its efforts to Americanize the new Louisiana Territory.

Thus, the novel explores the beginnings of a process of integration that the North was still trying to finish in the 1870s when Cable composed the novel. Frowenfeld arrives sick, having lost his immediate family to disease. His mission is to find, or at least found, a genealogy in the South in order for the South's integration into the Union to have its symbolic representation and justification, and the fact that "what Frowenfeld [learns] is never any new moral perspectives, but only a more detailed knowledge of the society he has come to join," signifies Cable's sincere offering of Frowenfeld as just such a symbol (Rubin 83); in the novel's conclusion he finds posterity and builds a successful business as an apothecary.

Lying on his sickbed shortly after his arrival, he sees the face of Clotilde, whom he later marries:

> He turned his eyes, and through the white gauze of the mosquito-bar saw, for an instant, a strange and beautiful young face; but the lids fell over his eyes, and when he raised them again the blue-turbaned black nurse was tucking the covering about his feet.
> "Sister!"
> No answer.
> "Where is my mother?"
> The negress shook her head. (12)

That his future wife is confused with his mother, sister, and a black woman is emblematic of the genealogical confusion that he will encounter in the Deep South and that if not sorted out, Cable implies, can potentially result in oedipal entrapment. His "perusal of this newly found book, the Community of New Orleans," and eventual mastery of the genealogical mysteries he encounters represent Cable's hope for a northern adoption of the Deep South's history with no attendant oedipal baggage (12). Frowenfeld steps into a world that Cable depicts without a center. There are only multiple margins: Frowenfeld is the marginalized immigrant; Honoré, f.m.c., the marginalized mulatto; and the French Creoles, the marginalized U.S. minority. Initially, Frowenfeld is aware that his own marginalization is akin to that of the mulatto (155), but, in the end, Joseph's successful romantic integration starkly opposes the mulatto's expulsion from the community. In other words, the novel represents the successful Americanization of the Deep South, centered on the healing rationality of the northern apothecary, at the cost of the expulsion of the history of miscegenation. Cable's novel does not satirize

"'Yankee' intervention in the South," as Gavin Jones argues, but rather furthers its assimilationist aims (259).

The structure of the narrative as detective story, clearly influential in William Faulkner's *Absalom, Absalom!,* indicates that Cable "recognized that the old forms of fiction were inadequate and that the complexities of southern life required a new and complex kind of writing" (Bendixen 25). For this he has been recognized as the founder of more morally complex Southern fiction (33). The fact that the crime is solved, however, suggests, as I will explore in chapter 4, that Faulkner rejected the ease of Cable's romantic solution and sought to retrofit the southern crime story investigated by the North in more tragic and oedipal terms. Frowenfeld and his northern cohort, Dr. Keene, sort through a multitude of stories, in varying degrees of dialect and narrative detail, that provide different versions of the family history. As in Villaverde's novel, the mystery of family secrets is represented as a visually impenetrable text. For Frowenfeld, the model reader, the tales of the family's past are "little more than a *thick mist* of strange names, places and events; yet *there shone a light* of romance upon it that filled it with color and populated it with phantoms. Frowenfeld's interest rose—was allured into the mist— and there was left *befogged*" (15, emphasis added). While listening to Aurora, "even in the *bright recollection* of the lady and her talk [Frowenfeld] became involved among *shadows,* . . . of hints, allusions, faint unspoken admissions . . . unfinished speeches" (96, emphasis added). As the reader listens to the narrations of the family past, at times told in difficult dialect or in elusive form, aural multiplicity curiously produces a visual confusion. That is, rather than presenting us with a modernist reading of narrative truth such as that explored by Faulkner, this plurality is filtered through an objectifying narrative gaze that helps the reader to gain control of signification in the novel. The function of the distance of the narrator's perspective is, on one hand, welcoming to the position of the northern reader vis-à-vis New Orleans, and on the other, useful for the southern reader who is perhaps too close and too familiar to be self-critical.

Honoré Grandissime explains to Frowenfeld why southerners refuse to listen to outside criticism: "My-de'-seh, it never occurs to us that in this matter we are interested, and therefore disqualified, *witnesses*. We say we are not understood; that the jury (the civilized world) renders its decision *without viewing the body;* that we are judged from a distance. We forget that we ourselves are *too close to see distinctly,* and so continue, a *spectacle* to civilization, sitting in a horrible *darkness*" (155, emphasis added). The emphasis indicates how the narrative's projected gaze intends to produce crucial knowledge of the Creole by making his blindness visible to the reader. We read and comprehend the darkness that impedes the Creole's ability to see himself because the narrative trains us much like Villaverde's to depend upon its visual guidance, casting "sudden flashes of light . . . upon dark places," to borrow from two of the chapters' titles, in order to expose the miscegenated genealogy of the Grandissime family. The visual fog that precedes these stories increases our dependence on the narrator by virtue of his ability to control the lighting on the New Orleans set.

For example, just as Villaverde initially conceals Cecilia's genealogy from the reader, Cable's novel opens with a masked ball where the novel's central cast of Creole characters portrays their legendary Creole ancestors: the Indian Queen Lufki-Hamma, the casket girl, the monk, and the French settler.[10] The narrator encourages the reader: "[B]ut all this is an outside view; let us draw nearer and see what chance may discover to us behind those four masks" (3). What little we learn in this opening scene is that behind these masks lie hidden kinship. Honoré, dressed as Lufki-Hamma, declares to Aurora behind her monk mask, "we will unmask to each other, and . . . find each other first cousins" (6). Behind his Indian mask, Honoré speaks to Agricola in the slave dialect, and Agricola insists on knowing who is behind the mask. Honoré responds rhetorically: "Don't you know your ancestors, my little son?" (3). Here Honoré bitingly suggests that both black and Indian blood are in his and Agricola's lineage, a fact denied by the Creoles in Cable's day.

The reader's visual training exposes the dark places in the Creole family tree, unveiling the contradictions of a society that insists on racial hierarchy while it simultaneously transgresses the very color line on which that hierarchy depends. Specifically, Cable exposes these contradictions by representing the arbitrary social and economic differentiations that the Creole society insists on between Honoré Grandissime and his mulatto half brother despite their almost twinlike appearances throughout the narrative. Similar to the early confusion between characters in Villaverde's novel, both brothers make appearances early on without the narrator helping us to discern between them. Distinguishing between them is the reader's, and Frowenfeld's, most important task in deciphering the Grandissime family history and is the key to the novel's romantic resolution.

Despite its careful control over visual readings of racial difference, however, Cable's narrative gaze is forced to borrow from the aural distinctions between the brothers' dialects in order to clarify for the reader their distinct identities and histories. This loan is the site at which Cable performs the exorcism of miscegenated cultures in the novel. Cable's racial ambivalence is apparent in the fact that even though the half brothers attended the same Parisian school, Honoré, f.m.c., can scarcely speak or spell English, while his brother is the only Creole in the novel shown capable of speaking standard English (Elfenbein 57). The linguistic whiteness of the white Honoré betrays traces of blackness around its edges, however, not unlike the edges of blackness that Villaverde's "knowing eye" traces on Cecilia's lips. As Jenny Franchot insists, visual markers of dialect, such as italics, "signal the transition from one language to another as a 'descent'; from the standard into the variant, from the naturalized imperial viewpoint into the marginalizes speech of the Other. In this way italics function as typographical equivalents of the stereotype" (514). When Frowenfeld argues that the darkness that haunts the story of the Grandissime family is "the shadow of the Ethiopian," Honoré lets traces of the African-infused Creole dialect appear in his speech for the first and only time in the novel: "'When I try sometimes to stand outside and look at it, I am *ama-aze* at the length, the blackness of the shadow!' (He was so deep in earnest that he took no care of his English.) 'It is the Nemesis w'ich, instead of coming afteh, glides along by the side of the morhal, political, commercial, social mistake! It blanches, my-de'seh, ow whole civilization!'" (155). And as the narrator earlier explains, even the Grandissimes have crossed the color line indiscreetly: "[T]he true, main Grandissime stock, on which the Fusiliers did early, ever, and yet do, love to marry, has kept itself lily-white ever since France has loved lilies—as to marriage, that is; as to less responsible entanglements, why, of course—" (22).

Cable's neglecting to name the act of miscegenation outright but merely suggesting it with the use of dashes, reminiscent of Villaverde's refusal to name the father outright, implies that Honoré is not as white as we may have presumed, but white enough that Cable's reader allows him to pass. Jones explains that "Cable's ambiguous allusions" were particularly threatening to the white Creoles because they "failed to set limits to the extent of intermixture" (247). And yet they also serve to mediate the assimilation, or passing, of Creole society into the Union. At one point the narrator seems to provide a cover for this passing when he declares that the appearance of the white Honoré (who does, in fact, have a measure of African ancestry) "was a dazzling contradiction of the notion that a Creole is a person of mixed blood" (38). Aurora Nancanou, Honoré's first cousin and eventual wife, and her daughter, Clotilde, also carry the suspicious mark of some distant act of miscegenation in their "black hair . . . [that] rippled once or twice" (140). Nevertheless, these suspicions of blackness are allayed for Cable's northern reader by the fact that they are so easily transformed into signs of a kind of European whiteness (Aurora and Clotilde are described as exhibiting "half-Gallic, half-classic beauty"; 139). If the colonialism of European culture historically was seen as the root cause of miscegenation in the Caribbean and the Deep South, Cable asks his northern reader to allow the more subtle signs of blackness to pass under the guise of Europe, since this is the Creole's best chance for integration into the Union. Ladd explains that the white Creole posed a threat in U.S. imagination because he was "someone who might look like an American and claim to be so . . . but who carries within him- or herself traces of the displaced and who might at some point act traitorously to undermine the progressive nation" (xv). The Creole's assimilation into the union simultaneously enacts the U.S. desire to offer itself as the "post" to European imperialism by symbolically reversing the direction of conquest and assimilation without confronting directly the Africanized sectors of the South.

Cable's offer of redemption for the South is facilitated by his narrative marginalization and eventual expulsion of the shadow half brother. Like Villaverde's María de Regla, however, he initially appears as the potential hero since he represents mediation between, and the confluence of, two conflicting cultures. He also conveys crucial knowledge of interracial and interfamilial relations to the reader. His identity lies at the borders between French and English, black and white, Creole and American; his letters are the most difficult narratives for the reader to decipher because they are written in the phonetically spelled and poorly learned English of a native French speaker. But like María de Regla, his linguistic and racial differences, although useful in helping the reader to recognize the kinship between the races within one family line, become too burdensome for the narrative to sustain their utility.

The entire subplot of Honoré, f.m.c., and his pursuit of the mulatto Palmyre's hand provides a shadow by which Cable's reader can measure the primary romances of Honoré and Aurora and Joseph and Clotilde. Louis Rubin observed Cable's "dangerous tendency" to be willing "to include side by side within one story a conventionally romantic love plot in picturesque setting and an urgent social commentary, without being greatly concerned about their interaction" (103; see also Richardson 8). What is dangerous about their interaction may be precisely what proves useful for Cable's purposes, however. The traces of Honoré and Aurora's blackness are eventually exaggeratedly "blanched" in contrast to this failed romance. Palmyre, we are told, is a relative of Agricola, possibly his daughter, and was once forced to marry a *bozal* slave of former African royalty named Bras-Coupé because of her infatuation with the white Honoré Grandissime. Bras-Coupé, a maroon, is killed when he returns to the plantation to demand that his wife be freed to go away with him. The narrator clearly associates Bras-Coupé's rebellion with the rebellion of Santo Domingo, and Agricola's denial of the slave's claim to a piece of the planter's genealogy and Bras-Coupé's death itself are attempts to excise from the family historical echoes of that rebellion. Although much has been made of Cable's liberating use of this story of African royalty in chains, its place in the narrative is essentially an interjection (it was, in fact, originally a rather unsuccessful short story that Cable resurrected for the novel). Although Cable portrays his colored characters sympathetically, "he also seems to feel a combination of fear of and fascination with their suppressed and animal-like sexuality and violence" (Campbell 168). That is, more fully rounded and humanized depictions of marginalized characters or pity for their tragic outcome do not translate into a sanctioning of blackness nor of miscegenation, as Elfenbein and others have assumed. It does signify Cable's willingness, so unusual for his time, to come to terms with the consequences of slavery, but in the end those terms relegate blackness and miscegenation to a permanent state of tragic exile in order to catalyze the white Creole romance.

If Agricola does not give black rebellion sanction through marriage, neither does he tolerate the milder form of resistance to his white planter ideology that Honoré, f.m.c.'s, marriage to Palmyre would signify. To the extent that he refuses to acknowledge mulatto rights, Agricola also disqualifies himself for integration into the Union. This is because, as Ladd argues, "black and mulatto characters are the post–Civil War white southerner's best tools for exploring the pressing issue of his or her own capacity for, and resistance to, assimilation to a national ideal" (80). Frowenfeld, on the other hand, encourages Honoré, f.m.c.'s, marriage to Palmyre because it would make the mulatto "a leader and deliverer of his people. . . . he understands [the colored population's] wants. He knows their wrongs. He is acquainted with laws and men. He could speak for them. It would not be insurrection—it would be advocacy"

(291). His role of advocacy never materializes because Agricola refuses the mulatto's request to buy Palmyre's freedom and to marry her, further marginalizing her into the role of the vengeful voodoo priestess. Marriage implies an audacious claim to social equality, but Agricola's denial paradoxically implies that he acknowledges his own paternity of Palmyre, his own act of miscegenation. Clearly he prefers this admission because, even if it is self-incriminating, miscegenation sustains a racial hierarchy from which he benefits.

The darker rebelliousness and sexuality of Palmyre is fueled by Agricola's duplicity regarding his own paternity and is only temporarily quelled by Frowenfeld's more rational advocacy of moderation, which is related directly to his ability to reject Cable's portrayal of her intensely sexualized personality (Elfenbein and Rubin). The stereotype of the quadroon's sexuality is not toned down but rather heightened and then ultimately dismissed as nonexistent by the northerner Frowenfeld (Germanic and Protestant) in order to criticize the moral weakness of the southern slave owner (French and Catholic). Cable creates around Palmyre a love triangle of the African and the two Honorés (one mulatto and the other a white Creole) in order to expose the covert operations of the slave owner and their dire consequences. Faulkner would later revise this triangular confrontation of the contradictions between marriage and racial difference when Thomas Sutpen tells his white son to prevent his mulatto son, Charles Bon, from marrying Sutpen's daughter, Judith, because Bon is a black man, not because he is her brother. In other words, Faulkner suggests that when miscegenation is the chosen demon of history, the result is the tragic insularity of U.S. postslavery culture.

Palmyre refuses Honoré, f.m.c.'s, hand because she wants "vengeance," not advocacy (291). The mulatto then spends twenty years funding Palmyre's eventual exile before he takes his own life. The tragedy of this subplot is that it unnecessarily drains the South of its wealth. The nearly $1 million he spends on Palmyre "is only a part of the pecuniary loss which this sort of thing costs Louisiana" (291). Cable criticizes miscegenation and the hypocrisies it necessitates because it drains the Creole patrimony, as it did Rosa's family, and weakens the potential for a strong postcolonial stance. Cable's implication is that the hypocritical miscegenator must be expelled, along with his mulatto kin.

These unfortunate outcomes are ultimately not tragic, however, because in their interaction with the romantic plot they reinforce the role of the "white" marriages of Honoré and Aurora and Joseph and Clotilde as the symbolic reunion of family and cultural differences, a reparation of financial loss within the white family, and the promise of a newly integrated and Americanized South. These marriages represent the cultural qualities of the South's plantation history that are salvageable and that can be welcomed into the Union. Cable was clearly aware of the profound debt Creole culture owed to African influence, as Jones persuasively argues, but it appears that although his portrayal of a hybrid Creole culture was unsettling to Creoles, the many "masked meanings" of the novel's Africanisms and its hints of miscegenation are not solely directed at exposing white Creole hypocrisy (Jones 261). They indicate Cable's preference for swallowing the bitter pill of a remote racial hybridity if it would mean an end to further obfuscations of racial and cultural difference in the South. These darker stories are not without a taste of Cable's criticism of racism or without a tinge of tragedy, but romance dominates the novel's conclusion, manifested in the nearly incestuous but ultimately redemptive marriages (Honoré and Aurora, it will be recalled, are first cousins, and Joseph almost mistook Clotilde for his sister and mother). This romantic collapse of the novel portends Cable's writing career, which increasingly found recourse to romantic and morally simplified views of the South under the pressures of the North's postbellum literary tastes (Kreyling). Despite what appears to be his attempt to broaden the boundaries of American culture, he repeats the cultural marginalization of the blacks and of miscegenation in a Creole context, expelling their more obvious markers beyond the newly reinforced bounds of a national community.

Both novels demonstrate both that plantation discourse had found its way into the work of some of slavery's most outspoken late nineteenth-century critics in the American South and in Cuba and that the search for postslavery autonomy from slavery's legacies would have to continue. They also demonstrate that U.S. and Cuban cultures, if not those of the rest of the Caribbean as well, took slavery as a common point from which they diverged in crucial ways. In the case of Villaverde, the cultures of the colored classes are the site of resistance to Cuba's colonization, because there we find the hypocrisy of the planter class exposed. They are also a dangerous site of desire, however. Leonardo's horrific discovery of the meaning of his incestuous desire for Cecilia is Villaverde's warning that the cultures of the colored classes, so attractive to the *independistas* of the late nineteenth century, could be an incestuous trap because those cultures are the offspring of Spain's enslavement of Cuba. Villaverde's imagined Cuban national identity is positioned rather precariously because the genealogy of the new nation cannot be disentangled from either Spain or the colored classes. The romantic conclusion to Cable's novel suggests that Cable felt a greater optimism about the possibility of integration, but his optimism is facilitated by the expanded frontiers of U.S. power and by his narrow conception of the differences that need to be integrated. Villaverde's entrapment is perhaps accentuated by virtue of the fact that Cubans, particularly those in exile who were witness to the impending encroachment of the United States in Cuba affairs, had no recourse to an expansive, externalized territory of imagined barbarism. As long as the United States imagined a "New South" beyond its borders, its internal contradictions would perhaps never have to reach their incestuous ruin.

In the U.S. cultural imagination, the incestuous implications of slavery's hidden genealogies surfaced later than they did in Cuba. Indeed, impending incestuous ruin is, in part, what Faulkner undoubtedly meant to expose some fifty years later in *Absalom, Absalom!*, when Charles Bon arrives to force a recognition of denied paternity. The parallels that we find between novels of postslavery in the Americas are perhaps ripples that, like Benítez-Rojo's description of *mestizaje*, "repeat their unknowns" (*Repeating Island* 26). As Faulkner's Charles Bon discovers, and Villaverde's Leonardo as well, genealogical searches into the origins of the Americas cause "incomprehensible fury and fierce yearning" because the centers of power, when they generate these searches, are always too far removed from the sites of their own misdeeds (*Absalom* 373). That is to say, postslavery national cultures simultaneously recognize themselves, and encounter a threatening difference, in the miscegenated cultures to which they have given birth.

3 Reading behind the Face

Martín Morúa Delgado, Charles W. Chesnutt, and Frances E. W. Harper

IN THE REALIST fictions of such writers as George Washington Cable and Cirilo Villaverde, as we saw, blackness provides the stepping stones to the construction of a new national identity, but ultimately the difference of blackness, Cable's "shadow of the Ethiopian," cannot be fully tolerated. As Kenneth Warren has observed of U.S. realism in the nineteenth century, "what began as an attack on slavery and caste threatened to metamorphose into an attack on the idea of African-American culture" (85).[1] Realism's attraction to local color was partly due to a white fear that hybridity and social equality might lead to a disappearance of the difference of blackness that would in turn signify the infiltration of an invisible blackness into the national family. The phenomenon of passing suggested that physical markers of race were insufficient and that some invisible blackness nevertheless persisted. Mulattoes, one step removed from passing, were useful characters to criticize racial prejudice, but any anxiety caused by their ambiguity had to be allayed by the narrative's "knowing eye" that traced the more subtle, but nevertheless knowable, differences.

Samira Kawash notes, as we saw in the previous chapter, that "while the implicit critique of the color line embodied in the mulatto might be a powerful one, in practice several strategies existed for recuperating the mulatto as evidence of the necessity of racial order rather than its negation" (133). As Thomas Otten also suggests, "to construct racial identity so that it can escape detection is to construct it so that it must constantly be worried about" (231). As the color line was explored and critiqued more aggressively, it became more necessary to identify the terms by which racial difference lay "inside a person . . . as an interior element, as a secret buried" (Otten 229). This fear of a disappearing space of difference was due to a number of factors, all of which contributed to the possibility of blackness becoming less remote and hence more mixed with white Cuban and U.S. culture: the collapse of slavery; the possibility of increasing and more varied social mobility, especially for blacks; and tremendous advances in transportation and technology, which threatened to make regional differences obsolete. As U.S. capitalism was busy industrializing the South and centralizing sugar mills in Cuba, black flight to urban areas proliferated and interracial contact between blacks and whites increased. To different degrees, then, both nations felt the need for legislation that would stave off the potential effects of this proximity by finding adequate legal definitions of blackness (Kawash 96). Even though Cuba advocated a graded color line as opposed to the one-drop rule and never saw the passage of laws quite as explicitly separatist as Jim Crow laws, postslavery segregation was not unknown in business practices and in public places on the island.[2]

Thus, realism contributed to each culture's need to codify differences politically, culturally, and socially. Warren notes that "as the realist novel sharpened its critique of social discriminations, it began to depend more heavily on the distinctions it challenged, especially with regards to matters of race" (84). Realism depends on regional spaces that are always different, and in the words of James Cox, "always ending. That is the fate of their imaginative space before the ever encroaching Union" (783). The local color of regionalism, then, can be read as the site of nation-making, of a negotiated inclusion and a backhanded exclusion of difference. And the difference most frequently exploited in realist fiction at the turn of the twentieth century in Cuba and in the United States is that of black cultural expressions that bear the mark of their African origins and hence constitute a potentially threatening alternative nation to the one ultimately formed by fiction. In the early decades of the twentieth century, both countries launched a vitriolic attack on Africanization, demonizing traces of African cultural practices as beyond the bounds of their democratic impulses. This literature was helpful in identifying those elements of Africanization that could be assimilated and those that could not.

This thirst for difference can also be understood as a longing for a society in which difference was less threatening because it was more easily identified and kept separate from whiteness. Arlene Elder has used a Salem witch trial as a metaphor for a postbellum racial epistemology in the United States. Cotton Mather warns his people that they cannot always trust what they see, that the Prince of Darkness can appear as an Angel of Light, and that therefore extreme caution must be exercised so as to avoid visual deception, to avoid permitting the presence of darkness among them. This is the kind of epistemological warning that Cable and Villaverde provide for their nations. In their outline of racism, they essentially redraw their own line between whiteness and blackness (although the line is different in each case) and warn that if their respective nations are not careful, they may allow the infiltration of racial pollution. Like Cotton Mather's warning, their position operates within an ideology of essentialized racial difference, pointing merely to the limitations of an untrained eye to perceive that difference. Elder explains that the rise of the Ku Klux Klan in the latter decades of the nineteenth century was a response to the discovery that eyes were insufficient to identify racial difference. As Eva Saks has demonstrated, miscegenation law in the United States during this same period wrestled with and reproduced an intense anxiety concerning the invisibility of race. This was also apparent, according to Verena Martínez-Alier, in Cuban legal debates about inheritance. The protection of white property that motivated much miscegenation law pushed the courts in the direction of genealogy as the determining factor of race and inheritability. However, "tracing the defendant's genealogy became the equivalent of a title search, the search for an authoritative representation of race" that remained elusive (Saks 52). The frantic attempts by whites to control the knowability and separability of race often led to simplistic solutions to racial categorizations, solutions that harked back to a mythical time under slavery when a black person was more simply identified as the one enslaved.

The writers discussed in this chapter—the Cuban Martín Morúa Delgado, and Charles W. Chesnutt and Frances E. W. Harper, both from the United States—expose the personality and limitations of white culture's gaze, which often masked itself in the guise of realism and which produced political, historical, and literary narratives to sustain itself. In their fiction, we see exposed the contradiction between realism's "democratic openness" and its tendency, as I have shown, to reify its subjects into inviolable categories of difference (Sundquist, "Realism" 502). In each case, however, this attack is launched by means of loosening the white reader's cognitive grip on the racial signifiers apparent on the black body and thereby transforming the terms on which racial difference is identified and imputed moral meaning. Although these texts ostensibly remain realist, this interrogation of the politics of seeing links them to the impulses of much postcolonial magical realism, which,

Stephen Slemon argues, "in its language of narration [reflects] real conditions of speech and cognition" (411). In other words, using a racialized language they have themselves inherited from slavery and colonialism, they interrogate the very production of knowledge and speech
about what we see and know. Even though their narratives sustain the
notion that racial difference is knowable, "the unity or density of [their]
. . . expression," in the words of Wilson Harris, "is paradox," because
their realism is "a cloak" that only faintly disguises multiple "layers of
reality" (*Womb* xvii).

This destabilization of the white gaze of realism is accomplished by
the authors' somewhat risky employment of the very narrative strategies
they wish to interrogate. Concerning this intention, Chesnutt writes:
"The subtle almost indefinable feeling of repulsion toward the Negro,
which is common to most Americans—cannot be stormed and taken by
assault; the garrison will not capitulate, so their position must be mined,
and we will find ourselves in their midst before they think it" (reproduced in H. Chesnutt 21). As Henry Louis Gates has argued about African American literature generally, these writers have a "complex and
ironic relation to their criticism. . . . [Theirs is] a literature . . . inextricably bound in dialogue with its potentially harshest critics" (*Figures in
Black* 26). These authors represent in many ways the very insinuation of
black culture into the mainstream that whites feared, a fear that motivated much realist fiction. My readings insist on the ideological complexity of this task, which is not unlike that of passing itself. The act of
passing clearly destabilizes the controlling mechanisms of white cognition of race since, like these novelists who write themselves into a white
public, a person who passes defies the color line that presumably would
have made his or her transition into a white world impossible. However,
passing also is a capitulation to those very mechanisms and is thus potentially complicit with the prevailing ideology since it accepts de facto
the color line. To the extent that these authors abandon representations
of a lived and historically conditioned blackness in the interest of exposing the social constructions of race, they leave behind viable forms of social, cultural, and racial difference within the national family, and their
insinuation loses its revisionary force because of its apparent collapse
under the pressures of white social power.

Nevertheless, in each case, the revision of the terms on which narrative communicates genealogical knowledge to the reader does more than
simply belie white claims of racial purity and genealogical rights to ownership. Rather, these writers open avenues for identifying alternative

claims on the national inheritance that are potentially inclusive of divergent genealogies. Their novels place the impersonal and omniscient narrative points of view we saw in the previous examples of realist fiction in the eyes of particular characters and thereby expose the political personality of such a gaze. They demonstrate how white genealogies have been constructed on the basis of the black family's being seen from the outside.[3]

Unlike much of the fiction that precedes the novels discussed in this chapter, the authors do not represent miscegenation as the ultimate taboo or evil for the polity or for the individual. Rather, as Heather Hathaway argues of mulatto writers, "the rejection of parental and spousal responsibility by the socially dominant, white, male miscegenator is the crime that cannot be excused" (164). Hathaway further explains that this denial of responsibility fragments the family because "the very life of a mulatto offspring confirms a blood tie, yet the exogamy taboo against acknowledging this tie prohibits that same relationship" (154). The refusal to grant to the child the paternal name, in turn, sets the stage for potentially realizing other, more pressing taboos, such as incest and fratricide. This denial is certainly central in the Cable and Villaverde novels discussed in the previous chapter, but the focus of those narratives is more intensely placed on the consequences of that illicit relationship, namely the racial differences that miscegenation threatens to elide visually. Cable and Villaverde lead us to believe that if paternal responsibility were accepted, it would make little difference, because the plague of miscegenation and its crisis of similitude have already been set loose on the polity. For both writers, incest is the potential punishment for miscegenation, a sin of the colonial past. Black and white citizens of the polity do not properly know their own kinship because their genealogies have been kept hidden and because they were crossed by the colonizer in the remote past. Liberation from colonialism, according to Villaverde and Cable, cannot entirely escape a longing for a "natural" order of racial separatism and the expulsion of the father miscegenator.

Because they are less interested in breaking the bonds of colonialism than in obtaining a rightful share of the national inheritance for at least the mulatto population, Morúa, Chesnutt, and Harper show that the secrets of affiliation that have caused familial and racial confusion are exploited by those with substantial social power; indeed, they show such exploitation to be the very means of sustaining that power. Rather than being exclusive of the father miscegenator, these writers are more interested in the need to be inclusive of the offspring. In other words, they suggest that the original sin of colonialism is not miscegenation but the disavowal of the mulatto offspring's claims to the national patrimony.

This chapter will explore Morúa's companion novels *Sofía* (1891) and *La familia Unzúazu* (1901), Chesnutt's *The Marrow of Tradition* (1901), and Harper's *Iola Leroy* (1893). In each novel, we find a father figure from the past, who, like the absentee slave owner, has failed to meet his paternal responsibilities; as a result, key genealogical truths have been withheld from his descendents. More important, however, we find a male character who, like the overseer, has stepped in to fill the void left by the absent father, a usurper whose substantial social power is sustained by his attempts to control the succession of property with a manipulation of public knowledge of the family's genealogical origins. These writers employ a variety of means, more modest than Cable's or Villaverde's, to help the reader gain proper cognition of genealogical origins, to provide the reader with needed knowledge by virtue of their emphasis on nonvisual kinds of cognition. They appeal to our moral, sentimental, and aural sensibilities to aid us in the pursuit of narrative and genealogical understanding. We are not trained to see racial difference and therefore to comprehend the injustices of the color line; rather, we apprehend those injustices by virtue of the failure of others to acknowledge kinship and of the pathos that results. We are trained to read character, to read behind the face, behind the facades of "race," good name, and reputation.

"Not Everything We See Is True"

Born of a Basque father and a free woman of color of the Gangá nation, Martín Morúa Delgado is a fascinating and troubling figure in the early years of Cuba's independence. He initially established himself as a successful journalist in the 1870s, when he developed his ideas concerning racial integration and offered redefinitions of the role of slaves and slave owners for a future independent Cuba. His interest in fiction began in 1886, the same year slavery was abolished in Cuba. Although initially an autonomist opposed to the independence effort, he eventually joined in the independence cause and spent 1882–1886 in exile in the United States. Morúa's fiction attempts to speak to the politically radical and largely black community of tobacco growers in Tampa, Florida, where he wrote the novel, and to Cuba's white Creole loyalists, in order to bring both groups to a middle ground of racial moderation in the interest of Cuba's political independence.

After 1898, Morúa became the first colored senator in the newly independent nation and a strong advocate of José Martí's revolutionary vision of racial democracy. Like Martí, he believed that black Cubans must unite with whites as "children of the same mother, the patria, Cuba" and must "become enmeshed with one another in a strong embrace [confundirse en estrecho abrazo]" in order to effectively "raise a hand and with a deadly and infectious pen, fatally wound father Spain" (*Integración* 52, 88). In no uncertain terms for Morúa, this unification necessitated the end of considering Afro-Cuban culture a distinct entity from what he saw as Cuban national culture. Philip Howard accurately concludes that Morúa's career as an essayist "reflects [his] internalization and acceptance of the racial inferiority of blacks constructed by whites and reinforced by slavery and the caste system" (168). This, of course, was prior to the 1930s and 1940s when, in the face of increasing Americanization on the island, writers such as Alejo Carpentier and Nicolás Guillén lauded Afro-Cuban expression as an icon of a resistant and independent Cuban nationality. Morúa has been seen as a precursor to the Afro-Cuban movement (Herrera McElroy), but if this is true, he is an example of how such appeals to a notion of blackness often serve nationalistic purposes while replicating the older forms of intolerance toward unassailable Africanized difference. Morúa ultimately does away with forms of blackness that are the products of marked cultural and historical experiences and that he sees as merely divisive.

Although as a senator he frequently fought for laws that would end discrimination in the workplace and elsewhere, he also fought tenaciously against the majority of Afro-Cubans who felt that the history of slavery and the continued legacy of racism since independence necessitated the formation of a political party dedicated to protecting the Cuban constitution's stance against racial inequality before the law. To form a party on the basis of racial considerations was, for Morúa, antipatriotic because it violated the raceless vision of nationhood most political elites ascribed to Martí. In Morúa's view, emancipation and independence had relegated racial concerns moot. To continue to talk of race was to succumb to the racist ideologies of slavery itself, since slave society had depended on the color line. For this reason he condemned any demands for the end of racial discrimination (Howard 194). Thus, when his Liberal party (then the political majority) authored a law to outlaw the Partido Independiente de Color (PIC; Independent Party of Color), formed in 1908 to fight racial discrimination, the law was named the "Ley Morúa" in recognition of its philosophical inspiration. While Morúa lay on his deathbed in 1910, the proposal was signed into law. Tragically, in 1912, the law was used as justification for the death of thousands of blacks who rebelled against it because the Cuban government refused to take any special measures to address the blatant social and political inequalities between blacks and whites. Indeed, Martí's vision of racial brotherhood had become the myth of Cuban nationhood; and to aver that racism remained a problem, as did the thousands of members of the PIC, was seen as tantamount to heresy and racism itself. The dogmatic view of a raceless nationalism led to justifications of official anti-black violence and government actions against the practices of *santeros* and *ñañigos* and against other elements of Afro-Cuban culture.[4]

For Morúa, lumping all colored people together on the basis of skin color alone was a "classification of slaveowning origin," and to campaign explicitly against public segregation was "just continuing the old slave behavior of begging masters for favors" (*Integración* 213; Helg 41). Morúa found commonality with Booker T. Washington, believing that "patience, work, and self-improvement" were the only ways to achieve equality (Helg 41). This was the cause of a sore disagreement with his archenemy within the Afro-Cuban political community, Juan Gualberto Gómez, who believed that black and mulatto Cubans needed to unite for political strength against persistent forms of discrimination. As early as the 1870s, Morúa stated his view that mulattoes should not be included in the same racial category as blacks because they essentially constituted a "new race, midway between blacks and whites" (Helg 40). Although he backed off from a strictly biological view of mulattoes after 1890, he never renounced this belief explicitly. For Morúa, the mulatto's "African mother" had relations with the "European father" in the interest of her betterment and in this way "fought against the exploitation perpetrated by the slave trade" (*Integración* 213). In other words, whitening is a justified step toward liberation from the legacies of slavery. Of course, what Morúa did not seem to understand was his own indebtedness to white conceptions of citizenship and civilization that were color-coded, not color-neutral as he believed. Like many white Creoles, he advocated what was essentially an evolution from black to white, which prominent mulattoes like himself evidenced and from which he personally benefited.

Though not necessarily the reason for this problematic view, his understanding of U.S. race relations helped support his notion that racial divisions were the natural result of being subject to outside powers like Spain and the United States and were therefore not endemic to Cuban life. He wrote in 1882, while in the United States: "Cuba is not North

America. In Cuba the white father has not disdained giving the sweet title of 'son' to the child of copper skin, the fruit of his African companion. The white father in Cuba has never considered that the tender being of intermediate blood would denigrate him by calling him 'father'" (*Integración* 88).[5] His fiction additionally suggests that racial difference itself is an invention of the colonial overseer. His view of race has been tempting for critics who want to see it in a postmodern light as a social construction forged by those in power. As a social construction, however, racial difference also becomes lived experience that shapes identity. That is, a color line, although arbitrary, conditions and shapes identity and the way in which we speak about race; therefore, although colonialism may cause racial difference, such difference cannot be easily demonized or mythologically separated from its resultant lived experience (Kawash 6). Morúa's view ultimately is of a raceless future, one in which talk of the persistence of lived racial difference must be silenced in order for Cuba to fulfill its national destiny.

The serial novels *Sofía* (1891) and *La familia Unzúazu* (1901) are set in the turbulent years 1878-1880, following the first failed attempt to establish Cuban independence and preceding the emancipation of the slaves. As such, according to Lorna Williams, they seek "to overcome the tendency to equate the signs of slavery with the signs of blackness in the interest of national independence" (*Representation* 198). It is significant that the second installment of the series, although published after independence just prior to the passing of the Platt Amendment, was in fact completed in 1895 just as the war against Spain was beginning. It is not entirely clear why Morúa was unsuccessful in finding a publisher before 1901, but we do know he intended to donate the profits from its sale to the cause of independence.[6] Read in this context, *La familia Unzúazu* in particular expresses postslavery yearning for an as-yet-unrealized Cuban nationalism. What is powerful about these novels, consequently, is their dissection of the construction of an exclusively white claim on *cubanidad* that Morúa believes has stalled political independence from Spain, even if in the process he also warns his white reader that until independence is gained, Cuba runs the risk of a further Africanization.

The father of the family, Sr. Unzúazu, is a slave trader in the Canaries (whence came Morúa's own white father) who dies shortly after his wife passes away and leaves to his son-in-law the care of three of his children. A fourth child, Sofía, is born to a different mother from the Canaries, reportedly a prostitute, who ends up in New Orleans. Unzúazu never explicitly names her as his child; he merely instructs all his children while still alive "to love each other as sisters [que se quisieran como herman-itas]" and his Spanish son-in-law, Acebaldo, to look after her (*Sofía* 212). After his death, the papers proving Sofía's white identity are miss-ing (although after Acebaldo later finds them he informs no one), and in the absence of a definitively documented racial identity for Sofía, Ace-baldo perpetuates the myth begun by his wife, Ana María, the eldest daughter, that Sofía has black blood. Claiming that she once heard her father exclaim to his friends that Sofía had her origins on the plantation, Ana María concludes that she is most likely the offspring of an unknown white man and a mulatto woman. Acebaldo, as a symbol of Spanish co-lonial rule not unlike Villaverde's Don Cándido, holds on to the inherit-ance that Sofía is due. The absent or unnamed father, rather than being the essential enigma to a mulatto's racial and social identity, as is the case with Cecilia Valdés, becomes in Morúa's fiction a space that is usurped by the ideological needs of the white plantation family to create the fictions of racial difference and slavery. The "fiction" of her race "is installed literally in loco parentis, a place [Acebaldo] can usurp because it is unoccupied" (Kutzinski 113). Deathly ill after childbirth, Sofía learns that she is the daughter of Sr. Unzúazu and a sister to the siblings she has served as a slave, notably to the illegitimate father of her child. This knowledge, in oedipal fashion, kills her. Morúa reveals Sofía's whiteness underneath slavery's rhetorical construction of blackness and exposes the need to move beyond colonial society's arbitrary categories of difference.[7]

In these novels, Morúa Delgado expressed his desire to rewrite the in-cestuous story of *Cecilia Valdés*. He was publicly critical of this work, particularly of Villaverde's use of realism, because he believed that real-ism did not allow the author the imaginative freedom to critique society. As a convinced naturalist of the Émile Zola school, he believed that fic-tion needed to condemn social ills emphatically. Of realism, he writes: "I detest that literary aberration known as the 'historical novel,' *an ambig-uous, amphibious creation,* that is neither novel nor history, and what's more, in its subtlety, it serves as a transparent screen that only partially conceals the imaginative insufficiency of its author" ("Las novelas" 35, emphasis added). He uses rhetoric normally found in diatribes against mulattoes to criticize the aesthetic practice of realism and its symbolic and social power to "pass" representations of customs and local color as real. Specifically, he takes aim in his fiction at realism's dependence on visual reliability for the success of its representations of society and of race and thus implies that white social power is allied to realism. The paradigm of miscegenation leading to incest takes on new dimensions here. Realism, although highly dependent on registers of difference for its representations of reality, also depends on verisimilitude and similarity between its representations and what might be perceived as real. Realism becomes a kind of insularity, a hermetically sealed world in which what exists and what we see coincide perfectly. According to Morúa's logic, the threat of incestuous realism is that it gives birth to mixed genres like the historical novel of Villaverde. Cuba's colonialism is a dependence on insular realism, which masks its ideological alliance with white society by pretending to provide direct access to reality.

As if to announce his intentions to parody Villaverde, Morúa begins *Sofía* with a description of the fictional city of Belmiranda that cannot help but recall Villaverde's tourist descriptions of Havana.[8] As the novel opens, the narrator exclaims: "What an enchanting sight! What a beautiful panorama! We are on the sea, at the entrance to a port on the north coast" (*Sofía* 9). Very intentionally, he opens our eyes to the city "from the point of view of a foreign observer," only then to abandon this technique and ascribe such ability to paint scenes to particular characters with considerable social power (9).

Morúa's characters, not his narrator, occupy positions of visual authority, particularly in regard to racial categorization. For example, Acebaldo influences public interpretations of race in mimicry of the narrator's descriptions of blackness in *Cecilia Valdés*. Before his fears are later confirmed, Acebaldo suspects that Sofía, the family slave, may in fact be the white sister of his wife and her siblings and may have some legitimate claim on the family property. To protect the patrimony of the slave trade from the threat of her striking physical resemblance to the family, he publicly denigrates her image: "Unable to stop himself, his face would lose its composed appearance and his personality would become bitter whenever the subject of Sofía came up, and he would then come undone with shows of antipathy against the girl, *painting her in the most detestable colors* [pintándola con los más detestables colores]" (49, emphasis added). Note here that the narrative trains us to read behind Acebaldo's composed facade; we don't see Sofía, but we read the signs on his face that betray his inner motivations.

When Acebaldo is murdered, legal truth proves vulnerable to similar manipulations of public perception. Initially many witnesses "saw clearly a mulatto fleeing and were sure that they would recognize him if they saw him again" (199). But when Acebaldo's body turns up with a "*ñañigo* stab wound," investigators convict the Unzúazus' slave, Liberato (198). Like Cecilia's birthmark, the wound initially appears to provide readable evidence of the instigator whose crime plagues the community. However, we doubt Liberato's guilt because the narrator reminds us that public opinion tends "to subjugate further, if that were possible, the disenfranchised [los desheredados], . . . either for being the most different in their obligatory social circumstances, or for their ethnic nature, or for both differences at the same time" (208). When the same stab mark turns up on the body of another murdered white man while Liberato is in jail, he is set free, and public confidence in visual evidence decreases. One witness to this second murder claims: "I would bet that it isn't a mulatto as people claim, but some white man, a noticeably white man, who was seeking revenge." Another confirms: "He must have been white; anyone can disguise himself" (282). Liberato's judge reminds the crowd that "not everything we see is true" (285).

What Morúa exposes here is prejudice, specifically that against the African presence in Cuba. Ñañigos were members of Abakúa secret societies of African origin who frequently identified themselves by means of secret signs and emblems (such as the one referred to in the novel). Prior to 1898, *ñañigos* were frequently targeted as suspicious proindependence rebels, and indiscriminate arrests increased after independence (and, interestingly, after Morúa wrote the novel) because of the suspicion that they were engaged in conspiracies against whites and against the government. Ñañigos, along with black *brujos,* were emblems of the Africanization of Cuba feared by most whites and many coloreds, including Morúa himself. Thus, in Cuba's effort to unify as a nation, these groups were frequently demonized for their radical cultural and religious differences from mainstream Cuban affairs.

Morúa demonstrates that the *ñañigo* functions as a circulating metaphor of white fear and suspicion of the Afro-Cuban classes, without any evidence of his identity or guilt. If the prejudice against *ñañigos* hurts anyone in Morúa's mind, however, it is the mulatto who is grouped together with *el negro.* Although Morúa effectively exposes how racism constructs meaning out of racial difference in order to sustain white privilege, he does not offer any radically divergent racial difference for comparison. In other words, race is, in these novels, an entirely empty signifier that never corresponds to an identifiable, historically conditioned signified. This problem is perhaps emblematic of Morúa's own difficult position as an Afro-Cuban politician in a mostly white government; he was painfully aware of whites' excessive fear and prejudice, and yet he was also threatened by an alternative black culture that resisted the Western ways he championed. Because of this, he was increasingly criticized by Gualberto Gómez and other civil rights activists after 1902.

Morúa's characters always fail to see essences beyond appearances, and this sets the stage for reputation as the standard of social value, a theme Morúa explores more fully in *La familia Unzúazu*. Those who obtain power in Morúa's Cuba are those who successfully manipulate public perceptions of truth and identity in order to establish a reputation, a tautology in which power is based on its perception and its perception on one's position of power. Plantation families like the Unzúazus perpetuate their status by reproducing social, racial, and genealogical myths.

In *La familia Unzúazu*, Liberato flees the home because Ana María threatened to punish him for his sexual advances.[9] Ana María's younger brother Federico, meanwhile, has squandered his inheritance and in desperation uses Liberato's escape as a way to extort money from the family. By threatening to return the slave to the plantation, Federico forces Liberato to write a ransom note claiming that he is holding Federico captive. Federico and his friend Perecito intend to recycle the threatening trope of an angry runaway slave in order to extort more money and to finance their extravagant lifestyles. Indeed, as members of the "idle youth of the city" given to profligate gambling and financial wastefulness, they represent the final decay of the plantocracy. In this respect they parallel Leonardo Gamboa from *Cecilia Valdés* and Chesnutt's Tom Delamere from *The Marrow of Tradition*. Because of Federico's financial needs, we suspect early in the first novel that he may have killed his brother-in-law and framed Liberato in order to get more money, having spent his inheritance in a matter of a few months. His behavior in the second novel helps to confirm this suspicion. The description of Perecito embodies the essence of this idle generation: "His was smooth and white skin; he had a hairless face with a good profile; black eyes that weren't pear-shaped but . . . round. . . . He had hair as black as his eyes that was pleasingly curly; a smallish mouth even though it seemed large because of the insinuating thickness of his lips, which often showed his healthy and white teeth envied by not a few beautiful women. . . . The popular Perecito . . . enjoyed showing off his round and pronounced womanish forms" (82–83).

The description resembles many of the racist stereotypes concerning mulattoes: the thick lips on an almost thin mouth, the black curly hair, and the emasculated, feminine aura. Here Morúa turns the trope of the emasculated mulatto on its head by creating symbols of moral decay out of the physical signs of racial mixture. And this decay is a function of the fact that these men have enhanced an already granted social privilege by means of distorting visual appearances. In addition to taking aim at a corrupted white elite, this implicates Afro-Cubans who might perform their racialized roles for their own social advancement but without merit. Indicative of his agreement with Booker T. Washington, freely given privilege here corrupts to the point of physically inverting or perverting prescribed social roles.

Manipulation of social categories and public perceptions is nowhere as powerful as in the uproar of erotic confusion Perecito and Federico cause by appearing at a local dance dressed as beautiful women. On the figure of the transvestite in turn-of-the-twentieth-century fiction in Latin America, Francine Masiello has written: "[T]he transvestite becomes both a perversion of the national plan as well as one of its disguised projects," and this is because "fashion underlines sharply these tensions of a marginal country on the road to modernization. . . . Fashion effectively opposes the law of inheritance" (11, 16). Perecito and Federico's immoral fashioning of their own privileges represents where the modern nation is headed if it is not wise to the ways perception can be manipulated to create black or white social power. The power to manipulate perception is the form of the plantation family's sustenance and the sign of their moral decay. Contrary to how Villaverde invoked the opposition between appearances and essences to talk about race, Morúa sees moral discourse as a way of moving beyond the discussion of race in the national debate, something he deems necessary because of his belief that culture and morality lie at the core of social inequality, not race and racism.

When Federico is killed at the end of the novel, we suspect that Liberato has finally taken things into his own hands and acted. If Liberato has fulfilled the assigned role of the conniving and violent mulatto, his action hardly suggests, as does his name, that he has been truly "liberated." Here Morúa faces a dilemma: either represent Liberato as the naive victim of Federico or as the vengeful mulatto who, in his own conniving, fulfills the role society has assigned him. This problem is really a symptom of a larger political misjudgment Morúa makes. In order to move beyond the discussion of race so that he can more effectively diagnose Cuba's moral ills, he neglects, even denies, the persistence of a historically conditioned racial difference in Cuba. In his extensive efforts to point out the hypocrisies of the white elite and the chimeras upon which their authority is based, Morúa has almost entirely neglected to represent black subjectivity that is not a product of white colonial corruption. To attack the use of visual signifiers as a basis for unequal racial and social classification is, of course, necessary initially. Clearly Morúa shifts away from representing Afro-Cubans as "constitutively other to an analysis of the relationships between the free and the unfree in a domain beyond ethnicity" (Williams, *Representation* 198). But going one step further, and denying any racial classifications as the basis for political representation, reproduced and confirmed the racism of whites who, with adequate social power, could control the terms of the struggle over signifiers. Essentialist conceptions of race were invoked by the racist pseudoscientists of the age, but when Morúa denies the right of those on the defensive end of such racism to counter with their own alternative classifications, he empties the ring of any opposition. Precisely because race is an empty signifier, its definitions are always contextualized by historical conditions and placed in fierce competition. A premature insistence on complete neutrality inadvertently blurs or entirely erases the historicity that has framed the debate in the first place; to refuse to grant blackness political representation is to end up with the race war of 1912.

By choosing a white protagonist who is blackened by those in power, Morúa exposes naked white social power. However, the white protagonist also serves as a warning against the threat of black contamination of whiteness as long as Cuba remains subject to Spanish colonial rule. Morúa implies that after full integration of the races, no difference will remain or at any rate be worth preserving in the interest of independence. Vera Kutzinski is rightly impressed with "the precision with which Sofía attends to the sociosexual construction of race in nineteenth-century Cuba and the consistency with which the novel links those issues to slavery and sugar production" (12). The mulatto figure, as it appears in much literature of Plantation America is, in the words of Hazel Carby, "an exploration and expression of what was increasingly socially proscribed" (89). However, Sofía's tragic ending, in which she simultaneously discovers that she is white and the mother of her brother's child, seems to warn against the dangers of arbitrary denotations of blackness and does not sufficiently guard against nostalgia for more reliable markers of difference. Kutzinski contends that "Sofía's genealogical whiteness of course breaks apart the unholy alliance of incest and miscegenation. Not only does racial purity offer no protection whatsoever against the dreaded possibility of incest in Sofía; ironically it creates that very possibility. . . . The desire for racial purity is revealed to be incestuous in that it is a (sexual) desire for someone of the same blood and social position" (129). Again the attack against racial essentialism and purity is clear, but Morúa's radically antihistorical critique advocates acceptance of past miscegenation in the interest of present national consolidation so as to prevent a more insidious persistence of blackness and racial difference. Cultivation or preservation of distinct ethnic histories after slavery becomes the new taboo. The implication is that the road to Cuban integration is through miscegenation and whitening and not through mutual respect for difference.

Morúa's reluctance to give historically derived racial difference representation in his fiction means that such difference can only be accounted for by moral corruption, and this can only be properly diagnosed through recourse to the science of medicine. Julio Ramos has demonstrated that legal and moral discourses came to dominate the discussion of Cuba's racial complexion in the nineteenth century and were frequently depicted as hygienic discourses that could diagnose and manage the "ills" of blackness in the interest of national consolidation and protection against the "plague" of Africanization (*Paradojas* 57). If the figure of the mulatto incites racist thinking to find a more interior and less visible marker of racial difference, medicine offers itself as a science of reading the body from the inside. We see this recourse to medicine in both novels from the previous chapter. Cable's apothecary, Joseph Frowenfeld, is an outsider who comes to look upon the body of Creole society and to provide possible cures for its ills. Cecilia Valdés, as a representative of Cuban contradictions, is sent to the asylum for treatment, following her mother. Morúa continues this trope in his fiction: The Unzúazu family doctor, Alvarado, "had as earnest an interest for the healthy preservation of the human body as he did for the betterment of the political and social health of his country" (*Familia* 136). The exceptional abundance of physical ailments that plague the Unzúazu family becomes in this paradigm the moral ailments that the body politic suffers. The doctor's intimate position within the family allows him not only to diagnose illnesses but makes him privy to family secrets, which are the essence of their moral illness. Ana María astutely insists that no doctor should help her sister Malenita during her pregnancy because doctors "are a bunch of blabbermouths who 'in complete confidence' proceed to tell all that they know" (86).

Alvarado, like the characters Gonzaga and his associate Fidelio, is less vulnerable to the white colonial manipulation of appearances. The three men are frequently found together discussing "the Antillean question" and seem to represent curative possibilities for the nation's perpetual corruption. Eladislao Gonzaga also has intimate knowledge of the family (he discovers the truth of Sofía's identity) due to his role as the family lawyer hired to straighten out their financial matters. As such, he is potentially a healer, particularly because "affected by the terrible experiences of exile, he had formed an *unimpressionable* character" (99). Gonzaga has learned from his experience with homelessness and exile to see beyond the exterior appearance of things, to withhold enthusiasm for any particular point of view until the proper information is made available. He understands that morality becomes like "an elastic belt, that each person employs according to his circumstances" (63).

The political prescriptions of Gonzaga and Alvarado appear, then, to carry the symbolic weight of Morúa's own agenda. However, due to their proximity to the family secrets, and their increasing involvement in the family drama, they too become tainted by the rampant corruption. Most significantly, Gonzaga fathers a child extramaritally with Malenita, which undermines his moral and political authority. Morúa warns that even the most comprehensive plans for national health, the most liberal intentions, should be held in suspicion lest they prove to be "a democratic spirit in form, but maintaining deep inside familial corruption, consecrating concubinage and stimulating vice with the excitation of feminine vanities" (227).

To account for the differences in Cuban society, Morúa must continually spread tales of uncontained moral contamination seemingly beyond his narrative control. It is as if the narrative, in its frantic drive to catalog and bandage the many moral illnesses that afflict the plantation family, has left behind the one character who might have offered some redemption: Fidelio, the mulatto activist who is undoubtedly an image of the author but who plays virtually no role in the family drama. The narrative itself, one might say, has become infected, tainted by the corruption it seeks to name, because it betrays its best intentions; it becomes obsessed with the need to spin off endless tales of intrigue and corruption. It is not hard to see why in Cuba the television soap opera *Sofía*, based on Morúa's novels, is currently enjoying national popularity. The only corrective for this obsession is that Morúa's representational dilemma implies that if there is to be a solution to the "Antillean question," it will have to come from a social perspective constituted independently of the legacies of the colonial plantation experience.

Looking with the American Eye

In Charles Chesnutt's *The Marrow of Tradition* (1901), two doctors are seated together on a train. Chesnutt writes: "Looking at these two men with the American eye, the differences would perhaps be the more striking, or at least the more immediately apparent, for the first was white and the second black, or, more correctly speaking, brown" (49). Chesnutt's writings consistently mark the tragedies that inevitably follow visual apprehensions of race, thereby reversing the direction of the gaze of white social power so that whites read themselves not as producers of racial knowledge but "as objects gazed upon, studied, and assessed by the African-American subject" (Knadler 429). He showed little faith that an "American eye" (the white gaze in the one-drop-rule society of the United States) that is trained to perceive differences could ever learn to see human equality beyond them. As in both Morúa's and Harper's writings, the seeing eye is not neutral, as Villaverde's "knowing eye" purports to be, but socially and culturally charged with various levels of self-interest. Chesnutt's "American eye" demonstrates, according to John Ernest, "the ways in which one's eye can be disciplined by culture—shaped by a history of social prejudices and racial domination—to see differences where others would see similarities" (*Resistance* 209).

Curiously, however, Chesnutt's pessimism regarding the unlikelihood that the "American eye" would ever learn to see beyond differences led him to argue for the eventual erosion of racial difference. In his controversial essay of 1900, "The Future American," he implies that as long as racial difference exists, there will always be those with American eyes who will create social and political inequalities on the basis of that difference. Cable, Chesnutt's one-time mentor and employer, had already declared the South to have been superseded by the "New South," which was Latin America and the Caribbean, regions that could carry on the legacy of hybridity that he so despised. As Chesnutt's argument implies, the paradox of Jim Crowism and of Cable's critique of it is that to denigrate racial hybridity is to convert it into the ultimate sign of blackness. As long as black and white were kept separate, whiteness could remain visible and, by virtue of the consequent invisibility of blackness, the reigning characteristic of U.S. culture. The more racially mixed regions of the South and of Latin America were the imagined sites of greatest blackness. Despite Cable's criticisms of Jim Crow legislation, the impossibility of literally casting the historical legacies of miscegenation onto Latin America means that segregation was the only logical outcome.

Segregation kept from the open and public view of white Americans a black South, wholly different from white America, which had not disappeared, as Cable's rhetoric might have suggested. What also complicated matters for Chesnutt was that Booker T. Washington, whom Morúa and other conservative Afro-Cubans in Cuba admired, had capitulated to the need for segregation and to the concomitant fallacious conception of white racial purity (Knadler 428). White eugenicists had long been arguing that a taboo against racial mixture was as necessary as public segregation because miscegenation "produced a degenerate mongrel breed" (Nowatzki 41). When Chesnutt witnessed American expansion into Latin America and the Philippines, he saw an opportunity to borrow from Latin American racial discourse and argue that U.S. denial of racial difference at home was only running the United States headlong into racial difference abroad and, sooner or later, that contact was going to lead to a thorough and permanent amalgamation and to the disappearance of the color line.

In his essay, he continues, the white race "will have absorbed and assimilated the blood of the other two races" (Elder 97). Whereas Cable proposed that civil equality would ensure that amalgamation would not occur, knowing full well that miscegenation was a principal fear in the public's mind, Chesnutt proposes racial mixing, in the Latin American mode, as the solution: Amalgamation, he writes, "has been going on peacefully in the countries south of us for several centuries, and is likely to continue along similar lines" ("MELUS Forum" 98). Without drawing any attention to the traditional views of Latin America as the barbaric racial nightmare that opposed the American dream of civilized segregation, Chesnutt insinuates into the American racial debate these regions of "the various peoples of the northern hemisphere of the western continent; for if certain recent tendencies are an index of the future, it is not safe to fix the boundaries of the future United States anywhere short of the Arctic Ocean on the north and the Isthmus of Panama on the south" (97).

Cable and Chesnutt's deliberations about the color line illustrate how the imagined boundaries of the United States shift according to one's position regarding the "Negro question." Chesnutt's "New South," as opposed to Cable's, is inclusive rather than exclusive of Latin America racial practices. He reasons: "[T]he adding to our territories of large areas populated by dark races, some of them already liberally dowered with Negro blood, will enhance the relative importance of the non-Caucasian elements of the population, and largely increase the flow of dark blood toward the white race, until the time shall come when distinctions of color shall lose their importance, which will be but the prelude to a complete racial fusion" (106). As Elder argues, this kind of reasoning clearly implies an ambivalence, not unlike Morúa's, toward the blackness of what Chesnutt called "genuine Blacks" that is symptomatic of his entrapment within the cultural logic of white America that constructed the color line in the first place. Cable and Chesnutt's shifting boundaries between the United States and Latin America appear to be symptoms of the same paradigm. If the disappearance of racial difference is necessary to national harmony, as in Martí's vision of a raceless society, the implication is clear: Blacks are radically different, their difference is threatening because it is inferior, and their difference must become invisible. This occurs either through segregation and by scapegoating the Other America or by idealizing the Other America and arguing for miscegenation, which will erase difference.

Curiously, Chesnutt is more reluctant to make this case for a utopian, miscegenated "America" in *The Marrow of Tradition,* perhaps because it concerns itself with near-to-home historical events whose conditioning of racial identity made a future beyond slavery's troubling contingencies seem too remote. Published in 1901, the novel is a fictional representation of the white supremacist race riots that took place in Wilmington, North Carolina, in 1898. Contemporary whites in the region saw an increasing number of blacks take positions of political and social power and work for greater racial integration and equality in the predominantly black town. In response to their quickly disappearing political power, many whites organized a riot that overthrew and disenfranchised black power by means of physical violence. Although the number of deaths was relatively small, thousands of blacks fled the region, and within two years they were no longer the majority.[10] In the very year that Chesnutt witnessed the expansion of the United States into territories of racial darkness to which he alludes, he also witnessed internal segregation and disenfranchisement, whose ultimate aim was the whitening of the United States. Rather than writing at a historical moment prior to violent racial conflict like Morúa, Chesnutt's fiction unavoidably responds to historical violence; his dream of future racial amalgamation was perhaps just that: a dream of escape from the reality of violent discrimination in the here and now.

In the novel, Mr. Merkell marries one of his slaves, Julia Brown, and although the relationship is publicly recognized as a common interracial liaison, its legality is kept secret for the sake of preserving Merkell's reputation and social standing. The documents that substantiate the marriage and declare Julia's daughter, Janet, a legitimate heir to a portion of the property are burned by Janet's white half sister, Olivia Carteret. The novel demonstrates the weakness of the written law, manifest in the marriage and inheritance papers, to overthrow white prejudice and social power. Major Carteret, Olivia's husband, is the surrogate father who, like Acebaldo, has stepped in by marriage to take control of the family's resources and genealogy and who subjugates the power of the law with his "gold pen" as editor of the town's newspaper. Chesnutt suggests that such power is forged by maintaining the appearance of legality while erasing black legitimacy. White prejudice dictates that "the lot of [Janet's] race" is the "social ostracism, social ruin" that accompanies "the stigma of a base birth" (*Marrow* 270). If kinship with the black race is legally acknowledged, people can allege that families such as the Carterets "had sprung from such a shocking *mesalliance*" (270). Like Cable's Agricola, the Carterets insist on the taboos of racial or genetic proximity (not unlike the taboos of miscegenation and incest) in order to sustain their social standing and to maintain social distance from their black relatives, the Millers.

As in the work of Cable, Villaverde, and Morúa, the streets provide opportunities for uncanny recognitions, both true and false, between blacks and whites and thus expose the instability of racial categorizations and white representational control, because streets are spaces of public domain, not of private, white control. Janet Miller explains to her half sister Olivia Carteret, "people have taken me for you on the streets" (328). On the eve of the race riot, Janet's husband, Dr. William Miller, disguises his mulatto coloring in the twilight from the whites who have seized the streets. He is successful because, as the novel shows, "all cats are gray in the dark" (225). Significantly, the narrative never engages us in the cognitive confusion of a witnessing moment that we experience with Cable and Villaverde's novels. This is because Chesnutt's realism does not reify, but rather shows the evasiveness of, difference. Racial similarity threatens the social order, but unlike in Cable's and Villaverde's novels, it is not a social order Chesnutt wishes to preserve.

In the novel, the black male servant Sandy, who works for the prominent Delamere family, is believed to have murdered a white woman named Polly and stolen her gold. On the night in question, Ellis, a young journalist and protégé of Major Cateret, witnesses what appear to be two versions of Sandy under a street lamp walking one in front of the other. Reminiscent of Morúa's Federico, Tom Delamere, the oldest son of the family, has incurred gambling debts and has stolen from and murdered Polly while dressed up as Sandy; hence, Ellis sees Tom-as-Sandy and the real Sandy on the same sidewalk. Ellis's cognitive confusion allows us to comprehend the insufficiency of visual identifications. We also understand that the black witnesses—Sara, the Delameres' maid; Josh Green, who spent that evening with Sandy; and Sandy himself—are all without the social power necessary for their testimonies to carry weight. Consequently, as in Morúa's novel, the murder of a prominent white allows us to appreciate how the truth is determined by a negotiation for white social power among various forces within white society.

In another curious parallel with Morúa's novels, the narrator's description of Tom is reminiscent of Perecito. Tom has a "symmetrical face, dark almost to swarthiness, black eyes, which moved somewhat restlessly, curly hair of raven tint, a slight mustache, small hands and feet, and fashionable attire. . . . But no discriminating observer would have characterized his beauty as manly. It conveyed no impression of strength, but did possess a certain element, feline rather than feminine, which subtly negatived [*sic*] the idea of manliness" (16). Chesnutt uses white racist rhetoric about mulattoes to indicate Tom's moral inferiority.[11] By contrast, the narrator notes that Miller's "erect form, broad shoulders, clear eyes, fine teeth, and pleasingly moulded features showed nowhere any sign of that degeneration which the pessimist so sadly maintains is the inevitable heritage of mixed races" (49). We are told that Tom Delamere, like Federico Unzúazu, is a "degenerate aristocrat" who possesses "a keen eye for contrasts" (95, 24). With an "American eye" that can discern subtle differences, Tom is able to manipulate racial categories, just as Federico and Perecito do. Tom, "a valiant carpet-knight, skilled in all parlor exercises, great at whist or euchre, a dream of a dancer, unexcelled in cakewalk or 'coon' impersonations, for which he was in large social demand," like Perecito, has a talent for deception and illusion that allows him to bluff in social settings and at cards, to play on subtleties of difference not normally noticed by others in order to survive financially and socially (96).

The community shows itself vulnerable time and again to the illusions of both social status and racial difference that Tom perpetuates. This preoccupation with seeing suggests that Chesnutt has not disavowed the idea of a corrective narrative training, but he does take it in a different ideological direction. His intention is to dissociate from the visual markers of race and genealogy their traditionally assigned social and moral meanings. That is, Chesnutt "responds to [his] cultural reality not by looking for new materials for the construction of identity but rather by reworking the available materials" (Ernest, *Resistance* 209).

Tom Delamere provides us with an interesting reading of how whites exploit black culture for survival and identity. In his personal writings, Chesnutt expressed concern that white writers, oftentimes from the North, gained considerable popularity from their representations of local color in the black rural South, representations Chesnutt believed he and other colored writers would be more qualified to produce.[12] The ability of Cable, Villaverde, Mark Twain, and other white writers to imitate the speech and style of black American culture could be read in this light as an unholy alliance that provided white cultural products, such as literature of "local color," a flourishing national identity. That Sandy is almost lynched because of Tom's mimicry suggests whence comes the guilt for which Sandy becomes the scapegoat; it is the dependency of white identity on an appropriation of its shadows. Chesnutt's aim, as Eric Sundquist argues, is to "expose . . . cultural segregation at work" in America, a process that draws false boundaries between black and white culture and seeks to conceal their interdependence and mutual influence (*To Wake* 396; see also Kawash 113).

Curiously, the interdependence in Chesnutt's novel does not seem to signify that the black and white families should be brought together into some kind of racial family reunion, as Chesnutt's "Future American" might have dictated. Although he shows that white social power is maintained by an imitation of black cultural expression, the novel's conclusion demonstrates that "the course of history . . . is altered when the black man refuses to imitate whiteness" (Knadler 436). Chesnutt's novelistic reconciliation between black and white cultural forces is a bitter disavowal of the significance of genealogical kinship and of color. Like similar choices faced by Don Cándido, Acebaldo, Agricola, and Faulkner's Thomas Sutpen, Major Carteret must choose between reasons of race and of kinship in order to preserve his family name. Chesnutt's exposure of the false segregation of the black and white families rejects both Villaverde's incestuously tragic resolution and Cable's nearly incestuous romanticized promise of black-white solidarity. Indeed, as I have shown, either resolution upholds the ideology of genealogy as legitimization, but in Villaverde's case its attempted erasure results in extramarital incest, while in Cable's in a restoration of property through marriage. Chesnutt moves us toward a notion of black-white affiliation that is based on ethical and moral values, not on genealogical affection and mutual claims to patrimony. He offers no false promise of a sentimental-ized family reunion between the races; rather, the best hope of reunion will be based solely on an acceptance of the moral responsibilities toward one another as fellow members of the human family.

The novel's focus on inheritance "scrutinizes the relation between property and the production and maintenance of white supremacy" that was implicit in the 1896 Supreme Court decision in *Plessy v. Ferguson,* which institutionalized segregation (Kawash 105). The Carterets find themselves forced to acknowledge their kinship to the Millers in order to obtain the doctor's help when their son and only heir falls ill. This irony displays clearly the dependence of the Carterets' social position on a false maintenance of separate genealogies between the races (Knadler 442). Because of past insults and the riot instigated by Carteret, which led to the death of the Millers' only boy, Dr. Miller initially refuses to help and appears to repeat Carteret's genealogical violence instigated against Miller's wife and son. In a desperate effort to soften their stance, Olivia admits that Janet is her lawful sister and therefore has a legal claim to half the Carterets' estate. The sin that plagues the polity is certainly not miscegenation but rather the fratricidal impulse of Jim Crowism, which seeks to erect white social power on the basis on black disenfranchisement. Chesnutt stages what appears to be a sentimentally charged ending to the novel in which restored kinship heals wounds and equalizes social wealth between the races. However, the entanglements of genealogy are perhaps too complex and painful to advocate a simple notion of interracial kinship. Genealogy is useful for him to expose the sins of Jim Crow, but ultimately for Chesnutt the wounds of segregation and of slavery will heal if we move beyond a social organization that follows the biological determinants of race and nurses instead the historical contingencies of ethnicity balanced with a common moral respect for difference. Whereas Morúa uses incest to expose the fratricidal impulse of racial categorization, Chesnutt reverses the sentimentality of family romance to expose the fratricidal impulse of segregation.

As in the case of Cable's Frowenfeld and Morúa's Dr. Alvarado, modern medicine stands as a metaphor for the narrative's own attempt to diagnose the ills of the body politic; physical ailments become representations of racial and genealogical secrets. Chesnutt's narrative, however, subordinates genealogical secrets to the "ideological significance that can be attached to [them], whether privately in the form of inheritance or publicly in the form of economic and political power" (Sundquist, *To Wake* 397). In Chesnutt's employment of the medical trope, the mulatto doctor's use of scientific knowledge on the white body potentially betrays his own wife and child, who have been denied legitimization and inheritance. Janet refuses Olivia's admission of kinship because it was "not freely given, from an open heart, but extorted from a reluctant conscience" (328). She explains that "now, when an honest man has given me his name of which I can be proud, you offer me the one of which you robbed me, and of which I can make no use" (327). Stephen Knadler rightly observes that Janet plays the "'untragic' mulatto" because she refuses to capitulate to the "structure as well as the content of race" (443). However, Knadler and Kawash want to reconcile the novel's conclusion with Chesnutt's essay "The Future American Race" by suggesting that the open-ended nature of the Millers' identity and of the final pages of the narrative point to an unrepresentable utopian future. I find no evidence in the novel to suggest that the future Chesnutt points to is anything but a radically historicized one, in which mutual respect for the differences that have shaped identity on both sides of the color line must be paramount and desire to erase those differences in an impatient rush to racial reconciliation must be resisted. Chesnutt suggests that if there is to be a reconciliation between the races, it must be based on a common, humane sense of mercy, not on a common genealogy. Kawash agrees that "justice cannot end the novel; in the cycle of violence, justice only produces death" (119). For this reason, he argues that Chesnutt discards the "ledger" mentality regarding racial justice. Dr. Miller decides to see the Carteret child because "Olivia was a fellow creature, too, and in distress" (*Marrow* 325).

The affiliative ties of the human family are substitutes for the genealogical ones whose meaning has been eroded by violence and injustice. Chesnutt demonstrates that the community and the family names blacks have had to build in response to their disenfranchisement cannot be revoked just to regain what has been denied. Like Morúa, Chesnutt argues for a conception of racial difference as a social construction, but unlike him, he perceives the political terror of wanting to erase, in the name of color neutrality, the history that has conditioned a black racial community. In his review of the novel, William Dean Howells complained that the ending was too bitter and did not leave the reader space for sentimental investment. Perhaps because he only could understand forgiveness in terms of capitulation to white genealogy, Howells missed the central message of the novel, complaining that there is "more justice than mercy in it" (qtd. in McElrath 497). Ironically, his review refers to mulattoes such as Chesnutt as "step-brother Americans," a term that, in its reference to a legally patched-up relation, is symptomatic of the very reason for Chesnutt's melancholy resolution (qtd. in H. Chesnutt 177). Joseph McElrath argues that Howells's reaction contributed to Chesnutt's increasing sense that the domination of the color line among even the most liberal white readers would make it impossible for him to remain on the fence: "[T]he 'not entirely white' author of 1900 had made it clear in October 1901 that he was on the other side of the color line, a 'negro'" (497).

Chesnutt learned that historical experience had shaped his nation's, and his own, racial consciousness more profoundly than his "Future American" had imagined. Instead of moving to a raceless future, the legacies of slavery and colonialism were progressively rooting the nation in its New World past. Chesnutt's mistake in "The Future American" was to assume that expansion in the hemisphere would facilitate more open and direct interracial contact. Indeed, on the domestic front, the result was quite the opposite: It caused racial retreat, at least symbolically, and thus further sustained white pretensions to racial purity. If his essay was prophetic, it was because, as Faulkner was to argue, the racial contact that imperialism facilitated would continually haunt the white home front not in the form of racial disappearance, but as disguised bigamy; the nation would continually propagate difference on the basis of its divided racial desires.

In my understanding, then, *The Marrow of Tradition* is a revision of "The Future American" because the novel seeks elected kinship rather than a biologically determined racial genealogy. Hortense Spillers explains that "kinship loses meaning since it can be invaded at any given and arbitrary moment by the property relations" ("Mama's Baby" 74). African Americans have frequently revised the meaning of kinship under these conditions because, as she notes, "the captive person developed time and again, certain ethical and sentimental features that tied her and him across the landscape to others, often sold from hand to hand, of the same and different blood in a common fabric of memory and inspiration" (75). What Chesnutt, and to a greater degree Harper, turn to is the obvious historical facts that racial difference exists independently of its symbolic value in the construction of white nationhood and that African Americans have developed models of family relations not based on genetically visible or socially upheld consanguinity.

"Seeing Things in a New Light"

As I argued in chapter 1, historical contingency is central to understanding the ideological dimensions of literature, and as we are beginning to see, each author is positioned in different ways according to race, gender, class, and nationality. We best see the narrative traces of these positions when the authors are juxtaposed with one another across those lines, and the relevant point is that no author is singularly positioned. Frances Harper, for example, makes "simultaneous appeal to different sets of historically and politically situated readers" (Foreman 332). She was accustomed to speaking simultaneously to different audiences throughout her prolific career (roughly from the mid-1850s to her death in 1911) as a poet, novelist, and political and religious activist on behalf of the black community and women's causes. The way her novel *Iola Leroy* (1891) speaks to multiple audiences is a textual admission that national consolidation does not have to occur under a singular genealogical model of the national family, nor should it. The novel interpellates divergent readers with the same signs and implies that national unity does not have to be founded on a unified reading but can be accomplished through metaphors that forge competing and overlapping imagined communities.

Harper's novel explores the challenges and obstacles that need to be overcome in order to "to bind anew the ties which slavery had broken and gather together the remnants of [a] scattered family," paradoxically proposing that slavery's legacies can be overcome if the black community will aggressively embrace slavery's historical contingencies (146). In this sense, Harper is a precursor to more recent postslavery writing. The scattering begins during slavery with Eugene Leroy, a Creole planter "deprived of his parents" at an early age, who fails to pass onto his children the social power attached to his name. Harper explains that his irresponsibility is a product of his own lack of family roots and thus introduces her main theme, the power of parental domesticity to integrate and sustain racial and communal identity: "[W]ithout the restraining influence of a mother's love or the guidance of a father's hand, Leroy found himself, when his college days were over, in the dangerous position of a young man with vast possessions, abundant leisure, unsettled principles, and uncontrolled desires" (61). He falls in love with Marie, one of his slaves, and sends her north to be educated as a white woman, since her coloring allows her to pass easily. When they later marry and return to New Orleans, he buries the secret of her racial identity from their neighbors and from their children, Iola and Nicholas. Lorraine, an old racist associate of Eugene's, produces false papers that substantiate in legal writ what he knows to be true about the race of his family members. With that legitimization in hand, Lorraine hunts down the children in the North, where they attend school, and sells them back into slavery. Later, during Reconstruction, Iola and her brother seek to reconstruct their black family.

Harper demonstrates that white prejudice has more power to circumvent the law than do those whose color allows them to pass as white. The promises of passing prove to be lies, since white power can counter with legal lies effectively enough to weed out even the whitest of Negroes; as long as the law is governed by prejudice, it will matter little that race can be invisible. Unlike Sofía, who is a white woman made into a slave, Iola lives a lie of whiteness until the law, dictated by white control, catches up with her. In both cases, white social power is exposed as that which arbitrarily imputes social and moral meaning to racial difference. In Harper's paradigm, because difference is not simply created but misappropriated by white power, constituent elements of black identity—beyond biology—remain behind.

Through Iola, Harper taps into white fears of the prostitution of young white girls, or "white slavery," in order to convince her white readers of the continuing dangers against black and white womanhood posed by slavery's legacies and by the persistence of the color line (Foreman 336).[13] Carby has demonstrated that nineteenth-century obsessions with protecting the purity of white womanhood were directly connected to postbellum fears of miscegenation and contributed to increased anti-miscegenation legislation (30). Harper reverses this threat by suggesting that it is in fact fear of blackness that most endangers womanhood, black and white. The point here is that while Harper's white readers were likely to find in Iola a message coded especially for them, her black readers would understand Iola as a sign of their own racial agency, as Gabrielle Foreman notes. Because Iola chooses blackness even though she is physically able to pass, she teaches that the meaning of racial difference is not simply determined by white society but can also be lived and nurtured.[14] Foreman argues that Iola resonates with the well-known case of Homer Plessy, whose light skin tested the color line but who was ultimately rejected in 1892 in his attempt to defy the color line by riding in the white section of a train. The rejection went to court, of course, and resulted in the famous *Plessy v. Ferguson* decision (1896) that led to formal and legal segregation. "Iola" was also the nickname of Ida B. Wells, a famous turn-of-the-century activist, and was a household name among many black communities (Foreman 339, 341).

The power of these associations to undermine the trope of the tragic mulatto cannot be underestimated. Rather than simply pointing to the injustice of the color line or the limitations of white cognition, Iola represents a call to return to the black community that has been forged under the weight of such absurd racist epistemologies and to further nurture racial integrity as an answer to white social power. In her long career as a public speaker, Harper frequently made reference to the story of Moses' encounter with the Egyptian who was found beating a slave and fellow Israelite. The story clearly offered an archetype of the need to sacrifice privilege and even nonslave status for the sake of uplifting fellow slaves and reintegrating the race (Foster 278). The mulatto's state is analogous to Moses' because of the ever-present temptation to move further into the white world and disregard the plight of slaves. Although Houston Baker has criticized the novel for being a "mulatto utopia" that reinvents white patriarchy under the new authority of the mulatto, Iola's purpose is precisely to reverse capitulation to racial disappearance (31). She is not the tragic mulatto because her father abandons her, or because she is not accepted by whites, but only if she fails to reverse the consequences of these actions by embracing her black mother. As Melba Joyce Boyd explains, "while [Harper's] characters must struggle with the ambiguity of their identities the resolution to the dilemma lies in political involvement to alter socio-economic structure that . . . benefits from such . . . divisions" (170).

Significantly, the basis of this call to nurture and restore blackness is not found in any biological or genetic notion of racial difference but rather in the contingencies of history that have shaped the memories, affections, and stories of an emergent racial community. Iola is not a Booker T. Washington–style "New Negro," as Otten contends. Harper clearly advocates the principles of self-help (including temperance, education, and spirituality) and accepts the inevitable conditioning of the history of the color line, but politically as well as in her fiction, she never accepts de facto segregation (Foster 219, 218). Otten claims that "there was no usable past available" to the "New Negro," but Harper insists emphatically that Iola uses the history of slavery and of the color line to reshape the black community (233). As Harper states in 1888, "let your past history be a stimulus for the future" (Foster 285). Unlike Washington's conception of race, which depended on acceptance of political inequality, hers depends on black protagonism; racial identity is not given or reified but chosen and reproduced.

Rather than confronting directly the abuses of the white privileged classes, as do Morúa and Chesnutt, Harper focuses on the urgent need to rescue and piece together a black genealogy scattered by the violence of slavery and the failure of Reconstruction. Like Morúa and Chesnutt, however, she begins by exposing the social power behind a gaze that can trace the subtleties of racial configurations on the body. This is apparent first in her metaphorical use of light and shadows. We are taught to read in the dark, metaphorically, but unlike the narrative training in Cable and Villaverde, the use of lighting highlights emotional states and familial status rather than racial and cultural identities. When the truths of genealogy are hidden, as in the case of Eugene's marriage to Marie, there are "shadows in the home," while light is associated with domestic peace (730). The narrator remarks that "the love and devotion of [Marie's] husband brightened every avenue of her life, while her children filled her home with music, mirth, and sunshine" (89). Iola's feelings for Latimer, a mulatto doctor, are described as "dawning affections," and when she decides to brood no longer about the past of slavery, "her face assumed a brighter look" (262, 195). Iola's brother Harry, who has grown up white, "sees things in a new light" when he decides to accept his black identity and to find his mother (124). Unlike Cable's use of the metaphor "the shadow of the Ethiopian," Harper is clearly conscious of the derogatory use of the word "shadow" for late nineteenth-century African Americans and attempts to redefine its meaning in the context of domestic sentiment (Ernest, "From Mysteries" 502).

Rather than training us to notice the subtleties of racial configurations on the body, Harper teaches us to read the pathos that lies beneath the surface of the skin. "Blood," historically the indeterminate metaphor for racial identity that whites frequently found recourse to when visual traces are found lacking, is the invisible carrier of a difference that the body can no longer sufficiently signify; it is, in Kawash's words, "the primary figure joining the visible surface of the body with its inner truth" (130). Even though it ultimately signifies nothing that can be verified, its unreliability paradoxically becomes a source of white social power since it cannot be questioned. Harper's fiction inscribes "blood" not with a biologically determined racial content, but with an emotional content that in turn connotes the agency of affection in establishing community. Iola's uncle Robert Johnson, for example, becomes excited when contemplating freedom from slavery, and "his heart grew buoyant with hope; the lightness of his heart gave elasticity to his step and sent the blood rejoicingly through his veins" (*Iola* 35). While Robert's friend Tom Anderson speaks of his need to remain with his mother rather than escape slavery with his peers, "a spasm of agony and anger darkened his face and distorted his features as if the blood of some strong race were stirring with sudden vigor through his veins" (29–30). His racial identity is linked to his fidelity to his mother. Whereas Villaverde sensed that the violence of slavery and colonialism was aimed at breaking down the power of maternity to forge alternative communities, Harper goes further to demonstrate that strength to do so is still available through a prodigal, not oedipal, return to the mother. We read on Tom's face the emotion of such a decision: "It was touching to see the sorrow on the strong face, to detect the pathos and indignation in his voice" (30).

In her essays, Harper repeatedly insists that "the work of the mothers of our race is grandly *constructive*" of identity, morality, and community (Foster 292, emphasis added). What is important about race, as the novel shows, is kinship and belonging, particularly in those cases where surrogate forms of kinship are needed to substitute for genealogical ones that are no longer viable after slavery; biology becomes subordinate to pathos and affection, which are the real determinants of community. Harper herself had direct personal experience with this: She lost her biological parents at the age of three, was raised by her aunt and uncle (from whom she received intensive training in speaking, writing, and political networking), and married a widower with three children in 1860, only to lose him to death four years later (Bacon 22, 31).

Whenever the novel provides physical descriptions of the various characters who lie on the color line, it does so indirectly, refusing to let our eyes rest on their conjured image. In particular, we hear and see Iola, most frequently, through other characters' eyes. Although Harper has been criticized for her use of the tragic mulatto, which in much nineteenth-century fiction played into white, and particularly white male, fantasies about racial difference, it is significant that she never positions Iola's features directly in our view.[15] We are aware that she could pass as white and that she is beautiful, but only because other black characters tell us so; when we do see her directly, we see only signs of her pathos. Harper revises the tragic-mulatto theme by refusing to eroticize the subject in the reader's eye.[16] The burden of the tragic-mulatto metaphor is additionally lightened by metonymical references to other stories of black genealogy that are not told in their entirety but whose presence constantly reminds us that Iola's is not the sole representative story of the black race. To be sure, Harper's use of dialect to suggest these stories as metonyms is highly stylized and framed by a standardized narrative voice (closely allied with Iola's) and therefore does not completely escape the grasp of white paternalism (Baker 31). But because she places those dialects in different contexts, is suggestive but not aggressive in those representations, and demonstrates how stories play varying ideological roles, her testimonial language refuses to reify entirely (Carby 74).

Harper comprehends that a visual epistemology that both identifies and eroticizes race, like Villaverde's "knowing eye," is intimately connected to white social power. Her positioning of this visual epistemology in the gaze of Dr. Latrobe, a prominent white doctor, manifests her critique of its limitations. Dr. Latrobe proudly claims to the mulatto Dr. Latimer that "there are tricks of blood that always betray [white Negroes]. My eyes are more practiced than yours. I can always tell them" (229). He, of course, fails to recognize that Dr. Latimer is himself one such man. Latrobe's name undoubtedly is meant to recall the prominent white family of the same name in Baltimore, where Harper grew up. The Latrobes were famous for siring successful inventors, well-known historians, architects, engineers, and military leaders in the Civil War. Indeed, as Ernest claims, in her parody of Latrobe and in the novel as a whole, Harper attempts nothing less than to identify the "conceptual boundaries of white culture" ("From Mysteries" 504). That Latrobe is a doctor also undermines the pseudoscientific discourse of white supremacy as well as that of white liberal postslavery nationalism, such as we saw in the previous chapter. Harper demonstrates that "the combined lights of the Northern and Southern cultures produce only ominous shadows, and argues that such shadows can be lifted only by those who stand beyond the cognitive limitations of these cultural systems" (505). And like Chesnutt's Dr. Miller and Morúa's Fidelio, Harper's Dr. Latimer is offered as a symbol of a black cognition that counters those limitations. In Latimer, she undoubtedly meant to evoke in readers the figure of George Latimer, who became somewhat of a cause célèbre among abolitionists when he was caught by his master after escaping to the North in 1842. His son, Lewis, also became well known as a legal witness for General Electric and "was heir to a hard-fought Black paternal legacy that provides a counter-story to the classic slave tale of white paternal abandonment. . . . [Lewis's father, George,] posed as his pregnant wife's master in order to escape slavery" (Foreman 343).

Visual failure to recognize race and genealogy does not merely signify the epistemological limitations of white culture; it signifies the contingency of history, which in this case is the violence of slavery on black families. Robert Johnson fails to recognize kinship in the face of Iola, his niece, because of the violence that has separated them and the time and experiences they have lived through independently of one another. Robert exclaims: "I have only a faint remembrance of my sister's features; but I never could recognize in that beautiful woman the dear little sister with whom I used to play. Oh, the cruelty of slavery! How it wrenched and tore us apart! Where is *your* mother now?" (142). Robert's hesitance to name their proper relationship solely on the basis of visually discerned kinship allows for other means of genealogical linkage to come to the fore.

He places more faith in the emotional memory recalled by a song Iola sings to him at his bedside in the hospital. When Robert is reunited with his sister Marie, a similar process of reconstruction occurs: "[I]t was almost impossible to recognize her brother in that tall, handsome man, with dark-brown eyes and wealth of chestnut-colored hair, which he readily lifted to show the crimson spot that lay beneath. But as they sat together, and recalled the long-forgotten scenes of their childhood, they concluded that they were brother and sister" (201). The telltale birthmark, although convincing, is not evidence enough for them to believe their kinship until the emotional memory of the past is mutually reconstructed through stories and song. Otten argues that "matters of identity and inheritance converge in the birthmark" and that perhaps the trope of the birthmark in Harper's work perhaps recalls the African tradition of seeing birthmarks on children as portents of future power (249). However, given the prevalence of this trope in fiction across national and color lines, and since the physical mark is ultimately disbelieved in favor of the power of song and story to forge affections, it seems more likely that the birthmark circulates as a sign of white (false) hope for the persistence of a reliable racial signifier on the body. Harper's conception of genealogy foreshadows the process by which Macon Dead pieces together the puzzle of his family past in Toni Morrison's *Song of Solomon* and highlights the fact that African history in the Americas is typically inaccessible by means of traditional or official historiography. Harper's use of the birthmark also curiously contrasts how Villaverde's Cecilia cannot be ultimately identified as Don Cándido's daughter until her birthmark is revealed, despite the fact that the truth of her genealogy was already available in the collective memory of the family, and in particular of María de Regla, the black wet-nurse.

Marilyn Elkins argues that "singing provides both the educated and the uneducated women with a voice that they eventually transfer to other, more public spheres" (48). Harper gives greater weight to memory, emotion, and song as the means of reconstructing the black family after slavery because visually discernable identities are always deceptive; the face and bodies are poor recorders, even at times disguisers, of familial affinities. Her narrative trains us to read as the former slaves do: to read behind the face, to see what the signifier hides in order to "circumvent the power of the establishment" (Elkins 46). Under slavery, the face of the master acts as a mask that attempts to hide its consanguinity, its brutality, and its knowledge, a disguise that is the source of the master's power. Another fellow slave with Robert, Aunt Linda, explains, "I can't read de newspapers, but old Missus's face is newspaper nuff for me" (9). Later, when Iola is teaching former slaves to read and write, "her face was a passport to their hearts. Ignorant of books, human faces were the scrolls from which they had been reading for ages. They had been the sunshine and shadow of their lives" (146). Harper's use of realism constantly lifts the veil of appearance in order to expose what lies beneath the surface and in the process heightens our understanding of the power of nonliterate forms of cognition. However, rather than simply inserting herself into that largely white tradition, she uses sentimentality to her own advantage in exposing the limits of white cultural understandings of the black community.

Like Villaverde's use of Leonardo as an example of a bad reader, Harper's Dr. Gresham, a white doctor who has fallen in love with Iola, observes that "it seems as if a whole volume was depicted on [Iola's] countenance. . . . It is a mystery I cannot solve." Foreshadowing the cognitive arrogance we see in the antagonists of Jean Rhys and Rosario Ferré, Gresham does not concede ignorance in response to this mystery; rather, he provides his own reading of her as an ideal symbol of black-white, North-South reunion, a symbol commonly forged out of the tragic mulatto in much literature of the period. He eroticizes the mystery of her face and wishes to marry her so as "to bury her secret in his Northern home, and hide from his aristocratic relations all knowledge of her mournful past" (118). Note that Gresham, not the narrator, proposes Iola as the metaphor for reconciliation. Harper allows us to see the metaphor of the white Negro, so common in much white literature, as a product of white ideology. We also see the limitations of that ideology: Gresham cannot read the face of Iola; he senses that there is a volume to read, but he cannot do the interpretation. Indeed, he is not even aware that she is a former slave dedicated to serving her people.

As in the case of Dr. Latrobe, Harper's reader sees Gresham's cognitive limitations and becomes suspicious of his prescription of racial disappearance to help cure the nation's racial illness. Harper offers the nurse as an even more powerful alternative to the doctor than Dr. Latimer. As Elizabeth Young explains, typically "the black nurse . . . brings the 'boys' of the wartime hospital to life," but Harper "transforms the category into a specific analogue for the black mother who finds in wartime an opportunity to seek both freedom and family" (281). Iola is a maternal stand-in for the black soldiers whom she nurses and is therefore the site at which they can regain a sense of racial belonging. In the grips of his war wounds, Robert Johnson experiences a momentary lapse of memory and "sometimes imagined that she was his mother, and he would tell her how he had missed her; and then at times he would call her sister," only to discover ultimately that his nurse is in fact his niece (139). The scene recalls Joseph Frowenfeld's recovery from the plague that takes the lives of his entire family; he confuses both his white and black nurse with his mother and sister. It also plays on the possibility of incest as a result of lost knowledge of genealogy. The difference is that in Frowenfeld's case, the nursing moment foreshadows and becomes the promise of national healing that his marriage to Clotilde would later signify, whereas the nursing moment here provides a recovery from what Young calls the "familial dislocation which often characterized the slave experience" (281). The near incestuous encounter becomes the possibility of family reunion, avoiding the fate of Villaverde's and Morúa's characters, and unlike the family reunification at the conclusion of *The Grandissimes* and its near-miss incest, this reunification brings together a black family divided by rape, slavery, and war.

Iola's refusal of Gresham's hand prevents her from becoming a mere symbol of white male liberal desire and works directly against the "popular racist beliefs that all mulattoes want to intermarry, and that they are intellectually superior to 'full-blood' blacks because of their partial white ancestry" (Nowatzki 49). As Claudia Tate contends, Iola's marriage to Latimer represents "the inalienable rights of black people as the consummated rights of families. . . . marriage and family life were not the culminating points of a woman's life but the pinnacles of a people's new beginnings" (126). Tate suggests that perhaps because of a critical preference for black male writings that confront racial injustice more directly, Harper has not received due attention. The marriage additionally signifies the subordination of Iola's ideology of racial salvation, of "uplifting the shadows" by means of maternal fidelity—her own prescription for the nation's ailments—and a perpetuation of the original plague of genealogical and racial dishonesty that Iola's father began. Iola refuses Gresham's offer because, as she explains, "I have resolved never to marry until I have found my mother" (118). By gathering stories and song in order to recover that matrilineal link, and by eventually marrying the mulatto Dr. Latimer, whose ideology matches her own, Iola represents a reversal of the trend toward racial disappearance. The novel demonstrates that the search for one's genealogical roots through the mother constitutes an acceptance of a historically shaped identity and the possibility of racial integrity. Harper's use of genealogy does not unveil blackness within the white family or deconstruct the established order, but discovers black kinship and reconstructs the black family on its own terms.

Despite apparent national consolidation following the Civil and Spanish-American Wars, colonialist ideologies from the period of slavery were disguised in new conceptions of the national family, and the political and cultural dynamics between the United States and Cuba provided the rhetoric that would blind them from these vestiges of colonialism. Some, in their eagerness to move beyond racial conflict, were tempted to elide racial difference altogether in order to arrive at a more facile solution to the painful problems of democracy in a former slave society. This is because Africanization, or what amounted to radical racial difference, posed a threat to each nation's family model and therefore frequently was made invisible to the nation's eye. In the case of the United States, because a white genealogy was the exclusive model, blacks were explicitly excluded from public space. Even in the case of Cuba, which like many Latin American nations chose a racially hybrid model, only those forms of blackness that could establish productive hybridity with white Creole culture found room in the national family.

The trap of Plantation America is that to ignore how history shapes the construction of race and the identity of individuals is to live a lie, but to forsake the responsibility of trying to move beyond the past is simply to repeat it. The authors in this chapter did not solve the race dilemma because they were not sufficiently listened to and, perhaps more important, because of their own entrapment between irreconcilable ideologies. Nonetheless, they did call attention to the role of white social power in the construction of race and they freed categories of racial identity from the prison house of visual perception; they were thus able to suggest what a future nation of blacks and whites might look like after the decline of such power. In the interest of the heirs of the plantocracy, the quest to define race would continue to exercise epistemological and, of course, political control in racial matters and to ensure that the black family did not find its legitimate place in the nation's soil. But it would also continue in the interest of those who did not yet have their legitimacy socially and politically established. By dismantling the effectiveness of visual control over the body as the racial signifier and by exploring alternative languages of the body, these writers helped to move investigations of national life in the wake of slavery away from sight and toward the sound and the signification of language itself. In their suggestive representations of alternative means of genealogical knowledge, and of the alternative meanings of genealogy, they opened the way for others to explore the sounds of narrative, music, and ideology as they resonate in the novel's form and in the construction of alternatively imagined national identities.

4 Between the Insular Self and the Exotic Other

Alejo Carpentier and William Faulkner

Though my *Flight* never pass the incoming tide
of this inland sea beyond the loud reefs
of the final Bahamas, I am satisfied
if my hand gave voice to one people's grief

—Derek Walcott (from "The Schooner *Flight*")

Postslavery Returns

In the wake of slavery, many regions of Plantation America were forced to make the difficult transition from an agriculturally based economy undergirded by a paternalistic plantation family model to an industrialized economy sustained by liberalist ideologies. As a result of the Spanish-American War of 1898, itself an outgrowth of the conflict of those ideologies, the United States brought to both Cuba and Puerto Rico, among other territories, the neocolonial strategy of absentee ownership along with new notions of egalitarianism.[1] Although such liberalist notions often won on the rhetorical level, their marriage to older, paternalistic ideologies was disguised when U.S. capitalism began to extend its influence first to the American South and then into the Caribbean.[2] It is important to remember that paternalism was not solely an ideology of the plantocracy, and nor was liberalism strictly an import from the North, which brought increasing technological innovations. The plantocracy itself was riddled by a contradiction regarding history's relevance to legitimacy; it was caught between the dream of ascendancy and that of descendancy, the dream of an economic rise from obscure origins and that of status determined by origin. The landed plantocracy in the Americas was, in essence, a class that sought to combine European models of aristocracy with the New World ideal of the rise of the individual.

As a result of modernization, the ideologies of the plantocracy escaped dissolution because they were integrated into the very institutional fabric of postslavery societies, and their contradictions were heightened. The paternalism of the landed classes was threatened during slavery from both ends, by bourgeois liberalism and by proletarian socialism. Once slavery was abolished, these classes found themselves in more direct competition with, and in many cases losing to, these two sectors. Consequently, they surrendered their "organic view of society and the idea that men were responsible for each other, while they retained the worst of their traditions, most notably, their ever deepening arrogance and contempt for the laboring classes and darker races" (Fox-Genovese and Genovese 398). The symbolic justification of the hierarchical, feudal, and paternalistic structures of the plantation family shifted from a private genealogy of the biological family to that of a public populist affiliation. The landed classes became in many cases wage earners, subject to the volatile economic changes of the early twentieth century with no genealogical hold on status and security. This, in turn, contributed to the growth of what Doris Sommer has called the "corporate nation," which represented "a father-figure of national proportions" to which these classes forfeited their authority (*One Master* 6).

Much early twentieth-century literature represents the failure of the generative impulse with stories of childless couples, orphans, and other family crises because modernization presented the challenging task of finding "new and different ways of conceiving of human relationships" in order to "substitute for those ties that connect members of the same family across generations" (Said 16). That process of substitution brought to the fore "institutions, associations, and communities whose social existence was not in fact guaranteed by biology but by affiliation" (17). Thus, the age of modernism saw the rise of a "compensatory order" in which subjection to the will of the community or cultural system that maintains a paternal power over its subjects replaces obeisance to a biological father.

As that "compensatory order" gained ground into the twentieth century, in literary representation the body became less reliable in making visible one's racial genealogy. Charles Chesnutt, Frances Harper, and Martín Morúa Delgado each hailed the loss of the plantocracy's control over the meaning and codification of racial signifiers but nevertheless remained bounded by plantation ideology, to a degree, in their obsessions with the visibility and readability of genealogical truths. As evident in the works of Alejo Carpentier and William Faulkner, by at least the

1930s genealogy was no longer merely indicative of social status, race, or even of national origins but of the economic, cultural, and political forces of modernization and neocolonialism. The body previously held the codes that, when read from the perspective of an outside eye, would unveil origins and thus grant the reader a measure of control over that knowledge. But in Carpentier's *El siglo de las luces* (trans. *Explosion in a Cathedral*) and William Faulkner's *Absalom, Absalom!*, boundaries of the body have become porous and unreliable indicators of origins.

Biological origins are always refracted through our cultural milieu; genealogy and race are merely metaphors for larger factors that constitute and constantly disrupt our identities. Those factors are neocolonial postslavery structures that, as my readings of Faulkner and Carpentier will demonstrate, place American identity in a negotiation between the insular self and the exotic other. Each writer explores the insular nature of the plantation household and the obstacles such insularity poses to understanding the range of identity in the postslavery Americas. They present the plantation's past as analogous to twentieth-century manifestations of imperialism in the Caribbean. They argue that plantations once imitated empires in that they brought into close proximity and into hierarchical relations otherwise foreign cultures and then expelled from the center of power the hybrid forms of culture that resulted. However, it is now the modern forms of imperialism that imitate the former plantation in a postslavery context.

Consequently, they question how the postslavery Americas can be free of the historical forces of colonialism and slavery without also being free of the forces of historical events altogether. If modernity is manifest in the desire to wipe out the past in order to create a new point of origin, what kind of modernity is possible for the postslavery Americas? Will not an effort to move beyond the legacies of colonialism and slavery (that the neocolonialism of the United States in particular has ironically transformed into the forces of modernity) paradoxically lead writers to simplify another past that is free of colonial chains—that of the African or the autochthonous—and that is itself antimodern and perhaps also ahistorical?[3] While Carpentier seeks a genealogy of the Caribbean island—a delineation of its historical and cultural place—that is neither incestuously sealed nor hopelessly scattered in reaction to dominant neocolonial forces, Faulkner raises the question of how an emergent imperial power, particularly one that has forged its authority in the wake of its own colonial and slave-owning past, decolonizes itself. Although the novels have different historical settings and geographical contexts, both explore the implications of the French and Haitian Revolutions in the extended Caribbean and expose postslavery nationalisms as reactively echoing historical change established elsewhere and as therefore potentially doomed to replicate slavery's structures. They describe a transnational postslavery identity riddled by the contradictions of egalitarianism and imperialism and inevitably condemned by its own historicity, its own enslavement to the history of slavery. Indicative of the respective geopolitical positions from which each author writes, historicity for Faulkner is an oedipal entrapment, whereas for Carpentier it offers prodigal, revolutionary possibilities.

Thus far we have seen attempts in postslavery writing to transcend the limitations imposed on historical memory by a dominant genealogy. By providing new witnesses to history and paradigms of representation, writers attempt to expose new truths that contrast what they insist are the illusory claims to realism of prior narratives. And yet we have seen that their success in representing new genealogical truth that escapes contingencies of former colonialisms is richly ambiguous. The new difference presented either collapses into familiarity and integration or remains exiled beyond the bounds of the imagined community. And the ontological position of the narrator vacillates between speaking from within lived historical experience or speaking to it as an isolated outsider. In his essay "The Two Relativisms," J. Hillis Miller calls this a distinction between constative narrative (wherein narrative effectively creates a new difference because it corresponds to an external reality or to the past) and performative narrative (where it collapses back into self-referentiality and sameness). He further argues that this tension reflects the dynamic between the taboos against too much difference—implied in the notion of miscegenation—and too much sameness, implied in incest.[4] It is, of course, the genealogical dimensions of this narrative vacillation that interest me here because they are suggestive of narrative's struggle against the contingencies of history. As such they are helpful in understanding Faulkner's depiction of the U.S. postslavery struggle as informed by oedipal and incestuous insularity (and as thus condemned, potentially, to the same story) and Carpentier's view of the Caribbean's prodigal desire for the exotic (which also condemns the subject, potentially, to a perpetual preference for a different story).

In that they represent a kind of hopeless redundancy in the search for origins, the oedipal and prodigal narrative paradigms signify the ambiguous survival of slavery's colonialisms. They represent, at both ends of the spectrum, the seemingly impossible task of encountering a postslavery originality. The search for originality can itself, in the words of Gabriel García Márquez, "become a Western aspiration" ("Solitude of Latin America" 90). Advocacy of imitation can inadvertently inject difference, while the promotion of originality may, in fact, replicate old patterns. For García Márquez, in Latin America, the "crucial problem has been a lack of conventional means to render our lives believable. . . . The interpretation of our reality through patterns not our own serves only to make us ever more unknown, ever less free, ever more solitary" (89). That is, if a New World language is merely performative and self-referential, and does not correspond to a New World reality, we will never escape foreign paradigms of thought and will never know ourselves. We will be trapped within Octavio Paz's labyrinth of solitude where foreign ideas, posing as universals, blind us to the "actual situation of our people" and sacrifice "reality to words." This is the kind of situation where, to revisit José Martí, "the colony lives on in the republic" (*Nuestra América* 13); that is, narratives do not display an awareness of their own ironic internalization of prior values from which they are ostensibly rebelling.

However, to insist that the dichotomy between exotic ideas and a local reality is clearly discernable is to risk a similarly blinding insularity. As Carpentier and Faulkner see it, if we are to escape the illusions of colonialism, we must never remain static at either end of the spectrum. Such perpetual movement provides the central tension in García Márquez's *One Hundred Years of Solitude* (1971), a tension between a flight ever outward and away from his fictional town of Macondo toward the foreign discourses of European culture and U.S. capitalism and the entrenchment of those who never leave. The two poles stand in a dialectical relationship with one another, and therefore identity is always under siege and under perpetual renegotiation. On one hand, Macondo's founder, José Arcadio Buendía, dreams of "a noisy city with houses having mirror walls," while on the other hand, José Arcadio's gypsy friend Melquiades prophesies that Macondo "was to be a luminous city with great glass houses" (*One Hundred Years* 32, 59). We are trapped incestuously by the opacity of our own image and our own thinking (hence the mirror walls that appropriately are seen in a personal dream). And yet we have the capacity to penetrate the outside and may be lured away by the promise of newness and freedom from the self (hence the glass walls that are appropriately seen in a prophetic vision). However, as José Arcadio discovers, the paradox is that in flight we will return "to where one had set out [regresar al punto de partida] by consistently sailing east" (14).[5]

Returning to one's origins is not only possible but inevitable. And in returning, the writer has the potential to recapture a local reality.

Much to the chagrin of his European and U.S. critics, García Márquez advocates this kind of solidarity with the local when he insists that "nothing has ever occurred to me, nor have I been able to do anything, that is more awesome than reality itself. The most I have been able to do has been to alter that reality with poetic devices, but there's not a single line in any of my books that doesn't have its origin in actual fact" ("Latin America's" 15). He concludes that "reality is a better writer than we are" (16). For him, the best Latin American literature has never been performative or self-referential but has constatively and honestly represented reality as it has unfolded for the writer.

García Márquez deflects intrusions of readers from dominant cultural centers by rhetorically positioning himself in perfect solidarity with local reality, or in Miller's terms as a writer of pure constative narratives, but this rhetoric somewhat problematically erases authorial performance. Paz depicts a less polarized scenario of the agency involved when the writer recovers origins: "[T]o return home it is first necessary to risk abandoning it. Only the prodigal son returns. To reproach Latin American literature for its uprootedness is to ignore that only by being uprooted can we recover our portion of reality. Distance has been the condition of discovery. Distance and the mirages that it created—there is no wrong in nourishing oneself on illusions *if we manage to transform them into realities*" (*Puertas* 16, emphasis added). Paz's final qualification is indeed the crux of the issue: Unless there is some way to transform quixotically into reality the illusions a prodigal distance provides, the lens by which the writer perceives a "native" reality will unavoidably reflect the very ideologies of the imperial powers that thus have forged their paternal authority. The question is whether the return to origins will signify an insular enclosure, repetition, an opening out, or repetition with a difference. In other words, is it a journey out of one's solitude (and hence a break with history) or simply a journey of one's solitude (and hence a mere confirmation of one's inescapable contingency)? Paz suggests, and Faulkner and Carpentier concur, that it is a rich combination of both.

Many New World exiles, from the Brazilian modernists to the Mexican muralists to Alejo Carpentier himself, have returned from Europe energized by a rediscovery of the native roots of their lands and the aesthetic possibilities such local realities represent. It was, in fact, Carpentier's return to Haiti that led to his own formulation of *lo real maravilloso* (the marvelous reality) of Latin America. While these artists and many of their critics have been eager to identify what constitutes a new paternal authority of national identity, they have been less willing to explore in their works the ideological complexity of such returns. We need to ask whether the returned exile injects new forms of colonialist ideology, or simply new forms of metropolitan dependency, into the national culture. Is what appears to be new and liberating merely a replicated, neocolonial sameness, and hence, an oedipal joke in that the populace is further blinded to the truths of their culture's genealogical roots?

The prison house of colonialism is that the tools of perception that might be brought to bear in discerning between colonial illusion and native authenticity are themselves of questionable origin. Some writers have resorted to nostalgia either for a nativistic authenticity that was prior to the arrival of the colony or, in the case of the Puerto Rican writer Antonio Pedreira's *Insularismo* (1934), for a pure cultural genealogy that is not corrupted by *mestizaje*. Pedreira believed that *mestizaje* was responsible for Puerto Rican insularity because it erased "almost completely the point of origin" (31). Between Spanish and African origins, the Puerto Rican personality "finds itself transient, in a pendulary action, leaping out and returning, in a coming and going, seeking a way, like a restless dove in flight. Confined between two types of opposing cultures, our people find themselves in a difficult period of transition" (75).

Although lamented by Pedreira, the lack of static and fixed origins for Carpentier and Faulkner becomes an opportunity to generate new identities. Rather than offering another, newer version of realism to counter the historical illusions of their precursors, they offer illusions—that is, their own aggressively imagined revisions of history—to counter realism's genealogical claims to origins. They call upon new witnesses to history, to be sure, but not because they have pretensions to historical revisionism but because, as Lois Parkinson Zamora describes the historical imagination in the Americas, "the anxiety of origins [becomes] an appetite for inclusion" (*Usable Past* 196). She further explains that in the New World where origins are often unknown, or even unknowable, this appetite creates "not homogenization or unification but the countenancing of multiple, coexisting, conflictual, unfinished histories" (196). The greater the bravado of their recourse to history, the more apparent the imposition of their own imagination onto reality becomes, and hence the more difficult it becomes to identify the distinctions between reality and their imagination. Whereas Pedreira is clearly disconcerted by the unstable movement of the subject between unknown origins, for Carpentier and Faulkner it is precisely in the perpetual and patient movement among the various origins of the Americas, between insularity and flight, where an American identity is created, not discovered. Like Paz's notion of transforming illusions into reality, Faulkner's and Carpentier's postslavery musings emphasize the autonomy of the postslavery imagination to imagine the past and negotiate identity in the movement among various origins.

A Prodigal Return

Carpentier, a writer of prodigious knowledge of European culture, was wary that Western culture had the power to veil a pure and original view of Caribbean reality. Published just three years after the 1959 Cuban Revolution, his *El siglo de las luces* (1962; trans. *Explosion in a Cathedral*, 1963) attempts to negotiate a way around the blinding power of imperial discourse by telling the story of the French Revolution's failure in the Caribbean. Carpentier's interest is representing the slippage between imperial discourse and island reality, or, in the terms discussed earlier, to portray the language of empire as performative. Important material from Caribbean history dating to the Age of Enlightenment and Revolution for him serves as an analogy to Caribbean's contemporary struggles with the paternalism of the United States. The years covered in the novel, 1789 to 1809, saw the groundwork laid for the emergence of Latin American independence due, in part, to the strange marriage of new forms of European revolutionary thought with familiar forms of European sovereignty in the colonies. What interests Carpentier about this period is the ways in which it reveals empire "as a translation system" of European values and policies, but one that translated unevenly and "transforms metropolitan democracy into pressures" of varying degrees from island to island (Stinchcombe 198). This discrepancy, as evidence of mistranslation, represents the possible delineation of a Caribbean identity that has anachronistically and wantonly cannibalized imperial discourse for its own revolutionary purposes.

As played out in the Caribbean, the French Revolution was "the first confrontation [of many analogous ones to come] between a democratic anti-slavery movement in the colonies and the politics of empire" (Stinchcombe 20). It provided the Caribbean with democratic ideals that eventually led to the temporary emancipation of the slaves in the French colonies and to the Haitian Revolution itself. And yet those ideals were imposed on the colonies in imperialist fashion. When Haiti took those ideals to heart and had to fight off French, Spanish, and British invasions in order to preserve freedom for its citizens, the imperial paradox had come full circle: "[T]he same international system that eventually abolished the slave trade, then even slavery itself on each empire's own islands, also isolated Haiti from the diplomatic system" (Stinchcombe 235). And, of course, the United States took an active role in Haiti's isolation until U.S. emancipation took effect in 1865. So the Western imperial governments that gave birth to and fostered notions of individual rights and freedoms proved intolerant of the Haitian Revolution simply because, after years of waiting on the French, Toussaint Louverture saw the need to divorce these egalitarian values from paternal imperialism.

Thus, the Age of Enlightenment in the Caribbean allows Carpentier an opportunity to explore the interdependencies of slavery and empire. He demonstrates how the plantation system depended on imperial capital and politics even though plantations were designed to be island economies. Arthur Stinchcombe observes in this regard that the plantation "as an organization of labor was connected to the world system by that system's finance capital part" and "had a political system among the capitalist oligarchy much like that of port cities of Europe"; thus, the plantation functioned as a "corporation" (61). In this way a story of the plantation's past has parallels with Carpentier's own time, during which twentieth-century U.S. corporate development intensified in the Caribbean. Carpentier further shows that, as Paul Gilroy contends, the "intellectual and cultural achievements of the black Atlantic populations exist partly inside and not always against the grand narrative of Enlightenment and its operational principles" (48). Although Carpentier is tempted to identify in black Caribbean resistance a core identity that is wholly other than European imperialism, ultimately his story of the impact of the French Revolution in the Caribbean tells of their dialectical relationship. And this raises the questions that pervades *Explosion in a Cathedral:* With what language, with what value system, can we identify the Caribbean difference Haiti embodies? How can a writer delineate that difference without also seeming to expel it?

When Carpentier began his career with *Ecue-Yamba-O* (1933), he found himself caught in this paradox. He attempted to unveil an autochthonous and autonomous Caribbean identity that successfully resisted neocolonial forces, but by the 1960s he claimed that the novel suffered a weakness of much regional literature of the time: an inability to liberate an authentic, autochthonous subjectivity from the grip of the outsider's view. That is, he lamented that his narrative collapsed into a mere performance of his own subjectivity. Although he had been exposed to Afro-Cuban religious and cultural practices as a youth and therefore felt qualified to document these cultural realities, he later "realized that everything deep, true and universal from the world I had presumed to paint in my novel had remained beyond the reach of my observation. . . . Since that time, I have little faith, every day less than before, in that literature which has presented itself, until very recently, as the most authentic of America" (*Tientos* 11). Carpentier became critical of the trend in Latin American literature to depend on the "naturalist-nativist-typicist-vernacular" of historical realism because "in very few cases it has arrived at the deepest, at the truly transcendental level of things" (10).

In 1949, when he formulates his theory of the marvelous reality of Latin America and the Caribbean, he remains insistent on being able to identify sites of difference. As he remarks in his famous essay "De lo real maravilloso americano," (1958; trans. "On the Marvelous Real in America") the Haitian Revolution represents "a history that is impossible to situate in Europe" (*Tientos* 115). For Carpentier, *lo real maravilloso,* America's marvelous reality, resists the discourses of Europe that seek to name and dictate Caribbean reality chiefly because of the presence of black culture and the New World's untamed natural world, which represent breaks from the continuum of European history (González Echevarría, "Socrates"). By virtue of its difference from Europe, *lo real maravilloso* provides the promise of escape from the grip of colonialism. As Carpentier's commentary about regionalist prose reveals, despite the distance he wishes to create between his work of the 1960s and that of the 1930s and 1940s, Carpentier did not abandon the aspiration that literature might somehow reach the transcendental essence of things.[6] The difference in his later novels, beginning with *El reino de este mundo* and more emphatically apparent in *Explosion in a Cathedral,* is that in them Carpentier acknowledges and exploits the baroque ironies that result from the writer's repeated failures to identify unambiguously the parameters of marvelous reality.

In *Explosion in a Cathedral,* he uses the conch shell as a metaphor for the kinds of baroquisms that paradoxically signify language's limitations in representing reality:

The snail [caracol] was the mediator between evanescent, fugitive, lawless, measureless fluidity, and the land, with its crystallisations, its structures, its morphology, where everything could be grasped and weighed.

... Esteban reflected on how, for millennium upon millennium, the spiral had been present to the everyday gaze of maritime races, who were still uncapable of understanding it, or of even grasping the reality of its presence. He [was] astonished by this science of form which had been exhibited for so long to humanity that still lacked eyes to appreciate it [sin ojos para pensarla]. What is there round about me which is already complete, recorded, real [definido, inscrito, presente], yet which I cannot understand? What sign, what message, what warning is there, in the curling leaves of the endive, the alphabet of moss, the geometry of the rose-apple? (*Explosion* 180)

The arbitrary fluidity of the ocean, similar to the lawlessness of European colonialisms, has clashed with the solidity of the islands to form the baroquism of the shell. The inability of language borrowed from European discourse to grasp Caribbean reality creates cultural practices that, like this shell, act as mediators between the two poles. The task for the Caribbean writer, then, is to create baroquisms like the shell by attacking the void created by the various absentee paternal cultures with all the force of language at one's command, by attempting to "name it all" (*Tientos* 37). Such audacity becomes, paradoxically, a humble confession of language's limitations before the primordiality of an American reality. Precisely because reality always offers surprises and exposes the limitations of representation, an American language must be audaciously baroque. Carpentier demands of great prose: "Show me the object; make it so that with your words I can touch it, evaluate it, feel its weight. . . . But the prose that gives a thing life and consistency, weight and measure, is a baroque, a forcefully baroque, prose" (*Tientos* 36).

Representation, for Carpentier, is procreation, or, in Miller's terms, it is performative not constative. But rather than falling into the very trap of colonialism's incestuously performative language, the spiraling of Carpentier's baroque prose indicates an awareness that language continually and unavoidably flees the objects it seeks to name, only to return and try to name them again. And when the object of language is history, the elusive nature of a New World history never fully enters into representation. Without pretending to a diachronic, Hegelian notion of historical evolution, Carpentier can passionately return again and again to the past and to notions of original authenticity in the New World as an escape from the trappings of colonialism. Roberto González Echevarría summarizes Carpentier's prose as "revolutionary writing in its etymological sense, in that it revolves around an absent axis that is constituted by the very movement of its periphery. If, in Hegel's famous dictum, world history is world judgment, in *Explosion in a Cathedral* history and judgment are one—writing is history" (*Alejo Carpentier* 253).

As the snail passage demonstrates, a baroque attempt to bring to life an object allows us to see much more than the object; it suggests what we cannot see. According to Carpentier, "baroque . . . is the language of those peoples who, ignorant of the truth, look for it eagerly. . . . Baroque, the language of abundance, is also the language of insufficiency."[7] We can read in Carpentier's excess of expression and of naming, in the morphology and architecture of the narrative, a metonymical representation of what we cannot see, of that marvelous reality untainted by traces of Europe that he cannot tell us. Raul Silva-Caceres explains that Carpentier "allows us to configure, by means of metonymic displacement, a profound *vision* of new literary objects" (495). The attempt to name everything, even at the risk of excess, prevents imperial powers from shrinking the Caribbean sense of self and limiting its freedom for expression, even if it also means that representations of that sense of self are always provisional, rhetorical, and ultimately performative, not constative, of the reality depicted. Carpentier always condemns his subjectivity to a position "of the belated outsider, despite his longing to discard his Western cosmopolitan perspective," because "only an alienated character . . . can rightly perceive the indigenous or native quality of the wondrous American real" (Mikics 386–87).

He avoids the illusion of a static, fixed originality because his narrative consistently moves between its performative and constative functions—between saying too much and saying too little—which is a tension between scattering and gathering, dispersion and cohesion, stagnation and nomadism, where both opposites at their extreme threaten to falsify the Caribbean self. Cultural stagnation can result from an excessive reluctance to cross cultural borders, but if those borders are too porous, constant contact with the world of empire can eventually erode the sensation of one's singularity. In Carpentier's world, reality is always refracted through lenses of geographical distance and cultural difference, making it impossible to see foreign objects as entirely other or autochthonous objects as entirely native to one's own land. Caribbean identity vacillates between the insular and antimodern temptation to insist regressively on its own autochthonous differences from modernizing powers and the endless temptation to chase and exoticize dominant, foreign cultural practices, ideas, ideologies.

Explosion in the Cathedral begins in the final years of the eighteenth

century, when the first signs of revolutionary change found their way
into the plantation system. As such, the novel explores the historical
roots of the plantation's adaptability to its challenges. The death of Sofía
and Carlos's father opens the novel and propels the newly orphaned
characters (the mother having already passed away) toward surrogate
affiliations. The father's absence represents the decline both of paternal
authority and of an economic system that thrived on the slave trade;
reminiscent of Villaverde's Don Cándido, the father had been an absentee plantation owner who engaged in mercantile activities. On their
own, the children are caught within a series of insular circles, abandoned
to run out the course of events begun elsewhere like "an island within an
island [ínsula dentro de una ínsula]" (14). Speaking of Carlos, the narrator observes that "islander" and "orphan" are synonymous:

> [H]e would be condemned to live in this marine city . . . where every pos-
> sible outlet to adventure was stopped up by the sea [con barreras de
> océano cerradas sobre toda aventura posible]; . . . finding himself . . . the
> victim of a father whom he reproached . . . for the crime of having died
> too soon. At this moment the boy was suffering as never before from the
> claustrophobia [la sensación de encierro] induced by living in an island,
> by being in a country where there were no roads leading to other lands
> along which to wander, ride, or make one's way, crossing frontiers. (14)

Without the father, they are beached on an island. If, as Stinchcombe observes, the relationship between empires and the islands "took place at
harbors and across beaches," to be stranded by the legacy of the plantation is also paradoxically to be made aware of transnational frontiers
that can now be crossed without the plantation father's authorial presence (39). At the same time that they become aware of their immobility,
the two children and Esteban, their cousin, are "overcome by an almost
sensual feeling of freedom"; unleashed are new desires for travel, experience, adventure, and sexual licentiousness (17).

This vacillation between insularity and flight results from the vacuum
created by the insufficiency of plantation discourse to serve as the paternal directive of Caribbean history; consequently, new forms of corporate
affiliation compete for the children's attention. A colonial executor steps
in as a surrogate "to be [the] father now," but he only offers them further isolation from both the slaves and the centers of colonial power.
Their hermetic vulnerability allows the French revolutionary Victor
Hugues to usurp the executor's surrogate authority and assume the "role
of the paterfamilias in the house" (35). His tales of adventure sharply

contrast with the literature of their father's library and draw the children outside the walls of the home. The decline of the organic view of plantation paternalism is facilitated by the arrival of a revolutionary element from the metropolis that speaks of new, democratic forms of political organization. So like the surrogate father who appears in the novels examined in earlier chapters, Hugues potentially drains the Creole family of its patrimony and of its potential for self-realization. The curious twist is the fact that, unlike the previous surrogates who step in to reinforce explicitly those structures that sustain the plantation, Hugues arrives ostensibly to offer revolutionary thinking that would do away with them. Carpentier's point is that plantation structures profited insidiously under the control of the French Revolution. The novel follows the vagaries of Hugues's political career, which merely postpone Esteban's sexual union with his cousin Sofía, a union that comes to signify a recovery of self-knowledge and a healing of the wound of their past dispersion. In the meantime, Sofía and Esteban are erotically and prodigally attracted to Hugues as an alternative "father" and as a foreign source of their own self-realization.

Hugues, on the other hand, proves to have committed the oedipal error in his desire to both control his destiny and ignore the historical difference created by the presence of blacks and a separate geography. As a colonial administrator of the French Revolution in the Caribbean, he has acted as revolutionary and tyrant, liberator and enslaver, because of his self-interested obedience to the latest, delayed commands coming from Paris. This has blinded him to the ways people, not policies, ultimately move history: "I thought I was controlling my own destiny, [but] *they*—the people who always make and unmake us, though we don't even know them—have made me take so many parts that I no longer know which one I should be playing. I've put on so many costumes I no longer know which is the right one" (333). Sofía remarks that the raw veal on his eyes, placed there in treatment of the "Egyptian Disease," makes him "look like a parricide in a Greek tragedy" (334). The father that Hugues has slain is not the father figure he replaced in Sofía's home, but rather what proves to be the real directive force of history to which Esteban and Sofía eventually ally themselves, that of the people. Carpentier implies that historical origins are not in the past or in possession of the policy-makers in metropolitan centers of power, but are always (re)constituted by the agency of contemporary peoples. Ultimately, a diachronic search for origins becomes a synchronic alliance with the social forces that metropolitan powers cannot contain and that shape the present and the future's possibilities. The implication, for Carpentier, is that history does not operate according to a rational order that stands apart from human agency or that therefore leads historical reconstruction into nostalgia. His is an existential view that history is what human agency shapes it to be in the present (González Echevarría, *Alejo Carpentier*).

Unlike Hugues, Esteban eventually discovers that the ideals of the French Revolution, even if they led to the abolition of slavery in France's colonies, cannot become the new paternal directives of the Caribbean because they have not emerged from the peoples of the islands and because continuing colonial status has been offered to the Caribbean under the guise of new freedoms. Initially he removes himself from the plantation home and from Cuba in order to pursue the center, the final Logos, from which emerge the discourses and ideologies that shape his world. As he brings himself geographically closer to the source of those revolutionary ideals, "one seemed to be in the midst of a gigantic allegory of a revolution rather than a revolution itself, a metaphorical revolution, . . . which had been made elsewhere, which revolved on a hidden axis, which had been elaborated in subterranean councils, invisible to those who had wanted to know all about it" (95).

Esteban acts at one point as a translator of revolutionary tracts, only to discover that they don't translate evenly. So the Caribbean, and other areas marginal to the French Revolution, prove to be shaped by specters whose origins have been rendered unidentifiable and ultimately irrelevant. Whereas in Faulkner, the Caribbean margins of empire never enter into full representation and are depicted as mere echoes of imperial fears, Carpentier centers his plot at those very margins where French imperial power never gains full representation; France only appears as "repercussions in the Caribbean" (González Echevarría, *Alejo Carpentier* 242). But Carpentier insists that this need not be a cause for lament since it is a sign of the failure of imperial discourse to control its own ideological meaning when it has been translated into the context of the Caribbean. Esteban's disappointment in discovering that his search has only encountered "the perpetually retreating line of the horizon" provides him with a crucial vantage point to see what he has left behind and renews his desire to return to his origins (299). At the heart of the revolution in France, he discovers his desire for his mother surrogate: "[H]e longed to lay his head in Sofía's form lap, as he had done so many times, in search of that soothing, maternal strength which had flowed from her virgin womb, as if she had really been his mother" (110).

Esteban embraces a new view of his origins, still rather diachronic, the only difference being that now, in his pursuit of the origins of power in the French Revolution, he becomes patriotically Caribbean. That is, he has changed directions and apparently found salvation in his new-found advocacy of Caribbean origins, but his understanding of historical origins and of legitimacy has not fundamentally shifted. He merely completes the other half of the prodigal journey by coming home. The story of the prodigal son is one of a return to origins, to be sure, but its applicability to Esteban lies in the fact that the prodigal son returns not to a redundant sameness (as does the unwitting Oedipus) but consciously chooses a redeemed sense of origins. This is what is particularly significant about his reunion with Sofía: It is incestuous—nearly a reunion with the mother—but because of his prodigal sojourns, it becomes a redemptive return to roots. And thus it is a return with the inevitability of a new departure, not a closure.[8]

Esteban's prodigal return paradoxically embraces not origins but anachronism and the differences that disrupt and disable the progression of a smooth historical continuum. Esteban becomes conscious of the Caribbean as both trapped and redeemed by history because it is freed by the impossibility of being able to trace origins and authority diachronically. Edouard Glissant explains that this historical trauma of slavery and colonialism in the Americas necessitates "the obligation to remake oneself every time on the basis of a series of forgettings" ("Creolization" 273). The chaos of cultural and historical change in creolization is precisely the source of its postcolonial power since it means that history cannot be predicted or controlled from the outside. Glissant adds that "imagining and recreating from *traces* of memory removes a person far away from systems, far away not only from ideological thinking but even more from the thought of any imperative system" (273). Esteban's creolized return opposes Hugues's devotion to an affiliative chain of command that insists dogmatically on an imperative system of unchanging power, wisdom, and authority foreign to the soil he occupies, that of the "incorruptible" French revolutionary ideals. When the leadership and the nature of the revolution change, he insists that the line of authority continues even if it cannot be seen. Even though he affectionately calls Esteban the "émigré," Hugues himself spends most of his time outside the country, never getting beyond the boundaries of his enlarged ego so as to accept his own historicity or to understand the world around him. Because he does not therefore perceive the anachronistic difference a Caribbean reality makes, time appears to cease its movement. That is why Sofía is overcome with "the horrible sensation that time was standing still" when she sees Hugues continuing his violence and spinning in a redundant circle of history (327).

Esteban forsakes the search for the origins of imperial discourse and begins a search for the cause of its failure, a search that begins with a sexual union with Sofía. First-cousin incest signals not an oedipal trap but a prodigal redemption because his desire for Sofía is a response to his disillusionment with his "father," the French Revolution and Hugues. As Werner Sollors has remarked, intragenerational incest "can . . . be represented as the victory of the revolutionary *fraternité* over the tyrannical father"; in this case, however, the empire-father is tyrannical because of the manner in which he imposes the idea of *fraternité* (*Neither* 319). Esteban and Sofía die not in the land of their origins but in what Carpentier finally concludes is the site of history's origins, in the Madrid streets where the people engage in struggle against the latest imperial manifestations of the French Revolution. This location is significant in that the conflict set a precedent for Latin America's wars of independence that were to come. As opposed to time standing still, they fight on a "Day without End," in an eternal present perpetuated by the activism of people, a day that remains ever the same in the sense that it is ever changing (*Explosion* 346). In this sense, their union joins the insular self with the self in flight.

The movement in *Explosion in a Cathedral* between a Caribbean revolution and a European one—between what Antonio Benítez-Rojo calls "nature and the folk tradition" and "the languages and episteme of Europe"—is an outgrowth of Carpentier's deep knowledge of Caribbean history (*Repeating* 2d ed. 275). The more he researched the history of the region, the more aware he became of both its singularity and its historical interdependency with Europe. The novel presents his more mature and self-conscious reflection on regionalism since writing *Ecue-Yamba-O,* in that it places at the center of its plot the search for regional authenticity, not some pretension as to what those origins might look like in narrative form. And he demonstrates that the search becomes a constant coming and going between the two poles. As Benítez-Rojo explains in his Lacanian analysis of Carpentier's short story "El camino de Santiago," "the circular . . . voyage between Europe and America . . . expresses not just the desire for the Mother within the Oedipal triangle, but also the search for the lost paradise of the Mirror Stage, where the Self and the Other compose the same body" (272). Although Carpentier insists on the permanent transience of Caribbean identity, he romances the possibility of the union between the insular self and the exotic other, a union that frames meaningfully the Caribbean's impossible search for origins. Esteban and Sofía escape the circular and repetitive patterns of plantation history—and the trappings of their own historicity—by foresaking the exotic frontiers that Hugues has represented and uniting themselves with the movers of history: the people. By implication, historical origins per se do not exist, but historical memory and contemporary social organization are things we create.

Rather than making an appeal to an ahistorical, mythical conception of the past that we see in much regionalist literature, Carpentier explores in *Explosion in a Cathedral* a representation of a densely, historically contingent past, that of the turn of the nineteenth century, in order to offer the possibility of the Caribbean's historical evolution toward a revolutionary, ahistorical future. This romance with historical evolution is not without its own risk, however, of prematurely identifying originality and authenticity. Derek Walcott has warned against those exiles whose returns are anything but prodigal. They make a "eugenic leap from imperialism to independence by longing for the ancestral dignity of the wanderer-warrior. Mysterious customs. Defunct gods. Sacred rites. . . . [T]hey are children of the nineteenth-century ideal, the romance of redcoat and savage warrior, their simplification of choosing to play Indian instead of cowboy, . . . is the hallucination of imperial romance" ("Muse" 22). Although Carpentier is clearly aware of this risk (and Walcott seems to believe Carpentier is decidedly not guilty of this error), the novel nevertheless is haunted by this kind of a romance.

Carpentier in his novel is undecided, ultimately, in his view of history. On one hand, he is attracted to Glissant's idea that creolization is unpredictable and deconstructive of colonial imperatives. On the other, he wants to locate and identify the source of that power as "the people" and thus exhibits an implied hope that he can predict the Caribbean's liberation from patterns of slavery's history. The risk is in mythologizing the historical purity of "the people," a risk he runs when he represents them en masse rather than representing them as individuals within historical process and seeing their already vacillating and ambivalent positionality vis-à-vis the West. "The people" seem to stand outside the deeply historical contingencies that otherwise act profoundly on the individual characters Carpentier does choose to represent. As soon as an individual enters his stage of representation, he or she is no longer original but swept up in the river of a priori historical process. In this marxist recourse to mythologizing the folk, history threatens to collapse back into ideological thinking where creolization is the power by which history, in the end, predictably evolves toward a better world.

This tension notwithstanding, Carpentier's reversal of center and margin turns us away from a fixation on empire as the center of historical change and allows us to see the desperation of colonial discourse to keep up with and manage the cultural change of creolization. At the transnational margins of empire, we see the empire's limitations in being able to replicate itself. Although he clearly began writing the novel before 1959, the Cuban Revolution no doubt also presented a tangible example, by 1962 at least, of a significant and marked difference from previous historical patterns in the region. It was a revolution to which he could return from exile and feel, in some measure, that he was joining history in the process of its being made, particularly in the revolution's successful resistance to U.S. imperialism and in its posture, by the early 1960s, as the ultimate "post" to Cuba's own history of slavery. These appeared to be differences from the old, familiar story of Caribbean dependency, differences that Carpentier, no doubt, hoped would be confirmed once they had repercussions beyond the island's shores. This context perhaps explains his desire to reconfigure, in Esteban and Sofía's union, the incest paradigm in Villaverde's island story and in Faulkner's triangular liaison among Henry, Judith, and Charles Bon. By resituating it in a transnational space marked by racial, political and geographical differences, the story of tragic and oedipal sameness, suffered under the insularity of narrowly nationalistic postslavery discourses, could be transformed into a story of redemption.

An Oedipal Return

William Faulkner's novel *Absalom, Absalom!* (1936) provides insight into both the solitude of the plantation and the flight of imperialism, in this case in the same geographical location. The postslavery South was riddled by the traditions of the plantocracy and by a new American imperialism whose first manifestation was the North's victory in the Civil War. In this sense, the Civil War was like the French Revolution in that it attempted to negotiate new democratic ideals in the context of slavery and an economy divided by varying degrees of metropolitan ties and by slave labor itself. Moreover, both wars saw an emergent imperial power impose those ideals and eventually emancipation against the will of the slave owners themselves.[9] Like Carpentier, Faulkner finds a tension in plantation history between egalitarianism (that welcomes difference) and paternalism (that controls it) and wrestles with the question of how to decolonize by separating the one from the other. The United States' particular problem is that it understands itself as both postcolonial and neoimperial.

Faulkner's strategy for confronting this contradiction is to reverse the empire-as-father paradigm and focus on the cultural offspring of U.S. imperialism. This is because the imperial mentality of the United States, as manifest in the character of Thomas Sutpen, has looked to areas such as the Caribbean to forge paternal authority and exceptionalism, a process that serves to veil its rather wanton appeal to the father cultures of Europe for models of social organization. U.S. imperialism resorts to an ahistorical rhetoric to describe its New World destiny, but underneath that rhetoric is an imitation of the historical role of an Old World father and a condescension toward its fellow nations in Plantation America. European culture is refurbished within the United States as the realization of the American dream, while Caribbean cultures—sibling rivals, as it were, in the struggle for cultural independence following the hemispheric history of colonialism and slavery—are denied their kinship. For Faulkner, there is no return from an exoticized father culture but rather a return of the exoticized bastard son-brother. U.S. culture cannot redeem itself from its oedipal attractions to Europe until it acknowledges its kinships with the exoticized fellow bastard sons and brothers of the postslavery Americas. Without such acknowledgement, Faulkner warns, U.S. culture will be doomed to the tragedies of insularity.

Like Carpentier, Faulkner restores Haiti and its black revolutionary resistance to a more central place in the imagination of the extended Caribbean. Also like Carpentier, he addresses the hemispheric dimensions of the plantation system, particularly its curious integration into the discourses of postslavery nationalism and imperialism.[10] His critique of U.S. imperialism demonstrates how the United States, from the end of the Civil War into the twentieth century, has been engaged in a long process of exorcism, expunging the ghosts of Europe and of the Caribbean from its own history of slavery. Such exorcism, however, has paradoxically led to direct exploitation of the West Indies à la Europe. Historically, the Deep South owed a tremendous cultural debt to the West Indies, to Haiti in particular, because of significant emigration from the Caribbean islands, especially following the Haitian Revolution (Hunt). The Louisiana Territory, especially the New Orleans area, has also retained much of that West Indian influence because it belonged to both the French and Spanish empires before it fell into U.S. hands. The pur-

chase of the territory was itself an indirect result of the Haitian Rev-
olution: When Napoléon was defeated by Haiti's revolutionary leader,
Toussaint Louverture, he gave up his ambition for an empire in the
Americas and shortly thereafter sold Louisiana to the United States
(Hunt 84). Such facts have been enough for some to conclude that the
Deep South represents the "northern extremity of Caribbean culture"
(Hunt 1; Ladd).

Because the Haitian Revolution represented a realization of every
slave owner's worst fears, however, the cultural indebtedness toward the
West Indies was quickly forgotten by the United States. As George
Washington Cable's fiction demonstrates, the Deep South attempted,
particularly after the conclusion of the Civil War, to refute the frequent
equation made by northerners between blackness, rebellion, miscegenation, and debauchery and the West Indies, Creole life, and ultimately
Southern slavery itself (Ladd 25). Northerners saw this cultural degeneration of the South as the result of European influence—particularly the
French notions of *egalité* and *fraternité,* which had become explicit platforms of the black rebellion of Haiti—that emanated from the Caribbean northward (Hunt 13). For this reason, Barbara Ladd argues, even
"white" Creoles posed a threat to "U.S. nationalism insofar as [they]
represented an intermediate stage between European 'encroachment' in
the New World and the development of a New World nationalism on
British foundations" (Ladd xv). Specifically, Catholic Europeanization
was targeted as the equivalent of Africanization and debauchery. One
northerner once remarked that "planters are 'prodigal sons,' who spend
their substance with harlots and riotous living" (qtd. in Hunt 6). The
hope, at least for the likes of Cable, was that such prodigal sons would
give up their European extravagance and Caribbean ways and return to
the Union where they belonged.

Cable called for the South to stop reading European literature and
striving to be distinct from the North. Essentially, he wanted the South
to incorporate itself into the North in order to be purified of its European and African elements. Curiously, northerners were, in some ways,
more familiar with the Caribbean and with Haiti than their southern
counterparts because, in the nineteenth century, those from the United
States who most typically gained economic advantages in Haiti were
New England shipowners (Stinchcombe 237). Cable's distinction between the South's affinities and its northern possibilities was perhaps a
false dichotomy. Faulkner insists that a prodigal return of the South is

impossible precisely because Cable's request for the whitening of the South represented the beginnings of an American imperial expansion modeled after Europe.[11] Similar to Faulkner's use of Shreve and Quentin, Cable structures the story of New Orleans in the context of a dialogue between two northerners, Dr. Keene and Joseph Frowenfeld, who try to piece together the puzzle of Creole history (Ladd). Postslavery aesthetics, for Faulkner, needs this representation of slavery's history as process, but it also needs to see the South's history in the context of the hemispheric, transnational history of the plantation, a history that the redemptive impulse of U.S. imperial discourse has attempted to transcend and eventually erase from its memory. Unlike Carpentier, Faulkner insists that there is no ahistorical escape from the legacies of slavery and the plantation and that therefore decolonization of the United States can only begin with a relentless encounter with those legacies in our contemporary circumstances.

The ahistorical, mythical dream in *Absalom, Absalom!* is, of course, Sutpen's design. Sutpen's rise from obscure origins in Tidewater Virginia to become a wealthy planter in Jefferson, Mississippi, is suggestive of the contradictory marriage in New World slave societies of an emerging liberalism with Old World paternalism (Railey 122). Faulkner represents a group that contradicted the myth of the Old South and the reliance of the landed plantocracy on a long-standing, well-established genealogy. Tidewater Virginia, whence Sutpen springs, was in the 1830s a region of considerable economic opportunity, where many poor white farmers were able to move slowly up the class ladder. This class, according to Faulkner, "lived remote and at economic war with both slave and slaveholder. When they emerged, gradually, son by infrequent son, like Old Sutpen, it was not to establish themselves as a middle class but to make themselves barons, too" (qtd. in Porter, *Seeing* 223).[12] Faulkner was bent on using this class as a curious case of what is most enigmatic about the very nature of the American dream—that is, its contradiction of a liberalism that championed individualism, social mobility, equality, and reward based on merit and a paternalism that upheld the hierarchical, static nature of plantation society. This dichotomy, according to Eugene Genovese, exemplifies the tense ideological opposition between the opportunism of the capitalist North and the fixed hierarchies of the patriarchal South that led to the Civil War ("Materialism"). What Sutpen's design exposes, however, is how interrelated the two ideologies had become and how they constitute a contradiction internal to the American dream forged in the latter decades of the nineteenth century: By what means can one rise without simultaneously repudiating those one rises above? If class differences are not natural as the plantation myth would have us believe, by what means are those differences maintained, since their ipso facto existence cannot be denied?

This marriage of contradictions clearly fueled much of America's self-fulfilling prophecy of Manifest Destiny, which pushed back its frontiers across the West, beyond the U.S. South to Latin America, and to regions beyond. The possession of land was crucial to the plantation owner and to the pioneer frontiersman as well, and that land was obtained by means of a paternalism engendered by market liberalism (Porter, *Seeing* 233).[13] Thus, according to Carolyn Porter, "the paternal authority of the state expropriated the land on which the paternal authority of the planter could then be exercised" on behalf of their new children, the slaves, who were brought in to fulfill their paternal longings (233). The vacuum creates not the absent father but the absent child, implying that U.S. culture is conditioned by its inability to establish and to see its effect on history.

This sharply contrasts Carpentier's depiction of a Caribbean awareness of being subject to prior events that, like an absent parent, are no longer accessible. The vacuum created by violence toward children that U.S. culture has "adopted" only promotes a greater longing for new subjects over which can be exercised paternal control. As Porter argues, the process moves on indefinitely, pushing the American dream in pursuit of greater territory. This dream, one might argue, has consistently resulted in the usurpation of the place of the father in other cultures without assuming paternal responsibility. The American dream erases genealogical ascent at the same time that it creates the need for descent.

As an embodiment of this dream, Thomas Sutpen outrages the population of Jefferson precisely because he arrives "with no discernable past" in order to "establish his descent" (9, 20). Despite his aberrant appearance on the horizon, however, he is altogether typical of the contradictions of the American dream. In archetypal fashion, he "tore violently a plantation" out of the earth; carved out an inheritance in soil, "which he took from a tribe of ignorant indians nobody knows how"; populated it with a wife and slaves; and constructed a "house the size of a courthouse" full of European wonders (6, 15). His "design" finds its incentive in his own encounter with the divisions of plantation society at the age of fourteen when he is turned away at the door of his father's employer. His was a fall from an edenic innocence where the land belonged to nobody and everybody and so the man who would go to the trouble and work to fence off a piece of it and say "This is mine" was crazy. . . . So he didn't even know there was a country all divided and fixed and neat because of what color their skins happened to be and what they happened to own, and where a certain few men not only had the power of life and death and barter and sale over others, they had living human men to perform the endless repetitive personal offices such as pouring the very whiskey from the jug and putting the glass into his hand or pulling off his boots for him to go to bed. (276–77)

These carved-out divisions among people are, of course, what Sutpen himself reproduces in his design to combat them. When Wash Jones, the representative poor white man who works for Sutpen, is denied entrance into the Sutpen house, the pattern comes full circle. Sutpen demonstrates that the contradictory impulses of the American dream simultaneously give new life to the genealogical dream of the plantocracy and to a new egalitarianism. Land division and ownership, in Faulkner's world, do not exist without a simultaneous division and ownership of people. The two concepts are violent and unnatural boundaries that establish "irrevocable demarcations" among people (247).

We learn from Shreve and Quentin's suppositions that this design, this dream of self-made manhood, begins with a crossing of irrevocable demarcations among peoples as well. After Sutpen's rejection at the door, he journeys to the West Indies, where he learns from his teacher who read it from a book that "poor men went in ships and became rich, it didn't matter how, so long as that man was clever and courageous" (302). Sutpen arrives in Haiti, a nation that constituted a realization of whites' worst fears for black violence and self-assertion. Historically, however, it was also a site of tremendous exploitation for economic gain and a cause for an intense and jealous rivalry among imperial powers in the Caribbean. Faulkner situates Sutpen and southern history into the middle of the multiple economic and political alliances of the plantation system in order to dispel notions of the South's exceptionality, and of U.S. exceptionality in general. The South's burden is, as Quentin hopes, not the South's alone, since it has emerged from a broader transnational and transregional space than the United States has typically acknowledged.

Faulkner's formulation of the "theatre of violence and injustice" that so intrigued Carpentier in his writing of *Explosion in a Cathedral* and *El reino de este mundo* portrays Haiti as an orphan of a violent marriage between Africa and Europe. Quentin's grandfather reports that Sutpen's Haiti is:

> a spot of earth which might have been created and set aside by Heaven it-
> self . . . as a theatre for violence and injustice and bloodshed and all the
> satanic lusts of human greed and cruelty, for the last despairing fury of all
> the pariah-interdict and all the doomed—a little island set in a smiling
> and fury-lurked and incredible indigo sea, which was the halfway point
> between what we call the jungle and what we call civilization, halfway
> between the dark inscrutable continent from which the black blood, the
> black bones and flesh and thinking and remembering and hopes and de-
> sires, was ravished by violence, and the cold known land to which it was
> doomed, the civilised land and people which had expelled some of its
> own blood and thinking and desires that had become too crass to be
> faced and borne longer, and set it homeless and desperate on the lonely
> ocean. (312–13)

Carpentier similarly places Haiti in the center of his plot, but in *Explo-sion* he reverses Faulkner's purely objectified view of the country. For Carpentier, Haiti is what creates the spiral of history because it is never contained by European discourse; it is the zero-point of difference that accounts for Caribbean echoes—its imitation but with a difference—of Europe. In Faulkner, on the other hand, Haiti is the repository of the contradictions of empire; Haiti's difference is sired by its darker side. The impulse of imperialism is to isolate (literally "to make into an is-land") those cultural "offspring" over which imperialism has exercised its paternal prerogative; these postslavery cultures of the Caribbean and of the U.S. South are left as bastard children condemned to live in soli-tude without a recognized genealogy. Faulkner additionally suggests that Haiti and the sea it inhabits have also come to serve as a scapegoat for the barbarism and violence of the United States' own slavery system.

The United States isolated Haiti diplomatically for close to sixty years, until 1862, and then occupied the country from 1915 to 1934, the occupation ending just two years prior to the publication of Faulkner's novel. Hans Schmidt explains that the precedent for the occupation was "the long series of guerrilla wars waged against alien races and cultures in western north America, the Pacific, and the Caribbean. The abrasive contacts with alien peoples outside the United States were being sub-jected to nativist and racist harassment marked by brutal treatment of Indians, lynchings of immigrants, Ku Klux Klan bigot-oriented exclu-sion and systematic suppression of blacks" (7). This externalization of

America's internal conflicts allowed American culture, if only temporarily, to forge images of itself that were decontaminated of the foreign
elements within the country. American presence in the Caribbean also
provided material benefits that were further fodder for sustaining the
American dream. Part of what Faulkner critiques in this novel is the fact
that, as Schmidt argues, "the occupation of Haiti was both a logical extension of America's quest for empire and a clear example of many of
the contradictions involved in that quest . . . the conflicts between American racism and rational progressivism, between democratic egalitarianism and military conquest" (17).

Faulkner critiques this unnatural demarcation between America and
the barbarism of the Caribbean by placing Haiti at the center of Sutpen's
design to rise to riches and subsequent tragic demise. He makes his
riches in Haiti in 1827 by courageously defying a slave rebellion and
marrying the slave owner's daughter. Faulkner commits an anachronism
in Sutpen's tale since slavery was abolished in Haiti after its revolution
ended in 1804, and there is some debate about whether this was intentional. What is of interest here is how this anachronism functions in
comparison to anachronism in Carpentier's novel. Whereas for Carpentier, anachronism is produced by the subjective agency of people at the
margins of empire, for Faulkner it is the product (conscious or not) of
the empire's objectifying gaze that symbolically orders time and marginalizes people. Imperialism does not operate according to a strict chro-
nology, as other writers and critics have assumed, but rather relies on a
tacit ahistoricism. To catch the empire at its game, to expose the empire's
anachronisms, genealogy and its strict biological and chronological
meanings become the necessary tools. Faulkner's anachronism allows
him to use Haiti as Sutpen's springboard into tragic contradiction (a
symptom, perhaps, of Faulkner's own ignorance,). However, it could
also be a symptom of Faulkner's desire to remind his readers of the
"theatre of violence" Haiti was projected to be prior to the Civil War
and, just as important, during the more recent U.S. occupation, during
which considerable debate took place about Haiti's ability to govern itself.[14]

With the wealth and slaves he accumulates in Haiti, Sutpen arrives in
Jefferson speaking to his slaves "in that tongue which even now a good
part of the county did not know was a civilised language" (67) and paying with a "gold Spanish coin" (38) for the deed to the land. The ev-
idences of his Caribbean connections become in the eyes of the local
population symbols of his having no past; they are foreign and therefore

enigmatically invisible. And as the plot of the novel bears out, those supposedly foreign aspects of this entirely "other" Caribbean culture are in fact the flowering seeds sowed by American greed. Sutpen's violent and relentless pursuit of his plan literally plants the seeds of his own demise on Haitian soil.

The haunting return to Mississippi of Sutpen's repudiated son, Charles Bon, forces a reconnection between imperialist "thinking and desires that had become too crass to be faced or borne" and the ideologue that produced those thoughts and desires (313). In an effort to rescue his own orphaned isolation and "homelessness," Bon confronts the father. He feels weighed down by an

> incomprehensible fury and fierce yearning and vindictiveness and jealous rage [that] was a part of childhood which all mothers of children had received in turn from their mothers and from their mothers in turn from that Porto Rico or Haiti or wherever it was we all came from but none of us ever lived in: so that when he grew up and had children he would have to pass it on too. . . . and hence no man had a father, no one personal Porto Rico or Haiti, but all mother faces. . . . all boy flesh that walked and breathed stemming from that one ambiguous eluded dark fatherhead and so brothered perennial and ubiquitous everywhere under the sun. (373)

The drawing of national borders is a dream of escape from the legacies of slavery's hemispheric history and leaves the citizens of the Americas like Bon: "*born into this world with so few fathers that I have too many brothers to outrage and shame while alive and hence too many descendants to bequeath my little portion of hurt and harm to, dead*" (385). U.S. culture, in its effort to throw off its father cultures and to maintain freedom from historical contingency, also fails to acknowledge its own paternity, its own fostering of "satanic lusts" in other lands that are comfortably situated beyond the frontiers of its "civilization." The failure to acknowledge paternity allows U.S. culture to assume Sutpen-like innocence and to propose a plan for the individual's rise, a pretense of self-made status that "innocently" ignores the divisions that have been created in order to sustain that rise. U.S. culture simultaneously pretends to have no father (since it denies its imitations of Europe) and, despite its need for symbolic descent, no son. Although ostensibly intended to promote a nation of brothers, this repudiation of genealogy creates a polity of Charles Bons who, rather than finding themselves united with their siblings, are mutually isolated, stranded by an un-

known history. And the plantation household is the primary manifestation of this isolation; Judith and Henry are "marooned at birth on a de-
sert island: the island here Sutpen's Hundred; the solitude, the shadow of
that father" (122). Sutpen's plantation offspring are unaware of their
kinship with the Caribbean and are incestuously bound to each other in
perpetual sameness. Faulkner shows that descent, as much as ascent, ties
one down to the responsibility of time and place and obstructs the tendencies of the individual to place the past and the future on a mythic, indeterminate scale in an attempt to stand outside history.

If Sutpen's design is founded on an ahistorical stance, Bon's return is
an attempt to force Sutpen's reentry into historical contingency, to bring
down his mythical project to confront its kinship with the demonized region of the Caribbean (Porter, *Seeing*). Bon's return breaks down the divisions between lands and people and the dichotomy between civilization
and barbarism on which Sutpen's design depends. He enters "a small
new college in the Mississippi hinterland and even wilderness, three hundred miles from that worldly and even foreign city [New Orleans] which
was his home" (89-90). His entrance into the family drama reverses the
terms of cultural difference, where he carries himself with the civilization
of Latin culture into the hinterland of Mississippi. His frenchified, cul-
tured manners "seduced the country brother and sister" much like Victor
Hugues draws Esteban and Sofía out of their insular, incestuous realm
with his worldly knowledge (114). Bon arrives like Sutpen "in the remote
Mississippi of that time . . . almost phoenix-like, full-sprung from no
childhood, born of no woman and impervious to time" (90).

However, his mysterious past and exotic power are, in fact, products
of his kinship with Sutpen and his family. Quentin's father observes that
the Sutpens "have not quite emerged from barbarism . . . [and] two
thousand years hence will still be throwing triumphantly off the yoke of
Latin culture and intelligence of which they were never in any great permanent danger to begin with" (116). The barbarism of the American
dream is the belief in the need for cultural purification from influences
considered "outside." After all, the dream of individual rise has been facilitated by its creation of, and intervention in, those cultural frontiers.
Charles simply presents himself as a mirror in which his distant family
can view their own contradictions. Latin culture is not, for Faulkner, a
repository for the crassness of U.S. thought that the nation cannot face,
as it is for Cable. Rather, he ironically points to the Latin virtues in
Charles that his southern protagonists, in their excessive fear of Latin affinity, are never in danger of possessing.

The erotic trio of Charles Bon, Judith, and Henry, although clearly the model for Carpentier's trio of Hugues, Esteban, and Sofía, differs because in *Absalom, Absalom!* the frenchified visitor brings a fragment of imperialist discourse back to its source. Bon's arrival on their cultural horizon is not, despite appearances to the contrary, exotic and foreign but all too familiar and incestuous. Unlike Victor Hugues, he has not come to play surrogate father in the wake of the plantation's demise; he is the bastard son of the plantation seeking recognition. In this sense, he embodies a piece of the fragmented, multiple cultures that have resulted from the imperialist expansion of the plantation system, and his return forces an oedipal confrontation of the contradictions of such an unholy alliance. Although he lures the plantation pair out of the household, ultimately they have no outlet from the solitude of the plantation precisely because imperialism has collapsed on itself. While Hugues is the empire come to find new children by offering liberal discourse, Bon is the colony that was never named as son by its new imperialist father-overseer to the north.

In his own erotic trio, Carpentier revises Faulkner's belief that colonialism acts as the pebble that causes the ripple effects of history. If there is a ripple effect in Carpentier's novel, it is double; the waves of historical force coming from the empire bounce off Caribbean solidity and return in new and unrecognizable forms. Hugues's oedipal mistake is to assume that empires direct history, and so even though he believes he emigrates from the center, he runs incestuously into an image of his own manic desire for historical control bouncing back at him. Carpentier suggests that the insularity of Faulkner's themes is related to Faulkner's failure to see the duality inherent in colonialism.

From Faulkner's point of view, U.S. culture does not allow for a prodigal journey out of the plantation's insularity because U.S. imperialism has already expanded the bounds of that insularity. His point is that U.S. culture perpetually blinds itself to difference by means of pretended incorporation of symbolic difference within its boundaries. This comes simultaneously with an expulsion of real difference beyond its borders that it then feels it doesn't need to know. The real Puerto Rico or Haiti will forever remain beyond U.S. insularity, and recourse to such realities can never entirely escape the expanse of imperialism's symbol-making reach. That is to say, Faulkner remains permanently skeptical of one's ability to cognitively grasp a new difference without it collapsing into a self-ingratiating mark of one's own civilization, and this is particularly the case when one is located within the center of imperial power. Carpentier's revision of Faulkner's critique suggests the need for an ounce of faith that real difference exists, and he argues that such difference, even if it cannot be captured entirely within representation, is signified by the slippage of language and discourse that is apparent on the margins of empire. Without such faith, Carpentier suggests that Faulkner potentially remains trapped within the insularity he critiques: no real Puerto Rico or Haiti, nor real blackness is rhetorically established, free of its symbolic function to critique imperialism and whiteness.

These differences notwithstanding, Faulkner and Carpentier both imply that the only escape to a postslavery openness would have to begin with at least a cautious openness to difference. Faulkner warns that decolonizing the United States is a treacherous endeavor because the combination of its impulses has already led to a throwing off of its fathers as well as its offspring for the sake of creating a perpetually redemptive brotherhood. As long as egalitarianism is allied to imperialism, the redemptive possibilities of incest that notions of *fraternité* have made possible are an illusion. Such a brothering of the United States has perpetuated the divisions of plantation life both within the country and in the U.S. relations to other nations to the south. So while Carpentier reverses the insular and incestuous stories of Villaverde and Faulkner to suggest the possibility of a prodigal progression of history, Faulkner cautions against the belief in the redemptive powers of the near-miss incest of first cousins we see in Cable and Carpentier. For Faulkner, this is again because within the United States, decolonization must begin with an acknowledgement that the United States, like Henry, has preferred the risk of incest to that of miscegenation. The United States has preferred to create arbitrary borders among postslavery cultures in the Americas and to deny kinship with them by means of its own imperialist pretensions, and this for the sake of preserving an idea of its own racial purity. To invoke Miller once again, this preference for incest also represents an arrogant belief in language's sameness, in its direct equation with that which it names. For both Faulkner and Carpentier, their criticism of this arrogance leads to a baroque narrative that, in its excess, continually acknowledges its failures.

The boundaries falsely drawn up between histories and nations are apparent in similar boundaries between the narrative voices that Faulkner represents. The various absentee fathers we have seen all acted on the pretense that their actions would have no historical impact. The children of such a father are stranded as orphans and must begin by tracing and reconnecting the past to the present in narrative. As Porter and John

Irwin have argued, when we attempt to narrate the past and to begin again the process of transmitting information from one generation to the next, we are also attempting to stand outside history, since a condition of our narration is the pretense of being able to stand as an outside observer of the events we relate (*Seeing and Being; Doubling and Incest*). In the act of narration, we cannot fail to expose that we seek to tell things we cannot possibly see. Although Faulkner's narrators reveal new truths about reality and about the past, they are also partial in that they are subjective voices speaking from and to particular historical conditions. The narrative informs us about reality but then it collapses back into performance. Faulkner's excessive recourse to testimonials about a story that has already happened shares much with Carpentier's notion of the conch shell and baroque writing. The stories must be excessive because, like the baroque, they always miss the mark. The story already exists, but as Carlos Fuentes observes, "the novelist, accompanied by the reader, searches for it and discovers it" (25). Inasmuch as testimony misses the mark, we must begin again our search for the novel and for a new witness, a new narrative voice that can account for the gap created by the previous one. As in Carpentier, history is made by the act of telling.

Narrative may expose our own contingency and historicity, as we learn individually from the various narratives, but it also exposes our dependency on each other in order to make a larger meaning. Sutpen's onetime intended, Rosa, cannot make meaning of Sutpen without Quentin, Quentin without Shreve, and all of them without the reader. For this reason, "the narrators cannot be divorced from the Sutpen story, [and] . . . the meaning of *Absalom, Absalom!* resides in their union" (Ruppersburg 83). The plot line that I have presented tells of the interdependencies of Caribbean and U.S. histories as constructed by Shreve and Quentin. Even though Shreve is "born half a continent apart" from Quentin, as Bon is from Henry, they are "joined, connected after a fashion in a sort of geographical transubstantiation by . . . that River which . . . is very Environment itself which laughs at degrees of latitude and temperature" (322). Together they abdicate individual responsibility for their story in the interest of their communal production of meaning: "That was why it did not matter to either of them which one did the talking, since it was not the talking alone which did it, performed and accomplished the overpassing, but some happy marriage of speaking and hearing wherein each before the demand, the requirement, forgave condoned and forgot the faulting of the other—faultings both in the creating of this shade whom they discussed (rather, existed in) and in the hearing and sifting and discarding the false and conserving what seemed true" (395).

The happy union of speaker and listener "overpasses" the barrier that keeps us from the past; it crosses the thresholds between the narrators and the events of the past. It is that moment—when our own historicity is combined with that of others—when we overcome our solitude in solidarity with others. Such solidarity is miscegenous, not incestuous, in the sense that it unites oppositions, brings together perspectives, and can thus laugh "at degrees of latitude and temperature." This happy union brings together the American plot with the Caribbean plot since neither can assume the absentee position outside historical responsibility. As the novel shows, it is a tenuous union at best, held together by means of a cautious openness and willingness to accept another's story as part of one's own. As soon as we pull back from that responsibility of listening, as does Shreve when he ultimately condemns Quentin to bear alone the story of the South, we leave open no redemptive passage for those histories that rightly deserve adoption, if not outright paternal recognition.

There is no basis on which we can escape the contingencies of slavery's history without perhaps rethinking, as Faulkner and Carpentier do, our confidence in identifiable boundaries between nations. Such rethinking, for Carpentier, highlights the transnational forces of the people at the margins of empire whose directive power surpasses that which emanates from metropolitan centers of power. In Faulkner, rethinking national boundaries means accepting that in solidarity there is no escape from the contingencies of colonialism and slavery because our historicity is made manifest in the stories we tell; if we listen to the stories from across the Americas, we can at least begin to construct a clearer picture of who we have been. These authors are engaged in the great struggle of the twentieth century to have the history of slavery behind us and to disentangle egalitarian ideals from the grasp of imperialism. They represent two extremes of incest and of reconciliation with history: a prodigal, spiraling return to one's origins or an oedipal confrontation with origins that, although tragic, offers new understanding. Although their resolutions are, at best, tentative, they set the stage for the postmodern investigations of postslavery writers, who, rather than struggling to free themselves from history, persist in excavating stories that the romance with history has left silent.

5 The Emancipation of / from History

Jean Rhys, Rosario Ferré, and Toni Morrison

The Contingencies of Narrative

With our understanding of how the modernism of Carpentier and Faulkner has tended to universalize the conditions of memory and narrative as existential, we can now examine the return to the specificity of sites of memory and of language production, the specific "cultural and political ramifications of geography" in Jean Rhys's *Wide Sargasso Sea,* Rosario Ferré's *Maldito amor,* and Toni Morrison's *Song of Solomon* (Barnes 150). Rather than simply appealing to voices on the margins of official discourses, these authors also work from an understanding of the various and competing contingencies of identity—gender, race, class, place—that shape the narratives of postslavery. They imagine a plural and shifting conception of identity and call into question the individualist assumptions by which postslavery imaginings have revised plantation and colonial discourses. While on one level they make crucial inroads to a male-dominated postslavery discourse by insisting on the significance of black and white women's experience for a viable postslavery aesthetic, they also revise our understandings of postslavery epistemology. Memory itself, they argue, is communal, shifting, and only temporarily situated in specific locations.

If, as I have insisted in previous chapters, plantation and colonial ideologies erase or disguise the historical contingencies that have given shape to the master's narrative, the key to its dismissal is speaking from and to circumstances that have been passed over. But this creates a rather interesting paradox: At the same time that these writers seek to use marginalized voices to substantiate their narrative authority, they must also disavow any conception of identity that would be static and fixed. It is as if the very witnesses they call upon must then be declared unreliable.[1] Plantation and colonial discourses pressure the marginal voice into a specific place, and thus the postslavery emphasis on place risks becoming complicit with those pressures.[2]

In their emphasis on the intersections of various racialized and gendered social positions within local plantation histories, Rhys, Ferré, and Morrison explore a postslavery aesthetic that moves not only between nations but among class, gender, and racial lines. Whereas Faulkner and Carpentier use testimonial voices and family relations to represent a variety of discourses emanating from different geographical sites and thereby expose the porous nature of national identity, these writers demonstrate that place is never entirely equal to geographical location. That is to say, where one speaks is as much conditioned by geography as it is by class, color, and gender; therefore, a deconstruction of nationhood, when it ignores these complexities, may only serve to reify intranational identities. To insist on a rigid conception of place risks romanticizing a notion of home and identity that ignores how slavery has alienated and displaced so many people (Davies 21). Identity and place are migratory categories not merely transnationally but also, because of various social differentiations, within a given geographical setting. Lee Irwin explains that when racial and gender differences are seen as "historically specific shifts in class and economic power," they cannot be as easily reduced to morally infused categories (144).

Additionally, in tacitly arguing for complexity of identity, these authors move beyond an oedipal replication of the master's discourse in two ways. First, they insist that an interest in patrimony has been a driving force of slavery and, most important, of the narratives that have attempted to tell its story. Numerous examples of this concern for maintaining the integrity of the patrimony and how such nostalgia limits the authors' ability to put slavery behind them have already been discussed. Rhys, Ferré, and Morrison imply that in order for the stories we tell about the past to move beyond an oedipal struggle with the burdens of slavery, our narratives must not be wedded to following the lines of inheritance, and we must be prepared to renounce our interest in maintaining the same uneven claims to land and property on which the system of slavery was based. Sutpen's need for slaves, land, and progeny constitutes the crude elements by which slave owners establish economic and social advantage and pass it on to the next generation. This is why, as I have discussed, genealogical claims became so important to the plantocracy; they were the means by which these holdings could be transferred within the family line. In the works studied in this chapter,

interest in patrimony ultimately proves to be an interest in self-consoli-
dation and separation from community and from ancestral memory. In
other words, because it seeks identification of an individualized self
through materialism, patrimony erases the constituent elements of the
self, the stories, ancestral memories, and communal relations that would
otherwise provide a broad web of possibilities of identity. Patrimony is
inherently interested in reifying boundaries around a hermetic self,
whereas the more collective conception of the self and of memory advanced by these writers is inherently transgressive of such boundaries
(Davies 17).

Carpentier and Faulkner insist on migratory explorations into the history of slavery so as to strike a balance between insularity and exoticism.
For Rhys, Ferré, and Morrison, however, such migrations are necessary
not because of the fixed paternal poles of plantation and colonial discourses but because of the migratory nature of identity itself. That is why
even though they write much about the place of the speaking subject, in
the end they are writing about positions that, in the words of Cynthia
Davies, "exist more in the realm of 'elsewhere' of diasporic imaginings
than the precisely locatable" (88). The difficulty academia has in cat-
egorizing, or properly situating, these writers is emblematic of the insufficiency of disciplinary structures to address the complexity of postslavery identities that their work represents. Where, for example, is the
proper place to teach Jean Rhys? In a course on feminism? On Caribbean
literature? English literature? Literature of the Americas? Could one con-
ceivably argue for the inclusion of *Wide Sargasso Sea* in a course on the
African Diaspora? And what of Rosario Ferré, whose career has moved
from Spanish to English? Is she a Latin American, Caribbean, or American writer? In what context can we properly address the complex relationships in these two women's work between the experience of women
and men, blacks and whites, and between geopolitical locations? More
work is also needed to explore the broad connections between Morrison's work, the African Diaspora, and other writings in the Americas.

The second reason these writers avoid the oedipal struggle with the
past is that the burden of slavery extends beyond its historical existence
to contemporary ghosts and its rhetorical survival in the narratives that
have attempted, in effect, to write slavery out of history. The oedipal error is to presume the present's unequivocal break with the past; it is to
fail to see that the burden of slavery is not the past itself but the legacy
of narratives that still provide room for the kinds of social, racial, and
gender divisions from which the slave owner, during another time, prof-

ited. In other words, history is merely a web of narratives that reflect what our values want to read into the past. These writers seek to disrobe plantation history from paternal authority. The problem, however, is how to deconstruct this history without simply assuming the same arrogance of historical authority and without undermining the legitimization of historical reconstruction. In the words of Laurie Finke, the problem for many women writers is that "if reality is nothing more than narrative we tell ourselves, . . . then these 'stories' can have no greater claim to inherent authority than the old ones feminists have rejected" (3). A postmodern alternative, in which a sense of the past disappears altogether, does not hold an attraction for writers trying to bring into representation that which has been erased in the historical imagination of their predecessors. Likewise, they do not want to repeat the mistakes of their predecessors by relying on an unexamined notion of history as a bag of facts, even if those facts are new.

These writers continue to explore Faulkner's argument that the contingencies of history do not consist of some original moment in the past but in the ripples of effect that have followed, demarcating the boundaries of our cultural imagination. Their novels further imply that the nature of Quentin's dilemma could also become the means of his salvation from the oedipal trap. The fact that memory cannot be contained within individual experience but has the capacity to shape a contemporaneous community of individuals who share common ancestral memories means that an individual's memories are essentially never individual property; the individual, then, has recourse to a community to lighten the burdens assigned by the past because of the collective and dialogic nature of memory and the language we use to represent it. Rather than confronting the ancestral past alone in a diachronic oedipal struggle, remembering becomes a way of reinstituting the individual as a member of a synchronic community. Therefore, if memory and the language used to represent it irrevocably reflect our present personality, then remembering the past can become a regenerative, creative process.

Narratives in this vein seek to emancipate themselves from history by imagining the emancipation of previously untold histories from within the plantation household. In jockeying between various unequal narrative positions, the novels unmask the construction of narrative authority and reveal that the stories each character tells are shaped by his or her social position and historical relationship to property, a relationship largely shaped by race and gender. They place the responsibility for the multiplicity of truth not on its existential elusion or its distance from us in the present but on the variety of social and historical circumstances that have emerged in the wake of slavery and that have placed the various members of a postslavery society in distinct relationships to one another, each with different investments in the stories they tell. Historical truth, for these writers, is itself historically and socially contingent (Gunew 65).

For this reason, the histories they deconstruct and reconstruct are always provisional because they never pretend to escape contingency and because they point to more gaps that will need filling with additional narrative voices. Lois Parkinson Zamora argues that this rather unapologetic, rhetorical use of historical narrative characterizes New World writing: "I consistently find that an anxiety about origins impels American writers to search *for* precursors (in the name of community) rather than escape *from* them (in the name of individuation); to connect *to* traditions and histories (in the name of the usable past) rather than dissociate *from* them (in the name of originality). . . . They are impelled . . . by the need to locate usable historical precursors and precedents. Their search for origins may be ironic and at the same time 'authentic,' simultaneously self-doubting and subversive" (*Usable Past* 5–6). Such writing, in a postslavery context, represents not a final, revised version of plantation history but history-in-process, one in which new, conflicting testimonies about the past are repeatedly interpellated. They demonstrate why our hunger for history must not be dismissed in the name of postmodern maturity but rather must be rigorously maintained as insatiable and ever searching.

This is despite the fact that Rhys, Ferré, and Morrison's respective novels each collapses into a kind of apocalyptic finality. Such recourse to apocalypse allows these authors to represent the driving forces of history-making. In this way, we gain both an understanding of history and of the means by which that historical meaning is generated. We come to understand that the conditions by which history is driven and by which it is narrated are one and the same; they are apocalyptic novels because, as Zamora explains, they make "the conjunction of meaning and ending its theme" (*Writing* 14). Paradoxically, they thereby express an "ongoing yearning after an imagined ideal" (16).

Testimonial Truth

Throughout this study we have seen examples of how novelists have portrayed various characters, both black and white, who have borne testimony to the injustices, the pain, and the evils of slavery and racism. By weaving into their narratives witnesses who have been traditionally silenced in official memory, they have sought to reopen for exploration the meaning of slavery's past in contemporary culture. We need only think of a few examples: Cirilo Villaverde's María de Regla, whose sufferings and knowledge of the Gamboa family history serve as poignant reminders of the injustices of slavery; William Faulkner's collection of testimonial narratives, which in their diversity insist on multiple understandings of slavery; George Washington Cable's representations of the various French Creole narrations of the Grandissime family history; Martín Morúa Delgado and Charles Chesnutt's use of crimes whose solutions depend on accurate eyewitnesses, when available, or on the necessary social power to forge truths to fit the crime. We have also seen that this use of testimonial truth serves a variety of purposes: It allows the narrative to communicate to the reader the evils of slave culture through the rhetorical medium of first-hand experience, and it argues implicitly for the need to hear a wider range of voices in order to understand history more adequately. These effects are achieved with the aid of a narrative structure that attempts to mediate the otherwise chaotic effects of these new voices and to establish a newly legitimated authority that can challenge the dominant cultural discourse.

Rhys, Ferré, and Morrison also give voice to previously silenced perspectives, particularly those of women, in order to convey new truths about the past. But as I have maintained, they demonstrate a more nuanced understanding of the ideological implications of narrative structure and representation. In the case of Rhys and Ferré, representations of individuals within the plantation household are not contained by an overarching narrative authority that aids the reader by means of its understanding the "truth." They are concerned with representing the act of representation itself by juxtaposing separate narratives that originate from particular individuals with differing social and racial status. Although Morrison uses an omniscient narrative voice, she is likewise interested in questions of narrative authority; by rhetorically juxtaposing other forms of narrative that are not literary, such as music and oral history, she achieves a similar effect.

Even though in these cases we find more evidence of intertextuality than in others in this study—evidence of the writer's explicit responses to texts that have come before—we find less evidence of nostalgia for a previous social or imaginary order. If these texts are nostalgic, it is for the future: Their abrupt interruption of multiple voices of the novel's conclusions suggests the need to seek additional witnesses, yet unheard.

Their simultaneous appealing to and turning away from the past indicate what Derek Walcott has called "the truly tough aesthetic of the New World," which "neither explains nor forgives history" ("Muse" 2). This is because "it is not the pressure of the past which torments poets but the weight of the present" (4). That weight is alleviated by an understanding that we can move forward from the past only by appealing to further witnesses in contemporary settings. In this way, the past is revised by virtue of an intimate interaction with present circumstances in order to release its future testimonial energies. Rather than seeing "language as enslavement" and therefore respecting only "incoherence or nostalgia" as a way out from the oedipal ties of the past, to borrow again the words of Walcott, these writers represent voice and language as rooted in the particularities of place; therefore, attention to the present and to what it can unleash becomes the solution to slavery's past (2).

In the discussion of testimonial language in chapter 1, I argued for the importance of understanding the personal and intimate language of the testimony as it stands in relation to impersonal and more public languages, such as historiography and nationalist discourses; testimonial language is metonymical because it always points to the experience of others who have not told their stories. Ferré, Rhys, and Morrison write about the historical and social contingencies of plantation society because they are aware that these contingencies have silenced some voices and thereby given others greater authority. By contrast, I explained how the slave master's narrative is metaphorical in that it attempts to substitute for the story of those who labor under the master. Economic and gender relations in slave society additionally helped to produce the metaphorical power of the master's language and to place testimonies from the margins in a metonymical relation to one another and to the historiography of the South. Rhys, Ferré, and Morrison, then, revise the history of slavery by focusing on the testimonies of those most marginalized by the slave owner—that is, second sons, blacks, women, and the working class—in each case including intimate testimonies that were implicit but largely silent in previous works. In the process, they expose history as an ongoing narrative that is always subject to contingency.

"There Is Always the Other Side, Always"

Jean Rhys's *Wide Sargasso Sea* (1967) attempts to fill in the blanks for the character of Bertha Mason in Charlotte Brontë's 1847 novel *Jane Eyre*. Picking up on Brontë's oblique reference to the madness of Bertha, who comes from the Caribbean, Rhys provides a full social and historical context in order to explain her seemingly irrational behavior. Antoinette Cosway, Rhys's recasting of Bertha, is an orphaned white Creole woman in the English colony of Dominica in the wake of emancipation. She is not, however, entirely taken from *Jane Eyre;* much of the facts surrounding the life Rhys imagines for her come from Rhys's own genealogy in the nineteenth-century planter class of the English Caribbean (Hulme 78; O'Connor 30).[3] This autobiographical dimension to Antoinette's story, among other reasons I will explore, suggests the need to rethink the novel as a simple, oppositional revision of nineteenth-century romance and English imperialism.[4] The materials from Rhys's own background no doubt provide authenticity to the blanks left by Brontë. However, her depiction of the subordinate role of the Creole woman does not entirely hold its own as a metaphor for the postcolonial subject.

My reading agrees with that of Peter Hulme, who asserts that Rhys is "fundamentally sympathetic to the planter class ruined by Emancipation" (73). There are, of course, similarities between colonialism and sexism that have been amply demonstrated by critics and writers alike and that are apparent in this novel, but the status of Antoinette and that of the English colonies do not always coincide.[5] Slavery placed its subjects in shifting relationships of power by virtue of its distinct positioning of Creoles, women, mulattoes, and blacks. Thus, Rhys's novel is perhaps less a postcolonial musing than an expression of the postslavery placelessness of the white Creole woman; while it clearly criticizes the legal and social power of men in the English colonial system—particularly regarding marriage—it also vacillates between a resistance to and nostalgia for empire and a concomitant attraction and repulsion toward Afro-Caribbean culture. This vacillation, which appears in other Creole positions we have investigated, typically depends on the points of comparison, the critical context, provided by the reader. If Rhys is read alongside *Jane Eyre,* her postcoloniality will emerge as dominant; read in the context of Caribbean literature, she may seem nostalgic.

The contradictory position of the Creole is represented in the very structure of the narrative, which moves between the points of view of Antoinette and her husband, Rochester, all the while haunted by the phantasmagoric presence of various Afro-Caribbean characters. But herein lies the difference between Rhys and the male Creole writers who preceded her: Rhys more consciously represents the distance between Creole and Afro-Caribbean cultures and therefore represents alliances between the two as tenuous and ultimately illusory. She provides a powerful deconstructive tool in resisting new constellations of planter hegemony, even when her own narrative authority tends toward nostalgia, by insisting on the fact that to every narrative position "there is always the other side, always" (128). This other side will always exist because of the ever-shifting political and aesthetic conditions of place that for each individual have a radical power to give shape to narrative truth (O'Connor 176; Emery 36). Rhys shows us a fragmented and multiple Caribbean history for which there exists no central narrative to control the telling of events (Howells 109). If there is always another side, then there is never a center position; this is suggested by the novel's title, which refers to the geographic space among Europe, Africa, and the New World.

Like other postslavery novels we have seen, the position of the post-slavery subject is an orphaned one. We meet the young Antoinette and her mother before emancipation, but once slavery is over and Antoinette has reached adulthood, her mother is dead and she has no parental directive. She is also similarly vulnerable, then, to the arrival of a surrogate father figure who can fill the void; hence, her marriage to Rochester. Despite the very palpable social power he yields over the family estate, however, his narrative never obtains a similarly paternalistic authority over the family history. Unlike Rhys's precursors, the narrative structure of the novel avoids filling in for paternal absence with an overarching narrative control.

Rochester, who is presumably the closest to this kind of authority, is decentered in at least two crucial ways. First, his voice is starkly juxtaposed against both Antoinette's voice (their narratives stand independent of a mediating omniscience to the point that his name is never mentioned; we only know his name from Brontë's novel) and the repeated references to Afro-Caribbean knowledge. Second, we learn that his authority is subordinate to the empire. As a representative of the second wave of English colonials following emancipation in 1838, he has no inheritance in England; he is sent to Dominica, marries into the Cosway line, and thereby obtains from Antoinette's stepfather, Mr. Mason, complete rights to her family's former slave estate. Rochester stands in a position of comparative strength, despite his weak position vis-à-vis imperial England, since as a male he can marry into Antoinette's property and wrest control over its value from her. Rhys explores postslavery social transitions and exposes how, as the empire accommodates itself to more viable forms after slavery, the struggle between white and black becomes ever more accentuated. Rhys exposes the particularly male construction of whiteness in this polarization and thereby demonstrates how the white woman fails to gain a stronghold on any meaningful social power. In this way, Rhys provides the historical and social material with which to recover the method to Bertha's madness. Ultimately, however, Rhys demonstrates that stories, lore, and songs are more lasting and powerful means of cultural sustainability than anything Rochester's colonial strategies can wage.

Rochester carefully follows a script laid down before him by his father. When he marries Antoinette, he is very conscious that he is playing "the part [he] was expected to play" as the white colonial marrying into Creole property: "Every movement I made was an effort of will and sometimes I wondered that no one noticed this" (76, 77). And yet perhaps because of his own awareness of the deception he engages in, he begins to suspect a slippage between that script and reality. The very presence of blacks suggests racial mixture—especially Antoinette's longtime family servant Christophine, her cousin Sandi, and her apparent half brother Daniel—and challenges the legitimacy of his claim to Antoinette's loyalty and consequently to control over the island and its history. Their difference increases his suspicion of his own dramatic irony. He remarks: "If I saw an expression of doubt or curiosity it was on a black face not a white one. . . . Curiosity? Pity? Ridicule? But why should they pity me?" (77). His inability to read the black faces, reminiscent of the white characters in the fiction of Chesnutt, Frances Harper, and Morúa who are attracted to but ultimately puzzled by black expressions, exposes the epistemic limitations of his "place" of social power in the second wave of British imperialism.[6]

Like his fictional precursors, he produces from the unreadable signs on black faces a perception of a "dominant 'blackness' everywhere," which he believes has contaminated the island and his investment in it (L. Irwin 155). Antoinette repeatedly reminds him that the black lens through which Rochester perceives everything, including her, stems from his profound ignorance of Afro-Caribbean realities and from his position as imperial outsider. When he receives a letter and later meets with its author, Daniel Cosway, Rochester's confidence in his knowledge of the family history he has married into is shaken. Cosway claims to be the part-black half brother to Antoinette by another mother and insists that the Cosways were "wicked and detestable slave-owners since generations" (95). He also maintains that Mr. Mason, who had brought Rochester into marriage with Antoinette, is "a sly man and he will tell you a lot of nancy stories, which is what we call lies here" (98). Cosway further dislodges Rochester's confidence in another previously reliable source when he tells Rochester that Antoinette "talks sweet talk and . . . lies" (125).

The suggestion of miscegenation in Antoinette's past begins to loosen Rochester's confidence in the truth and in his own imperialistic script. He is no longer certain of Antoinette's own racial identity; he thinks he notices signs of her own possibly mixed racial heritage and kinship with the black servant Amelie: "Perhaps they are related, I thought. It's possible, it's even probable in this damned place" (127). In the final moment of their conversation, Daniel tells him, "you are not the first to kiss her pretty face, my sister" (126). Rochester associates this hint of Antoinette's transgressive sexuality with miscegenation and incest once he learns that Antoinette has had relations with her part-black cousin Sandi Cosway. Amelie asserts: "I hear one time that Miss Antoinette and . . . Mr. Sandi get married, but that all foolishness. Miss Antoinette a white girl with a lot of money, she won't marry with a coloured man even though he don't look like a coloured man. You ask Miss Antoinette, she tell you" (121). But as Christophine explains to Antoinette, "the man hear so many stories, he don't know what to believe" (114).

The rich suggestiveness of stories and truths fills Rochester with an anxiety about his own legitimate claim on the estate that can only be calmed by a greedy appropriation of what lies on the "other side." Indeed, from the beginning, he is attracted to Antoinette and the island because they are mysteries: "[I]t was a beautiful place . . . with an alien, disturbing, secret loveliness. And it kept its secret. I'd find myself thinking, 'What I see is nothing—I want what it *hides*—that is not nothing'" (87). And yet with each act of possession, enigmas remain behind and mark the limitations of his appropriations. Amelie, for example, is a kind of darker twin to Antoinette, and when she suggests both by her appearance and her tales the possibility of miscegenation in the family line, Rochester takes possession of her. He "looked into her lovely and meaningless face," which precisely because it is illegible becomes all the more alluring (139). He makes love to Amelie only then to find her "skin was darker, her lips thicker than I had thought" (140). Here Rhys provides an insightful interpretation of the white male miscegenator's original desire for the black woman, which Lorna Williams has argued is often clouded with mystery in tragic-mulatto fictions. His racism continually seeks more signs of blackness because he wants to appropriate the "other side" of his power. Desiring blackness is a function of his insatiable greed, which cannot be content with the limits of his own understanding.

Nevertheless, Rhys's novel repeatedly demonstrates that the appropriation of land and of people during and after slavery fails to subsume the religious practices, stories, and music of the Afro-Caribbeans and the natural world itself. And thus with each passing effort to further appropriate these sites of difference and mystery (the very sites of simultaneous attraction and anxiety for Rochester), the master's narrative must resort to new and more desperate measures of control. In this sense, we can understand Antoinette's meaning when she remarks that the days following emancipation "are forgotten, except the lies. Lies are never forgotten, they go on and they grow" (131).

We learn, for example, that Rochester is haunted by the songs he hears among the Afro-Caribbeans and from Antoinette herself, and he desires to demystify the sounds and language of the Creole world: "all day [Antoinette would] . . . try to teach me her songs, for they haunted me" (91). Our prior introduction to these patois songs in the first part of the novel establishes them as omens or riddles that tell the very story of abandonment Rochester will fulfill, one that is basic to the structure of Caribbean colonial history: "The music was gay but the words were sad. . . . 'Adieu.' Not adieu as we said it, but *à dieu,* which made more sense after all. The loving man was lonely, the girl was deserted, the children never came back" (20). So Rochester's attempt to appropriate the mysteries around him is an oedipal investigation into his own crimes; despite his belief that he pursues an understanding and control over otherness, essentially he chases after vestiges of his own colonial story.

We perceive this oedipal irony rather poignantly when he listens to Daniel Cosway's complaint of having been cut off from the family inheritance because he claims he is the mulatto son of Antoinette's father. He explains that "They call me Daniel . . . but my name is Esau" (122). In a moment of self-pity, Rochester drinks rum, writes a letter to his father, and comments that the rum "is mild as mother's milk or father's blessing." Rhys portrays Rochester as the unknowing Jacob, the second son who ultimately obtains the inheritance due not only to Daniel but to his own brother in England as well. Antoinette also accuses him of perpetuating the truth the patois songs prognosticate: "I thought you like the black people so much . . . but that's just a lie like everything else. You like the brown girls better, don't you? You abused the planters and made up stories about them, but you do the same thing. You send the girl away quicker, and with no money or less money, and that's all the difference" (146). Even though this second wave of British colonialism is supposedly postslavery, in essence it represents more insidiously disguised expansions of the same stories. Rochester is a mere repetition of the pattern already established by Mr. Mason, who also married into Antoinette's mother's property, because he resorts to neocolonialist strategies, or to the same lies Antoinette describes, in order to reinforce the structures of slavery (Barnes 154). Mason's strategies led to the insurrection of the blacks who burned Coulibri, the original Cosway home; Rochester's will lead to the burning of Thornfield Hall, his residence in Brontë's England.

Nature is similarly beyond Rochester's capacity to control or to know. He refers to the "inexorable sound" of the rain, which was a kind of music, "a music I had never heard before" (90). He remarks that "I understood why the porter had called it a wild place. Not only wild but menacing. Those hills would close in on you. . . . Everything is too much. . . . Too much blue, too much purple, too much green. The flowers too red, the mountains too high, the hills too near. . . . A bird whistled, a long sad note." (69–70). And his response to nature's extremity and melancholy is again to want to penetrate its meaning and discover the secrets it holds regarding the history of the plantation. Rochester observes overgrowth on a path that appears to lead to plantation ruins: "The path was overgrown but it was impossible to follow it. . . . How can one discover the truth I thought and that thought led me nowhere. No one would tell me the truth. Not my father, nor Richard Mason, certainly not the girl I had married. . . . There had been a paved road through this forest. The track led to a large clear space. Here were the ruins of a stone house and round the ruins rose trees that had grown to an incredible height. . . . Under the orange tree I noticed little bunches of flowers tied with grass" (104). Rochester's conflates here the mysteries of Afro-Caribbean culture (signified by the bound bunches of flowers), the truths of the history of slavery, and the potency of nature. Nature, then, is simply a signifier of the lies that have buried historical truth.[7] When he asks Baptiste, one of the black servants, about the meaning of a road and ruins and about the existence of ghosts or zombies in that location, the answer is repeatedly and tersely: "No road" (106).

As is true for Antoinette, Rochester's access to the truth about himself is blocked by his family's lies and by an evasive Afro-Caribbean culture. But because he is male, through a fortuitous inheritance he is able to recoup the social power necessary to prolonging a confrontation with the oedipal nature of his investigations. Rhys emphasizes the threat to Rochester of oedipal tragedy when he complains: "And do you think that I wanted all this? I would give my life to undo it. I would give my eyes never to have seen this abominable place" (161). But rather than facing the truths obscured in the songs and hidden in nature, including his own desire for his father's death, he denigrates and objectifies Antoinette as the madwoman in the attic. He responds with acts of tighter cognitive control to the possibility that Antoinette's secrets and those of the Caribbean cannot be known. We hear his mind pushing itself to assume this arrogance: "*(But it is lost, that secret, and those who know it cannot tell it.)* Not lost. I had found it in a hidden place and I'd keep it, hold it fast. As I'd hold her" (168). Remaining in love with Antoinette would signify his subordination to his father's deceptions. At the same time, if she becomes "black" in his eyes (which seems to happen every time he tries to control her), he has committed miscegenation. Hence, he insists that she be removed from the place that has caused him so much anxiety, and he has no intention of allowing her the role of the English wife; she must remain placeless, in between. Rhys reconfigures Brontë's depiction of his bigamous marriage to Jane Eyre when he returns to England as also oedipally incestuous, since it vindicates him socially and economically once his father dies. That he goes blind from Antoinette's actions is, by Rhys, reconstrued as his oedipal punishment.

He demands that Antoinette become his marionette and sing the songs the "rain knows"; he assures her that he will "listen to the rain" and "to the mountain bird." In this way, he creates the illusion of having taken possession, through Antoinette, of the Caribbean's mysteries, and he can mute out the self-incriminating story of abandonment that was once contained in the songs. He tells her insistently: "Do not be sad. Or think Adieu. Never Adieu. . . . And you must laugh and chatter as you used to do—telling me [your stories]" (168). He hopes that these appropriated songs and stories will correspond to a new place, but this irreparably contaminates Antoinette's own sense of place. She declares: "Do you know what you've done to me? . . . I loved this place and you have made it into a place I hate. I used to think that if everything else went out of my life I would still have this, and now you have spoilt it. . . . I hate it now like I hate you and before I die I will show you how much I hate you" (147). Her madness, then, is a product of the radical displacement his arrogant presumptions have caused.

Although Antoinette's narrative and Rochester's knowledge are often construed in parallel terms—as the unwanted child, as the one lied to— Antoinette provides us with the other side of what Rochester knows. Most significantly, unlike her husband, who refuses to accept the ever-present existence of the other side of what he knows, Antoinette "was

undecided, uncertain about fact—any fact" (87). Whereas from Rochester's point of view, the island of Dominica and its history seem "quite
unreal and like a dream," Antoinette declares that to her England appears equally unreal (80). Rhys implies that there is always the need for
another version of the same story and that the truth is always undermined by its darker and unknown side. Rochester is not unaware of the
other side, but he greedily presumes that it is knowable and something
to be subjugated. Antoinette, on the other hand, declares frequently her
own ignorance about herself and about others, a cognition that the
novel ultimately values as more truthful. Antoinette explains to Rochester that a patois song was "about a white cockroach. That's me. That's
what they call all of us who were here before their own people in Africa
sold them to the slave traders. And I've heard English women call us
white niggers. So . . . I often wonder who I am and where is my country
and where do I belong and why was I ever born at all" (102). Unlike
Rochester, she sees her story contained in the songs, and such understanding paradoxically results in an awareness of one's ignorance. When
he reprimands her for promising Baptiste that he can come to England
with them, she apologizes: "No, I had no right, I am sorry. I don't understand you. I know nothing about you, and I cannot speak for you"
(171).

Rhys exposes the instability of cognitive certainty by this juxtaposition of overlapping voices that tell of the same events and yet tell separate tales. By representing the slippage that occurs between varying locations of speech, she does not represent that other side per se, but the
fact that the "other side" always haunts what one knows. For this reason it is problematic to complain that Rhys consistently seems to be
placing Afro-Caribbean culture in the space of the other, or for that
matter to argue that she unequivocally represents an authentic Afro-
Caribbean subjectivity. Curiously, critics have made both arguments
rather vehemently. Angelita Reyes, Lee Irwin, Mary Lou Emery, Wilson
Harris, and Kevin Magarey are among those who have highlighted the
Afro-Caribbean symbolism employed throughout the novel and the
ways in which Antoinette's status is akin to that of the former slaves. For
example, they point to her traversing the ocean in a kind of reverse Middle Passage, after which she must assume a new name. Moreover, these
critics appear to be more persuaded by the authenticity of such black
characters as Christophine.

Maria Olaussen has strongly argued, however, that many of Rhys's
representations of blackness are tools for Antoinette's strategic escape

from white femininity and that they are not unlike stereotypical constructions of black sexuality (including Amelie as the black whore and Christophine as the Aunt Jemima figure) of the nineteenth century, which helped to bolster notions of white Christian femininity. She states that equating the status of the white Creole woman to slavery "disregards the actual, historical institution of slavery as experienced by black people under the domination of their white owners. That these white slave owners could also be oppressed and excluded by metropolitan politics and the fact that patriarchal oppression took on a specific meaning for a white Creole woman still do not make her share the experience of slavery" (69). My own position is that Rhys tries to represent Antoinette's need and desire for blackness as escape, but ultimately Antoinette is aware of the ironic limits of such a project (unlike Rochester). Therefore, Rhys's representations of blackness are not constructive of whiteness but serve to deconstructively expose white colonial dependency on Afro-Caribbean culture.

If Rhys were to flesh out the subjectivity of Afro-Caribbeans more completely and assume the narrative responsibility of always capturing the essence of the "other side," she would be guilty of Rochester's presumptuousness. She uses the references to Afro-Caribbean songs and other lore as phantasms, not as fixed subjectivities, that destabilize Western cognition; they are the repositories of what European imperialism cannot contain, what it cannot understand about the colonized or about itself. Rhys seems to argue that one cannot wage an anti-imperialist literary campaign without some self-incrimination. In one sense, then, Gayatri Chakravorty Spivak is correct in stating that "no perspective *critical* of imperialism can turn the Other into a self, because the project of imperialism has always already historically refracted what might have been the absolutely Other into a domesticated Other that consolidates the imperialist self" (272). Spivak reads Christophine—correctly, I think—as a character that ultimately cannot be contained by the novel, but Spivak seems to betray her own thesis since Christophine then suggests a subjectivity that is, in fact, resistant to the containments of the narrative.

Rochester identifies Antoinette with blacks and with obeah, but Antoinette remains aware of her own distance from them. This is particularly apparent in her failed attempt, with which Rhys frames the novel's beginning and conclusion, to ally herself with the blackness of her black childhood friend Tia. Their separation at an early age (and the fact that Antoinette's scar, thrown by a stone Tia throws at her head, heals so as not to spoil her wedding day) facilitates Antoinette's marriage to Rochester and her eventual exile in England (Olaussen 78–79). Rhys marks the limitations of Antoinette's resistance to English colonial discourse, since it requires solidarity with the Black Caribbean, which remains beyond her own symbolic and cognitive grasp. Antoinette quips that Rochester has participated in "obeah too" because he has insisted on changing her name both by marriage and by calling her Bertha in an apparent attempt to "make [her] into someone else" (47). Antoinette seeks Christophine's aid in using obeah to cast a spell on her husband to make him desire her as before, but as Sandra Drake remarks, the irony is that "Antoinette wants to use the spell to complete her assimilation to England and to whiteness" (104). Ultimately, her very use of obeah provokes Rochester to take her away to England and lock her up. The more black she tries to become, the more easily he can identify her as mad, a discourse of madness that in turn legitimizes his appropriation of her family's estate and that of his father. Precisely because she desires obeah for the purposes of assimilation into the British Empire, it seems unwarranted to neglect, as Drake does, the additional irony in Antoinette's apparent union with Tia in the novel's conclusion. Among other critics, Drake insists that in Antoinette's final resolution to burn down Rochester's property and throw herself into its flames and into the imagined arms of Tia, Rhys uses Afro-Caribbean symbolism to demonstrate Antoinette's ultimate union with the Black Caribbean.

To be sure, Antoinette identifies with Tia and with all of the Black Caribbean, but she has recourse only to a fantasized reunion with Coulibri and with Tia since Rochester has taken her away from all points of self-reference and self-knowledge, even, as she remarks, a looking glass by which to contemplate her image (180).[8] This absence of self-referentiality has been her history. In the novel's beginning, after Tia throws the stone, she contemplates Tia's tears, commenting that it was "as if I saw myself. Like in a looking-glass" (45). Rochester sees her as a black woman, and yet when she contemplates Tia as her black "twin," she only sees Tia's rejection of her, an image of her failure to unite with the Afro-Caribbean world. Only moments after she decides that "this is where I belong and this is where I wish to stay" in Christophine's presence, she requests obeah in order to win Rochester's love back.

In the novel's ending, she dreams that her act of arson is a reunification with Tia. The dream serves as an anticipation of the dual role as black and madwoman scripted for her by Rochester's and Brontë's tacit colonialist discourses; in anticipating her role, the dream retroactively recovers a measure of Antoinette's agency. Antoinette is imprisoned by colonial discourses of madness and blackness, yet she is neither mad nor black.[9] This apocalyptic closure of colonialist discourse and of Antoinette's existence demonstrates the historical conditions that have shaped her existence. By destroying both herself and the estate at Thornfield (the patrimonial center of Rochester's pain as the second son and ultimately his means of escape from his own oedipal trap), Antoinette rejects patrimony as the colonial discourse of white malehood that has determined her history.

In the wake of slavery, many white writers, as we have seen, have attempted to overcome the epistemological trap of resisting contingency with a symbolic union with blackness. Unlike these writers, however, Rhys acknowledges the unbridgeable gap that lies in between. In the earlier examples of Cable, Villaverde, and Faulkner, this symbolic appropriation of cultural blackness does not provide an effective escape from the historical and social conditions of the whites. Rhys's narrative irony suggests that this attempted union is a response conditioned by the history of slavery rather than an escape from it. Rhys does not claim that she somehow has escaped the contingencies—cultural, historical, and otherwise—that have conditioned her representations of the white Creole woman, but by exposing the other side of both narrative authority and claims on social and legal legitimacy, she provides a powerful tool by which we can examine how and in whose interest historical truth is constructed.

"Everything That They Relate Is Gossip, Lies, Unabashed Slander, and Yet It Is All True"

Like *Wide Sargasso Sea,* Rosario Ferré's novel *Maldito amor* (1986; trans. *Sweet Diamond Dust,* 1991) examines the strategies by which neocolonial forces reemerged in the wake of slavery and also how the marginalized sectors adjusted in order to sustain their struggle for equality. Ferré has explained that she intended *Maldito amor* to be an "anti-regionalist novel [anti-novela de la tierra]" ("Entrevista" 248).[10] She takes aim at fiction writers, not historians, who have nurtured Puerto Rican historical imagination. Although the art of fiction is to lie in order to tell the truth, Ferré insists that fiction lies sometimes simply to lie and that the revisionary task is to resurrect the ghosts, Rhys's "other side" of foundational fictions, in order to expose lies as the basis for the construction of national identity (Gutiérrez Mouat 287). In other words, she exposes history and the historical impulses of fiction as patriarchal rhetoric and reality as "corrupted by mythification to the point that the past exists only as myth" (Acosta Cruz 24). In her introduction to the Spanish edition of the novel, Ferré chronicles the Puerto Rican cultural imagination of political leaders and novelists since the nineteenth century, a history that has idealized "the romantic life of the hacienda and its male owners," and explains that her work attempts to "parody that vision of history and of the master's life on the hacienda, to wrest from that myth its power to confer authority and identity" (*Maldito amor* 10).[11]

In the early decades of the new century, American investors in Puerto Rico aggressively bought land owned by local families and began sugar production on a previously unseen scale. Consequently, many families, having once owned slaves (before slavery was abolished in 1873) and controlled their own economic well-being, found themselves with smaller pieces of property and less control over their own familial status. The traditional *hacendado* structure began to change into that of the *ingenio,* a transition from a personal, paternal, and hierarchical authority to "an impersonal corporation made up of hundreds of shareholders" (Umpierre 28).

One of the great ironies of the U.S. invasion of Puerto Rico is that it brought greater educational opportunities for the masses and increased employment for women, two consequences that went against Spanish colonial tradition.[12] Those most opposed to the presence of the United States and its modernization of Puerto Rico, including such intellectuals of the *hacendado* class as Salvador Brau, often became the most nostalgic about Spanish colonial rule because they paradoxically believed that Puerto Rico's national personality was most evident. According to Angel Quintero Rivera, such nostalgia elided the pressing class and race conflicts in Puerto Rican history by romanticizing the integration of races and believing it was facilitated by the paternalism of the old hacienda system. Such rhetoric celebrated Puerto Rico's Catholicism; the position of the woman in the household previous to the arrival of U.S. factories; the preindustrial labor of the country; and coffee plantations, which, in their minds, opposed the sugar industry's growing political and economic dependence on the United States. This set the stage for an emergent populism in Puerto Rico that sought to regenerate a popular faith both in the past traditions of the local plantation and in the governmental institutions that stood in their stead as repositories of national patriotism.[13] In particular, it gave new life to the metaphor of Puerto Rico as a "la gran familia puertorriqueña," which, according to Quintero

Rivera, was essentially a return to the "feudal mode of production" of the plantation. The plantation originally provided a "paternalistic conception of the homeland as a great family—a hierarchical family to be sure, led by an acquisitive father, the *hacendado*—but a family nevertheless, constituted by a common citizenry" (*Patricios* 47).

In literature, these protonationalist ideologies were manifested in a Puerto Rican version of regionalism, a literature that represented the infirmities of the national spirit that had resulted from U.S. mechanization of the island economy. From the late nineteenth century through the 1930s in particular, writers such as Manuel Zeno Gandia, Enrique Laguerre, and Antonio Pedreira took on the task of rescuing in the Puerto Rican imagination a sense of national tradition based in the *hacendado* model of the "great family." Most frequently, the sugar-plantation regions along the coast were depicted as the sites of the greatest racial, social, and natural erosion, in contrast to the internal, mountainous regions of the coffee plantations, where many of the pre-1898 values apparently could still be found.

Like many literary forms of regionalism in Latin America, according to Carlos Alonso, this literary tradition developed in response to, and attempted to cure, the crisis initiated by U.S. encroachment throughout Latin America, and yet the works of regionalism tended to "reenact that crisis in their own rhetorical structure" (7).[14] Alonso explains that "the attempt to produce a text of autochthony places the writer in an eccentric perspective with respect to his or her own cultural circumstance" (6). This means that "affirmations of cultural autochthony exhibit simultaneously two irreconcilable attributes: an essentialist, ahistorical conception of cultural identity, and an explicitly historical agenda for facilitating the imminent manifestation of that essence" (11). Thus, despite the regionalist writer's intention to speak from within the native essence he or she depicts, he or she is placed outside that essence and his or her work is therefore expressive of and conditioned by alienation. Therefore, regionalism cannot cure the degradation it depicts because it needs a disease in order to establish its anti-imperialist authority.

Puerto Rican literature is no exception; the authority forged by regionalist writers and critics alike depended heavily on representations of the trauma caused by colonialism.[15] Consequently, regionalism was a viable tool for the *hacendado* class, particularly for the men, since they established the authority by which to name Puerto Rico's illnesses and thereby were able to set about curing them. No need for substantial social change would ever be exposed. If we follow Alonso's argument, we come to the conclusion that such writing is a kind of paternalism itself, since it relies on the eccentric and ahistorical position of the writer who, by virtue of a disguised position outside history, can offer cures with no account of his or her own historical genesis. Postslavery regionalism, as Ferré demonstrates, is essentially a nostalgia for the paternalism of the plantation; paternalism recycles itself by an eternal recourse to a diseased past for which it continually offers itself as a cure.

The narrative structure of *Sweet Diamond Dust* parallels the social and historical changes in Puerto Rico over the twentieth century and reflects upon the conditions that helped to produce the various platforms for Puerto Rican identity. Throughout the early 1900s, debates raged about the future of the workers, the island, and Puerto Rico's cultural and political allegiances, and we see in Ferré's novel representations of the various platforms within the declining plantation-family model. Her rigorous association between narrative voice and social position within that family structure informs her strategy, which Sidney Mintz identifies as a Puerto Rican propensity for "historical reconstruction" (56–57). Historical reconstruction and interrogation are, as Josefina Ludmer has observed, the means by which marginal voices such as Ferré's challenge the authority of the dominant class. The strategy, in Ludmer's argument, is to focus on representing the "specific positions occupied by women" and other marginalized subjects in order to tell new stories ("Tretas" 54).[16] In other words, like Rhys, Ferré argues for a conception of voice as deeply embedded in, and reflective of, place and social context.

With respect to Ferré, the term *marginal* must be used somewhat cautiously. She is, after all, the daughter of one of the most powerful figures in recent Puerto Rican political history, a sister to the owner of the island's chief newspaper, and a descendant of the very *hacendado* class with which she argues in the novel. It is perhaps her proximity to the power nexus of her own family and her awareness of her position as a woman within that nexus that qualify her voice as marginal. That is not to say, however, that her novel contains no evidence of her own distance from the positions of resistance that she represents. As I insisted with Rhys, the context in which Ferré is read produces various and contradictory ideological readings. Now that Ferré has enjoyed success as a writer in English and has recently publicized her political change of heart regarding Puerto Rican status (she was a longtime proponent of independence and is now pro-statehood), it becomes even more imperative that we have the adequate linguistic and transgeographical context by which to assess her oeuvre.[17]

Ferré begins with Hermenegildo's narrative, which is representative of the nostalgia for pre-1898 paternalism offered by Pedreira, Brau, and others. His is the very model of the *novela de la tierra*—novel of the land—which Ferré sets about deconstructing. Not only is he apparently in discursive control over the meaning of his friend Ubaldino's life—his prototype of the anti-American paternalistic hero—he is also the proprietor of Ubaldino's will. Ubaldino's story takes place in the post-1898 town of Guamaní, a fictional representation of the city of Ponce, which many landowning families (including Ferré's) left when they could no longer compete with the American capitalists for ownership of the region's numerous sugar mills. Hermenegildo's narrative is interrupted and finally dismissed as various players in the history of the plantation tell their versions of Ubaldino's family history.

Like historiography generally, Hermenegildo's fictional memorial is characterized by its attempt to speak impersonally in the name of a larger whole. But again, this is not a fictional lie that tells the truth; rather, it attempts to elide permanently the social differences that, if pursued, would lead the reader into other histories. The "we" of Hermenegildo's account are the possessors of a collective national memory, but by the end of the first chapter, his inclusive "we" betrays him: "Well-to-do families lived in elegant houses, with wood-carved lace fans. . . . At that time, Guamaneños of the upper crust all belonged to the same clan. There were blood ties among the most distant families, and *we* always gave one another financial and moral support, so as to better manage *our* sugarcane haciendas" (*Sweet Diamond Dust* 6; emphasis added). The impersonal and disinterested "we" quickly breaks down into a personal and interested one, that of the plantation owners.

In the narratives that follow, Ferré exposes the interest of Hermenegildo's false plurality in keeping the Diamond Dust property away from women and illegitimate children in order to forge a "legitimate" national heritage. Her narrative performs what Finke has called "dialogic criticism," which involves unmasking monologic language of the powerful as illusion (17). This mask is akin to the split consciousness of regional literature described by Alonso; it attempts to speak from outside history and from outside the region in order to represent an autochthonous local color.

The failure of Hermenegildo's narrative to trace the patriarchal line of legitimate authority is also its failure to sustain itself as an official history. Ironically, Hermenegildo's novel is the only narrative in quotation marks—a redaction that assigns his voice the responsibility of time and place and thus marks it as rhetorical rather than metaphorical. It also places his language in a prior and more broad discourse of testimonial language about plantation history. This serves to represent the testimonial force that follows as a series of voices that are, in the words in Ricardo Gutiérrez Mouat, "implied presences [ínsito] in other voices and in the end work themselves free from their predecessors in order to reveal themselves in their own integrity" (292). This process of one story giving unwanted birth to another is what ultimately will disable master narratives, since they rely on the silent "implied presences" for the construction of their own authority; they contain the seeds of their own deconstruction. Ferré lifts Hermenegildo's narrative out of the context of a struggle for national identity vis-à-vis a colonial power and exposes how, when placed in a context internal to the social dynamics of the island, the otherwise revolutionary rhetoric of the Creole male nationalist carries particularly oppressive ideological baggage. This comparative reading, which should remind the reader of Villaverde and Cable's Creole imaginings, perhaps suggests that my reading of Cable and Villaverde mimics the writers in this chapter in terms of how they read for the ellipses in the representations of the nation that precede them.

An examination of the narrative of Titina, the last slave from the plantation days, illustrates these deconstructive powers of testimonial language. Like all the narratives from the various members of the family, hers is not in quotation marks, which suggests that these alternative narratives of the family history incorporate Hermenegildo's within their own boundaries rather than the other way around. Her narrative is motivated by her interest in a piece of the estate, which she claims Ubaldino had promised her before he died. This begins a series of claims on the estate made by subsequent narrators. Because of Titina's intimate position within the household, she has privileged information about the family history. Titina's mother suckled Ubaldino; Titina ate from his plate and silver spoon; and she has heard most of the intimate talk between the family members. Unlike Hermenegildo, who attempts to hide the specific time and place from which he speaks, Titina refers to her intimate proximity to the speech she reports, bearing witness not just to the information she relays, but to her own accountability for that information. Explaining his anti-American sentiments, she claims that "Ubaldino wasn't just going to let the newcomers [U.S. capitalists] take away what it had taken him years to rescue from the wrong hands, as he used to say to me *when I poured out his coffee in the morning*. . . . For one must be a generous host to them, he'd say to me *as I handed him his hat and his briefcase,* but one must never bed with them" (23, emphasis added). She explains that *Manifest Destiny* and other words were "part of the vocabulary with which he damned the heavens every morning, as he shaved, washed his face, and combed his hair *before the mirror I held up to his face*" (22, emphasis added).

The real mirror being held up to her master's face, however, is Titina's testimony itself. Her testimony is a language that is always expressed in the context of her economic and social situation and is thereby empowered to unmask the supposed universality of Puerto Rican patriotic rhetoric; she reveals it to be merely an expression of Ubaldino's own social and economic situation. Ferré embeds the *hacendado*'s national discourse within an account of the labor relations that make that discourse possible in the first place. Titina's speech reverses the metaphorical erasure of labor relations in the master's narrative described by Elizabeth Fox-Genovese. Just as the slave master claims "I ploughed my field," we can imagine Ubaldino, were he relating the events of that morning, saying, "I poured myself a cup of coffee," or "I got my hat and briefcase." Titina's narrative is not so dishonest; she cannot avoid revealing those relations, since they provide the stuff of her narrative. Once Titina suggests the possibility that Ubaldino's son, Nicolás, was murdered by someone in the family, Hermenegildo has to confess: "Every family in Guamaní hides a skeleton in the cupboard and Ubaldino's is probably no different. But it's better to forget these unhappy events, erasing them with the edifying accounts of his heroic exploits. Every country that aspires to become a nation needs its heroes, its eminent civic and moral leaders, and if it doesn't have them, it's our duty to invent them. Fortunately this is not the case with Ubaldino, who was truly a paragon of chivalrous virtue, and whose story I have already begun to relate in my book" (24–25).

Ferré's fictional introduction of a previously silenced voice forces the nationalist discourse to confess its lies even if it doesn't make the truth any clearer. Hermenegildo confirms Ernest Renan's claim that "forgetting, I would even go so far to say historical error, is a crucial factor in the creation of a nation" (11). Hermenegildo's reaction to a history he can't control parallels Rochester's increasing desire to possess what the other side hides. Arístides, the second and less-favored son, provides further allegations that elicit in Hermenegildo the same cognitive thirst we saw in Rochester. Hermenegildo remarks: "His tale had a feverish aura about it that proved contagious" (51). He is interested in the truth only because, like Rochester, he wants to know what lies beyond his discursive control so that he can know what appropriative strategies will rein in those truths, strategies Ferré here reveals as lies.

Titina's story clearly evokes the need for further investigation, which Hermenegildo at first pursues but, like Rochester, eventually abandons. In this evocative sense, we can say that Titina's narrative functions metonymically; unlike the master narrative, her story suggests rather than hides other possibilities. For example, in a chapter from Hermenegildo's novel that immediately follows Titina's testimony, we hear Ubaldino's father, Don Julio, conversing with his sister-in-law while Titina serves him a cup of coffee, just as she had Ubaldino. Because her position within the plantation family economy privileges her with what Hermenegildo regarded as a "totally different explanation" of the events he relates, her shadow presence in this subsequent chapter destabilizes and decenters the narrative. He investigates Titina's allegations, exposing himself and his reader to further versions of the family history normally marginalized in a national romance such as his own. Each narrator discloses to Hermenegildo new information that portrays him or her as marginal to other, more powerful voices concerning the future of the family estate. As the narratives progress, they perform their own forms of exclusion and oppression, like Hermenegildo, in the interest of obtaining a piece of the inheritance.

The novel represents the competition for legal authority by which to lay claim to the patrimony and to the truths of the Puerto Rican family history. Essentially, "the structure of *Maldito amor* resembles a lawsuit at the base of which is Doña Laura's will. The narratological function of Don Hermenegildo (to be the narrative director [narratario] of contradictory stories) coincides with the legal attributes of his character [as a lawyer]. . . . But the lawyer assigns himself the role of judge . . . when he pronounces himself in favor of the interests of the hacendado class" (Gutiérrez Mouat 293). As Hermenegildo attempts to seal hermetically his account by playing the dual role of lawyer and judge, the witnesses continue to proliferate.

Arístides has married into the American family that is buying up the local sugar mills, so his interest is to justify turning the estate over to the Americans. Unlike the first-born, Nicolás, who is educated in Europe, Arístides receives an American education at home and in English. He advocates an Americanized and modernized vision of his country's future and dismisses the European claim on Puerto Rican nationality by portraying Nicolás as an emasculated homosexual whose death was a suicide. Because of sympathy for American culture, he exoticizes but ultimately wishes to expel from Puerto Rican culture its history of miscegenation. He suggests that Nicolasito, Nicolás's son, is a genealogical nightmare, a monster produced by the confusion of the plantation and therefore an illegitimate heir to the property. He conflates confused paternity (and the possibility of miscegenation) with incest since, as in the case of incest, Nicolasito represents "the interruption or entanglement of genealogical discourse that disqualifies the most basic categories of social organization" (Gutiérrez Mouat 294). Nicolás's son was "his father's child and his mother's grandchild, his brother's child and his brother's brother, his son, his brother, and his nephew all in one" (49).

Arístides's particularly "American" rejection of the plantation's confused racial genealogy parallels a similar desire to whiten the mill's sugar. He advocates the white sugar, the "diamond dust," produced with the aid of U.S. technology, as an alternative to the brown sugar produced by many Creoles. In a further attempt to denigrate the hacienda's legacies of racial mixture, he initially is seduced by the mulatto Gloria and proudly proclaims his virile sexual relations with her, but he ultimately wishes to destroy the family will in which his mother, Laura, bequeaths the property to her. He claims that Nicolás died in despair upon learning of the numerous progeny that Ubaldino supposedly sired with black women.

Laura, who married into the family from a lower-class background, struggles as the household matron against the tradition and strength of the patriarchal order. She lays claim to being half owner of the property and therefore to legal authority to pass it on as she pleases. From her we learn essential details of the family history, apparently repressed since Spanish rule of the island: Ubaldino was not a strong leader; his father Don Julio was a horse tamer and a black man, a fact that denigrates the family's Spanish claim to purity of blood. Laura's vision of national identity celebrates Puerto Rico's possibility as a gateway between North and South America, between English and Spanish heritages, and between the black and white races. This was, in fact, a popular position in the 1920s and 1930s in the polemical debate over Pan-Americanism throughout the hemisphere. Laura explains:

It's our island's destiny to become the gate to South as well as to North American, so that on our doorsill both continents will one day peacefully merge into one. And it's for this reason that I'm set on leaving Diamond Dust to Gloria and to Nicolasito. . . . From the very first day of Gloria's arrival at our house, I was very much aware of her constant visits to the waterfront canteens and bars, where she soon became a sort of legendary prostitute . . . and thus, Nicolasito can be said to be the child of all. In her body . . . both races, both languages, English and Spanish, grew into one soul. (76)

In an interesting, vengeful twist to the de la Valle family's pursuit of genealogical purity and in contradistinction to Arístides's Americanized denigration of Nicolasito's origins, Nicolasito becomes the ideal recipient of the patrimony precisely because we can't be sure of his genealogy. Laura's genealogical discourse combats the ideology of *limpieza de sangre*—purity of blood—implicit in both Hermenegildo's Creole narrative and Arístides's advocacy of the United States. Laura explains further that Gloria will sell the estate piecemeal to support those going and coming from the mainland United States. So we move from Hermenegildo's rather consolidated vision of the great Puerto Rican family to a radically dispersed family line that is no longer recognizable. The irony is that Nicolasito is likely the son of Ubaldino and Gloria, since, Laura explains, she allowed Gloria (who came to take care of the ailing Ubaldino) to sleep with Ubaldino in order to shield herself from his venereal disease. By implication, Laura's vision of Puerto Rico as the bridge between cultures is facilitated by a prostitution of the land and the culture.[18] This vision clearly disputes the discourse of genealogical purity and unequivocally advocates openness as an answer to the plantation's solitude, yet it still proves to be a discourse that upholds racial hierarchy. While it appears to be a benevolent offering of the patrimony to the mulatto prostitute and her offspring, Laura's discourse is guilty of paternalistic racism through her use of the mulatto woman's body as a shield by which to exact revenge on Ubaldino and his family.

Because of this apparent competing self-interest that ultimately conflicts with both Arístides's and Gloria's narratives, it is hard to argue that Ferré is exclusively interested in exposing the collective force of women's narratives that categorically resist masculinist discourse. While it is certainly true that Laura's narrative works against Hermenegildo's patriotism, so does Arístides's, and it is clear that Laura's narrative is equally infected by political interests that have rather unfortunate implications for Gloria. What we have in this proliferation of narratives is a synchronic and metonymic reconstruction of history that represents women as part of a larger "dialogic criticism" of history from the margins. As we attempt to move back into the past, once the narrative authority to do so is decentered, then we find ourselves moving across the social landscape in search of more and more "partial positions [that] may be related to contingent wholes," each one competing for that central authority but also made suspect by the ones that will certainly follow (Zamora, *Usable Past* 208).

Until the final narrative, by Gloria, then, it appears that the cumulative effect of each testimonial is to serve the function of Rhys's other side; each is implied by, and works against, its predecessor. As the testimonies accumulate, so does our appreciation both of the ways in which people lie—lies being the real national heritage—and of the metonymical power of competing narratives to create expectations of additional witnesses to counter what has been said. However, when Gloria declares the end of Hermenegildo's novel (and of his life, for that matter), rejects the will, and burns the hacienda (with Hermenegildo caught inside), the metonymical impulse of Ferré's work implodes. Unlike Antoinette, who cannot but self-immolate in her act of textual revenge, Gloria stands outside the history/hacienda she burns. She is also, as Gutiérrez Mouat reminds us, the madwoman in the basement, not in the attic. As such, she represents the foundational level of Puerto Rican society, that of the Africans, according to the argument of José Luis González.[19] Ferré adds to González's argument by implying that black female subjectivity is the radical and ultimate witness to the struggles of Puerto Rican nationalism.

Once again we are left with a kind of apocalyptic total closure when we might have expected, given the structure of the novel, an open-ended finish to the postslavery struggle for historical truth and authority. Ferré has acknowledged that Gloria's truth claims seem to violate the conditions of truth that the novel has established.[20] We cannot escape the feeling in the novel's conclusion that we have finally discovered the real story of the family and of Nicolás's death. How is it that Gloria's narrative assumes the authority to tell the "truth" that overarches her particular circumstances within the plantation family? Does Gloria escape the trappings of the history she relates by means of a recourse to a mythical ahistorical space? Ultimately, these questions raise the larger concern of how we can reconstruct a more honest history, from the margins, once we have become aware of how social and historical conditions inevitably shape the "lies" we tell.

Ferré offers Gloria's position as a possible resolution of this dilemma because she is the most marginalized, she is the most used by the family, and, like Rhys's Antoinette and Morrison's Milkman, she rejects patrimony. Once an individual totally renounces patrimony, Ferré suggests (by using an unrepresented future tense and not by a reversion to a mythical past) that there is no need for further narrative.

The irony here is rich, since we arrive at this point after discovering the unveiling powers of deeply historicized testimonial voices as they stand within particular social and historical circumstances. But perhaps, as Ferré herself has observed, this paradox is symptomatic of an irony she describes as "the splitting in two of the creative consciousness, a cleavage in which the writing self breaks into an historical empiric self, as well as into a linguistic self" ("Ire to Irony" 901). She explains that because of our increased awareness of our own historicity in the moment of writing, "it has become increasingly less possible to speak of human experience in historical terms, . . . and we become progressively ironic as we realize the impossibility of displaying our historic self. . . . [Paul de Man] argues, that it's just as we develop a type of language which does not want to say what it says, that we finally can say what we want to say" (901). Gloria's ultimately triumphant and truthful narrative is a logical contradictory outcome, a hall of narrative mirrors, as it were, of a hyperawareness of historical contingency.

If we examine how the song lyrics of "Maldito Amor" shift throughout the novel, we find an additional clue to Ferré's apocalyptic meaning. In the second chapter, we learn from Hermenegildo that the couple who are to give birth to Puerto Rico's hero Ubaldino, the Spaniard (so we're told) Don Julio Font and the Creole Doña Elvira de la Valle, have fallen in love. When Don Julio is away, Elvira sings:

> Your love is now a songless bird
> Your love, my dear, is lost in my heart
> I don't know why your passion wilts me
> And why it never flamed! (9)

Here Ferré reverses the terms of the foundational romance of nineteenth-century Latin American literature, which, according to Doris Sommer, imagines national reconciliation and consolidation through natural affections. What gives birth to the nation is not affection but disaffection and the violence that is needed to cover it up. (We later learn that Don Julio beats his wife and has perhaps sought his own social betterment through marriage.) The nation is born out of disenchantment when one discovers there is no object worthy of one's affections but rather a void that can only be filled with stories.

After Gloria sets fire to the hacienda, Ferré reverses the meaning of the lyrics of the song:

Your love is a bird which has found its voice
Your love has finally nested in my heart
Now I know why it burns
when I remember you (85)

The implication is that as long as we continue to draw national and cultural boundaries, love of nation will remain a bitter and cursed love, more *amor maldito* than *maldito amor,* as Lourdes Martínez Echazabal observes (501). That is, a patriotic love is not cursed simply because it can't find the object of its affections but condemned, by its very nature, to fail. There will always be the need for someone new to tell someone else that something different happened; in other words, the birds will continue to sing. If there is to be any fulfillment of our longings for national and cultural origins, we must content ourselves with an incessant need to read yet another witness to history.[21] The burning of plantation property is represented in the novels of several of her precursors, including Laguerre, René Márquez, and Faulkner, but Ferré's representation of arson is a nod to the future rather than a redemptive return to a prior era (Gutiérrez Mouat 301). Because there is no one to follow or contradict her, Gloria's testimony is the most powerfully suggestive of future, not past, possibilities.

Ferré's novel does express nostalgia for the truth, but unlike the *novelas de la tierra* she rejects, it is a nostalgia for truths yet to be revealed (Friedman, "Missing Contents?" 242). This is particularly evident in her verb tense: "Facts have a strange way of facing down fiction, Titina, and if Don Hermenegildo's aborted novel was to have been a series of stories that contradicted one another like a row of falling dominoes, our story, the one we've taken the authority to write, *will eradicate* them all, because it *will be* the only one in which word and deed will finally be loyal to each other, in which a true correspondence between them *will finally be established*" (82, emphasis added). What remains at the end of the novel is a haunting disappointment that Ferré offers no grounds to believe that Gloria can legitimately establish her authority outside the history she narrates. Ferré uses the mulatto woman, nevertheless, as her means of imagining an escape from the history of the plantation, and this decisive break with the past has greater emphasis in her own English translation than in the original Spanish (the above citation is absent in the Spanish). Rather than finding justification for Gloria's stance in the historical conditions of the plantation in Puerto Rico, the context of a decidedly more Anglo reading audience empowers Ferré to imagine this escape. One is left wondering if writing in English with awareness of the possibility of a more white-identified readership enables Ferré to grant Gloria's narrative this transcendent power. Does the broader U.S. readership that her English translation has interpellated shield her accountability for portraying, like Laura, an exoticized and ahistorical mulatto feminism?

"You Just Can't Fly Off and Leave a Body"

If the apocalyptic closures to *Wide Sargasso Sea* and *Sweet Diamond Dust* are any indication, Rhys and Ferré do not entirely escape the oedipal implications of their attempts to emancipate themselves from history. Their difficulty is in finding the narrative structures to represent stories beyond the reach of the historical structures that originally represented their containment. Toni Morrison concurs with Ferré and Rhys: The delimiting nature of the history of slavery is not merely the weight of events that have come before but what was erased in its telling and retelling; in Morrison's case, she attempts to liberate the history of blacks from the expansive and all-inclusive reach of white imaginings of slavery's past. One of the chief reasons that Morrison, in her quest for historical transcendence in her novel *Song of Solomon* (1977), more successfully moves beyond the structures of the oedipal story is her more broadly conceived notion of testimonial language as transindividual and translocational. It may seem odd to categorize this novel with the others in this study, since it does not deal as directly or explicitly with slavery, the plantation, and black-white genealogies (and it deals with these subjects less than Morrison's *Beloved*), but precisely because it self-consciously and radically departs from those paradigmatic structures of postslavery, *Song of Solomon* provides special insight into strategies for emancipation of/from history.

The novel clearly responds to several literary precursors, but here I will focus on its response to Faulkner's implied reading of black history in *Absalom, Absalom!* I do so ultimately to establish important transnational parallels with Rhys and Ferré; such synchronic connections are vital in considering Morrison because of the novel's themes and her own, justified distaste for any diachronic classification of her writing:

Our—black women's—job is a particularly complex one. . . . We have no systematic mode of criticism that has yet evolved from us, but it will. I am not like James Joyce; I am not like Thomas Hardy; I am not like Faulkner. I am not like in that sense. I do not have objections to being compared to

such extraordinarily gifted and facile writers, but it does leave me sort of
hanging there when I know that my effort is to be like something that has
probably only been expressed perhaps in music, or in some other culture-
gen that survives almost in isolation because the community manages to
hold on to it. (qtd. in Duvall, "Morrison" 6)

As I will demonstrate, her recourse to music and community liberates
her from any kind of Bloomian anxiety of influence and allows her an
interplay with Faulkner and ultimately with slavery's history, without
placing her in subordination to the past.[22]

Her novel engages in exposing the other side of Thomas Sutpen's
story by situating Milkman Dead's search for genealogy and identity in
the context of the rural South that was once dominated by families like
Sutpen's. Milkman's grandfather, Macon, purchased a piece of land ad-
jacent to the plantation household of the Butler family shortly after
emancipation. In what appears to be an allusion to Sutpen's European
purchases, their house is similarly furnished with "pink veined marble
from across the sea," and they hired "men in Italy to do the chandelier"
(*Song of Solomon* 247). Like Faulkner's Sutpen, who appears abruptly
on the horizon in Jefferson, larger than life, and with "no discernable
past," and who "tore violently a plantation . . . apparently out of nothing" (*Absalom* 6,9), Macon arrives "out of nowhere" and "tore a farm
out of a wilderness" (*Song of Solomon* 235, 293). His success on the
farm was "a sermon" on the American dream: "'You see?' the farm said
to them. 'See? See what you can do? Never mind you can't tell one letter
from another, never mind you born a slave, never mind you lose your
name, never mind your daddy dead, never mind nothing. Here this here,
is what a man can do if he puts his mind to it and his back in it. . . . Grab
it. Grab this land! Take it, . . . buy it, sell it, own it, build it, multiply it,
and pass it on—can you hear me? Pass it on!'" (293).

Morrison places the story of Milkman's genealogy as a kind of Rhy-
sian "other side" of Sutpen's story. Sutpen begins his life in a world
where, like this edenic beginning for Macon Dead, "the land belonged to
anybody and everybody" (*Absalom* 276). But like Macon, Sutpen falls
into a country that was "all divided and fixed and neat with a people living on it all divided and fixed and neat because of what color their skins
happened to be and what they happened to own" (276). Morrison's But-
lers, representative of the plantation legacy that Sutpen comes to epito-
mize, find Macon's success an effrontery to their own economic survival
after emancipation. Deciding they need his property, they shoot him in

front of his two children and take possession of the land. Unlike Sutpen, whose claim to the land depends on a white son whom he loses, Macon's claim to the land is deracinated by an act of violence that deprives his posterity of their father. Faulkner conceives of the "design" of white male social power as founded on a contradiction that proves to be genealogically sterile, while Morrison exposes that complicit with that design is a violence that deprives African Americans of their ancestral ties to the land. Hence, Faulkner's is a story of a man who cannot insert himself into history through his posterity because he forsook his own past, while Morrison's works backward; it is the story of a man who discovers his own historicity by availing himself of the contemporary circumstances shaped by the death of his father.

Morrison clearly nods to Faulkner, but only by reducing him to the same phantasmagoric presence the emancipated stories had in her literary precursors. In other words, Faulkner is no more of a presence in her literature than the black history of postslavery is in Faulkner's work. Morrison reads Faulkner in the same way Homi Bhabha claims she asks us to read her: "The critic must attempt to fully realize, and take responsibility for, the unspoken, unrepresented pasts that haunt the historical present" ("The World" 450). When Milkman arrives, like Quentin, at the door of the Butler plantation household and discovers the ghostlike Circe—an analogue to the slave Clytie, who survives after more than forty years within the Sutpen mansion—he is able to obtain from her key knowledge regarding his family's past, including his grandfather's true name.[23] Morrison asks us to imagine that Clytie stood at the doorway of the Sutpen household as the holder not only of the Sutpen family secrets but also of the family secrets of the black lives, which were irrelevant to Quentin and apparently to Faulkner in his representation of southern history. Morrison's work exposes Faulkner's view as a uniquely white understanding of the South in that Faulkner seeks to understand slavery's history by means of "playing in the dark." His recourse to what she calls an "Africanist" presence serves to perpetuate an eternal return to the white father's story (*Playing* 5). This implies that the oedipal dimensions of Quentin's struggle are not existential but historically based in the white conventions of the plantation.[24]

Morrison ultimately resists the burden of the Sutpen saga by telling a different story altogether: that of the black community's struggles against continuing oppression following emancipation, the failure of Reconstruction, and the flight to the urban North. She unwinds that history by moving back across black postslavery geography, from the

North to the South, from the outer margins of plantation history, not to the plantation per se but to the communal places of genesis that have given shape to contemporary black identity. This movement across a variety of locations speaks to the variety of situated strategies by which black culture has responded to its repeated deracination, and it also demonstrates that distinct locations correspond to the distinct but overlapping stories Milkman hears about himself and his past. Milkman discovers the permeable boundaries of his individual self; his being is made of the constituent elements of places his family left behind. He learns that he has been created from a dynamic process of making and remaking community according to the demands of place. Milkman's story "enlarges the orbit of geography for Afro-American identity and performance" where "past and present—African and Upper Michigan—are fused in a temporal resonance that shapes the novel into the song of a heritage" (Dixon 136; Barthold 174).

Initially, Milkman is vulnerable to an oedipal fate. Repeatedly in the novel, we see attempted flights from history becoming as much of an obstacle to individual and communal emancipation as history itself. Milkman's story is set in motion by his great-grandfather Solomon's attempt to emancipate himself from slavery and fly back to Africa. In turn, his grandfather sought a similar flight from the conditions of the postbellum South in his attempt to pursue property freely. In each case, however, the failed attempt to secure personal freedom from a history of oppression becomes an added burden for the next generation. Macon Dead Jr., having witnessed his father's murder, "paid homage to his own father's life and death by loving what that father had loved: property. . . . He loved [property] to excess because he loved his father to excess. Owning, building, acquiring,—that was his life, his future, his present and all the history that he knew" (300). Macon Jr.'s manic pursuit of ownership and economic gain is simultaneously an attempt to break from his painful past, and, as Milkman concludes, it is the very "measure of his loss at his father's death" and a function of his own entrapment in a history that he cannot escape (300). Like Oedipus, the trappings of Macon's birth are evidenced most clearly in his pursuit of freedom from them. He instructs his son to "own things. And let things you own own other things. Then you'll own yourself and other people too" (55). His past harms him and his son precisely because he seeks freedom from it and from responsibility toward his community. He is literally making money, but as his name implies, he is spiritually "makin' dead" because of his exploitation of the community in the interest of individual betterment.

The pattern of flight from responsibility—from the insurance sales-man who lands on the pavement to the flight of Solomon, who leaves be-hind twenty-one children—is repeated anew in the story of Milkman. His circumstances weigh heavily on him; his father's designs for him, his mother's incestuous clinging, Hagar's manic desire for him, and the weight of Guitar's politics all create his desire "to beat a path away from his parents' past, which was also their present and which was threaten-ing to become his present as well" (180). Macon's parents make manic efforts to free themselves from their past, only to have their past loom ever larger and threaten to swallow up any sense of independent exist-ence Milkman might have. His very assertion of his identity—"'I'm a Dead! My mother's a Dead!'"—rings sadly true. Thus, when he learns that there is gold in his aunt Pilate's house, he sees it as the key to "com-plete power, total freedom, and perfect justice" (185). Once he is on his journey south in search of the gold, "in the air, away from real life, he felt free, but on the ground, . . . the wings of all those other people's nightmares flapped in his face and constrained him" (220). Milkman re-peats the story of his great-grandfather, who gained freedom in flight at the cost of abdicating his family responsibilities.

Pilate represents the ethical position that Morrison offers as an alter-native to this flight, namely, that one gains the greatest freedom from a full acceptance of responsibility toward the past and toward one's com-munity. Pilate can fly "without ever leaving the ground" because she un-derstands long before Milkman that "you just can't fly off and leave a body" (336; 332). For this reason she carries with her the bones of her father; she accepts the responsibility for the death of a man she and her brother encountered in the woods as children because, as she says to Milkman, "the dead you kill is yours. They stay with you anyway, in your mind. So it's a better thing, a more better thing to have the bones right there with you wherever you go. That way, it frees up your mind" (208). Unlike Milkman and his family, she does not spend her life in search of freedom from the responsibility of a painful history by means of material acquisitions but in search of the freedom of responsibility.

Despite the belief of some critics that Morrison's work represents a postmodern disavowal of the past, it is clear both in the structure and theme of *Song of Solomon* that, as in Harper's *Iola Leroy*, a return to historical contingency, to an acceptance of one's place within history, is a critical strategy for individual and communal liberation. That return, as Theodore Mason explains, is facilitated by speaking and listening to sto-ries and sounds: "Vanity [of self-absorption] is alleviated ultimately by the power of the story properly considered and by the *historicity of comprehension*. . . . Stories facilitate . . . an essential commonality between teller and listener" (182, emphasis added). The exchange of language, of stories and sounds, is the process by which we make and remake ourselves communally and by which we continually resituate ourselves into history. Morrison examines the same question Faulkner and Carpentier wrestle with regarding the relationship between the storyteller and history in the narrated story. They agree that in allowing the storyteller to step outside history and objectify it, storytelling temporarily removes him or her from history, but the difference for Morrison is that storytelling also involves a listener who is deeply drawn into history. This aspect of storytelling is what Mason refers to in the phrase "historicity of comprehension." The dilemma of whether the storyteller oedipally flees or prodigally returns to history is here exposed as a narrowly individualistic conception of the construction of historical memory, because ultimately storytelling's significance is its power to forge communal, dialogic engagement in the making of historical meaning, a call and response of individual and community in which both are equally subject to the transformations of identity that result from such engagements.

Mason asserts that Milkman's illness is a blindness to his own historicity that is a kind of deafness to the web of stories in which he finds himself. Rather than realizing the potential of his own participation in the making of his history, he has turned a deaf ear to a past he sees as threatening and essentially as radically apart from himself. Once he opens his ears to stories, riddles, fables, however, he gains a more fluid understanding of his agency within time. Mason explains: "A story is 'dislocating' because it has the capacity to pull us out of one particular place in time; but it is more importantly 'locating' since it allows us to fix that place within the larger continuum of human history" (185). By coming back again to one's own historicity between intervals of temporary transcendence—a dynamic facilitated by exposure to stories of others—one exercises human agency within history.

Pilate provides Milkman with a model of how to relate to the past. Like the names of her male relatives, her name is potentially self-defeating. She carries her name in a tiny tin box hung from her ear because it is the only word her illiterate father wrote in his lifetime. Keeping the name on her person, and in particular near her ear, allows her to bear its meaning not as contained in the literary sense of the word but in the story of illiteracy and orality behind it—how her name is ironic because of her father's illiteracy and his misreading of the world. As she explains to Milkman, "everything bad happened to [my father] because he couldn't read. Got his name messed up because he couldn't read" (53). Pilate's father, also Macon Dead, is given this name by a drunk Yankee who, after emancipation, misheard the information given him. This postslavery renaming is reminiscent of Rochester's "obeah," manifested in his linguistic power over Antoinette and suggestive of the reassertion of white supremacy following slavery, a second major rupture, as it were, in African continuity (the first being the Middle Passage, where slaves either died or, if they survived, were given new names and new languages).[25] Pilate's brother and nephew abandon community and appeal to material ownership in order to escape the irony of their names, but their behavior only fleshes out that irony. On the other hand, Pilate directly opposes the biblical character of the same name who wiped his hands of responsibility for Christ's death because she accepts responsibility for others.

Language is a crucial battleground between white social power and black identity and history. In the hands of white society, written language threatens the survival of a memory of black history, but Morrison emphasizes the signifying power of the black community to overturn the inscribed meanings of language. The Post Office declares officially that "Mains Avenue" is "not Doctor Street," a name the community used to commemorate the "first colored man of consequence" (329). The community's clever response is to rename the street "Not Doctor Street," resulting in the punitive measure of sending letters thus addressed to the "Dead Letter Office" (4). In other words, white society intends the death of signification in black cultural expression. As the community's signifying implies, there is no inherent meaning in language, but language gains meaning in its social context and the intended direction of its use. William Handley explains that rather than signifying slavery's history of loss as a debilitation of language, postslavery representation for Morrison "relies on the regenerative sound of words, on language as productive force rather than as prison house" (694). Names, which blacks get "the best way that they can," according to Guitar, are signs, not of identity, but of a history of struggle over signification and against historical erasure (*Song of Solomon* 88).

Morrison does not portray this struggle as a binary opposition between oral and written language but emphasizes the interplay between the two as a means of liberation and survival for black memory (Clarke 265). Names, stories, and words only become "dead letters" when orality concedes victory to the written text. And because oral language is so much more apparently communal in nature, it will lose its power when language users, like Macon and Milkman, cease to understand their relationship to community. The written text, the assigned word, in a racist society becomes one-dimensional, dead to plural meanings. The written word masks the context of its utterance, hiding the place, time, and identity of the language, while orality has a testimonial function in that it bears witness to those very localities and has the potential to expose others that are hidden behind the written word as well. Pilate places her written name in her ear so she can presumably listen to the sounds of language that will provide knowledge of place. To prevent the erasure of their history, these characters learn to read names as a story of naming, as keeping "alive the complex, painful, disorderly . . . reality of human experience (Byerman 117). If becoming literate means that they read the letter merely as a sign of meaning, they discover that the meaning assigned, as in the case of Milkman Dead, spells their own social death. But if they know how, as Pilate does, to unread—to see the letter not as a sign of meaning, but as a misassignment, as a substitute for sounds, a song, a story that is not there, and therefore as a sign richly encoded with communal memory—then a sense of history can be recovered and maintained.

Song of Solomon does not represent a plurality of individual, competing voices, and yet it clearly represents a new departure from the old stories. Morrison proves that the key to the emancipation of/from history is not in narrative structure per se or in obtaining the "right" witnesses, but in a reconceptualization of memory itself. Witnesses of history may be called forth to tell new stories, but what guarantee is there that they will not be subsumed again under the rubric of a master's discourse, newly expanded to encompass its latest challengers? Reading a name as a story of struggle over the power to name involves understanding the communal nature of language and memory.[26]

Milkman frees himself from the oedipal prison house of his own name as soon as he abdicates, like Gloria and Antoinette before him, his interest in the freedom of ownership. This means that he must also abdicate his desire for an escape from the communal responsibilities implied by his own historicity. As he moves closer to his family origins, he loses his clothes and is thus stripped of the trappings of class. He also goes beyond the realm of official history by searching for locations such as Shalimar, which are off the map. After he abdicates his interest in patrimony, he is able to hear the suggestive nature of words, to link and associate synchronically across time to different words in order to move back diachronically through time and discover his genealogy. He begins to thirst for what names hide:

> He read the road signs with interest now, wondering what lay beneath the names. . . . How many dead lives and fading memories were buried in and beneath names of the places in this country. Under the recorded names were all the other names, just as "Macon Dead," recorded for all time in some dusty file, hid from view the real names of people, places, and things. Names had meaning. No wonder Pilate put hers in her ear. When you know your name, you should hang on to it, for unless it is noted down and remembered, it will die when you do (329).

Milkman's thirst for what language hides opposes that of Rochester and Hermenegildo because he abandons his search for patrimony. Rochester and Hermenegildo seek the "other side" of what they know because they need to create a monologic and impersonal discourse that escapes the contingencies of time and place and can thus authorize their control of the estate. New versions of the past therefore only cause greater anxiety and more obsessive acts of control. Milkman's openness to new narratives is more akin to Carpentier's Esteban, who learns to disavow Europe's monologic view of Caribbean reality. He learns to ask: "What is there round about me which is already complete, recorded, real [definido, inscrito, presente], yet which I cannot understand?" (*Explosion* 180). As discussed in the previous chapter, this attitude is what gives birth to a New World baroque expression, because it prioritizes a subaltern reality that one must assume can never be satisfactorily named. Morrison has likewise claimed that "language can never live up to life once and for all. Nor should it. Language can never 'pin down' slavery, genocide, war. Nor should it yearn for the arrogance to be able to do so. Its force, its felicity, is in its reach toward the ineffable" ("Nobel Lecture" 321).

Unlike Carpentier's model, however, *Song of Solomon* demonstrates that what can fill the void is not a return to further outbursts of the same language but a diversification of the very conception of language in order to include orality, tales, rhymes, and song. Milkman welcomes each new association of word and sound he is able to make because he knows that his knowledge needs to be unlearned. By association and suggestion, and because of his constant geographical relocations, he is able to make cognitive leaps that are also aural leaps: from "Shalimar" to "Solomon," "Sing Byrd" to "Singing Bird," "Jake" to "Jay." He eventually links himself genealogically to the flying African figure in the children's rhyme and by implication to a broader diasporic geography and community that encompasses "KiKongo and Greek, the Islamic and the Judaic, West Africa and Cuba, priestly exile and burning love within the mother's home, biblical fable and Morrison's own family biography" (Benston 104). Milkman discovers in the "Song of Solomon" a story of flight from history, but the song itself is a language that ties that story down, returns Shalimar to the ground in the form of a song in the mouth and ears of the children who have been left behind; it is the flight's remainder, and as such, it prevents such flights from leaving, irreparably rupturing the community. It is a grounded, communal language about the various strategies of managing one's own deracination, a language of ancestral memory, unbounded by nation, idiom, or place.

Like Rochester's image contained in the Creole songs, Milkman's own image is signified in the sounds and narrative structures around him. However, even though his journey clearly provides an oedipal structure—after all, he discovers that his is the name contained in the omens, stories, and sounds he investigates—his fate is not one of horrific discovery of his own hopeless insularity. This is because he genuinely embraces the other side, or underside, of language as well as the new affiliations between speaker and listener that language inherently creates. He does not find himself trapped within a diachronic oedipal struggle with his genealogy, because he is also simultaneously discovering his synchronic affiliations. He is not interested in appropriation but in learning from the dislocation of stories how to relocate his self-understanding more accurately within history. Like Hermenegildo and Rochester, he listens to what appears to be a cacophony of lies told by various individuals speaking from their disparate circumstances and points of view, but these are not stories in competition for patrimony as in *Sweet Diamond Dust*. They are the sites of folk memory, riddles in nature and in songs, where the fragments of experience, in the aftermath of slavery, have been deposited.

As we saw in the previous two novels, reading a plural and fragmented history becomes a metonymical search. Milkman hears one story, and "each story . . . reveals a new mystery and then calls for another story" (Fabre 108). In the process, the investigator or listener becomes implicated in the story, ultimately reading his or her own destiny. In this sense, the listener becomes an agent of his or her own history, since, as Mason reminds us, "the story 'is' in some important sense the history we experience" (185). Not only does Milkman discover himself in the rhymes and riddles he uncovers, but he in turn includes his and Pilate's stories in the song he refashions. Milkman's authorship of his own song demonstrates the interactive and interdependent nature of cultural preservation in which "deeds generate songs, songs generate deeds in an uninterrupted act of creation" (Fabre 113).

When Milkman voluntarily turns toward Guitar to surrender, he surrenders himself to the stories that have oppressed him, to his own inevitable and irrevocable historicity. His actions, like those of Antoinette and Gloria, ultimately join the story scripted for him; he is reunited with the story of Shalimar, the flying African (Milkman, by implication, also leaves behind kin in his abandonment of Hagar), and with Guitar's calculated plans for his death.[27] Thus, like the apocalyptic endings of Rhys and Ferré's novels, Morrison also brings "narrative closure and historical disclosure" together in the final page (Zamora, *Writing* 16). But because Milkman anticipates that script and wills himself to act in accordance with it, he is not subsumed by it but rather shows himself liberated: "For he knew what Shalimar knew: If you surrendered to the air, you could *ride* it" (337). Like Ferré, Morrison also implies that history is driven by the slippage between word and deed, since the narrative and Milkman's history appear to come to an end at the moment when his deeds unite with the stories that have defined him. But since we know that word and deed do not always correspond, and that therefore stories are in some essential sense always going to lie or miss the mark, there is always a give and take, an interplay between our attempts to transcend history (when we listen) and our return back (when we speak). For Morrison it is in that give and take that community and identity must be perpetually renegotiated if they are to survive in a meaningful way.

What the writers in this chapter so consciously explore is the implicit impulse of the majority of postslavery writers. In their collective imaginings regarding slavery and its legacies, postslavery writers demonstrate the value of an ongoing and diversified interplay of stories that both reflect and shape that history. They write about slavery because the stories we tell and the memories we preserve keep us in history and also allow us the potential to reshape it in an act of ongoing reconstruction of a more truthful history and of a more truthful "we." When we, as readers, follow their lead across borders and languages in pursuit of more diversified stories about slavery's past, we make their dream of an unbounded community a greater possibility.

Conclusion

RATHER THAN diminishing in scope and intensity with greater distance from slavery's history, postslavery literature in the Americas has, in fact, seen an increase over the past few decades in many nations. This study, as I have maintained, is only a sampling of comparative understanding that can be gained by looking across the literary landscape of postslavery Americas. Other countries will offer different insights, particularly those such as Brazil, where the racial paradigm does not follow the black-white binary but is posited as a triple combination of Native American, African, and European; or Trinidad and the Guianas, where East Indian and other Asian peoples were also introduced into the plantation mix. Given the variety of racial and colonial histories throughout the Caribbean; the Caribbean coasts of Mexico, Central America, and South America; and nations such as Ecuador, Uruguay, and Peru that also saw slavery, there is indeed much work to be done. That work needs to begin, I believe, with the most recent resurgence of postslavery writers throughout the Americas.

Some of my readers are surely disappointed that I did not treat the unique contributions of poetry, or the important work of particular writers, such as Wilson Harris from Guiana; Juan Bosch or Blas Jiménez from the Dominican Republic; Charles Johnson, Langston Hughes, Robert Hayden, or Zora Neale Hurston from the United States; Jorge Amado or Graciliano Ramos from Brazil; Venezuela's Romulo Gallegos or Juan Pablo Sojo; Martinique's Aimé Césaire or Edouard Glissant; Guadeloupe's St. John Perse; St. Lucia's Derek Walcott; or countless others. I confess my own weakness in not being able to tackle more than I have and look forward to future revisions of our postslavery understanding. I am particularly intrigued by two novels that I consider to be among the most extraordinary New World writing regarding slavery:

Texaco, by the Martinican Patrick Chamoiseau, and *Divina Trace*, by the Trinidadian Robert Antoni. These novels exhibit engagement with many of the issues I have covered (they share with the novels in this study a profound interface between historiography and testimonial language), but they add the elements of irony and humor, which results in a kind of liberating and paradoxically sobering flippancy.

The literary outpouring is not limited to fiction and poetry, of course, but has also found its way into nonfiction. We have seen an increased interest in genealogy in such works of nonfiction as Shirley Taylor Haizlip's *The Sweeter the Juice*, James McBride's *The Color of Water*, and Edward Ball's *Slaves in the Family*, which in the context of the United States represent an understanding of the interdependency of black and white cultures. Indeed, the general increased interest in genealogy and family history throughout the Americas is bound to continue unveiling the interdependency of races and ethnicities in the creolization of New World societies. Additionally, the enormous outpouring of historical and sociological studies of slavery and its legacies in contemporary politics and cultures in Brazil, the Caribbean, and in the United States amounts almost to an obsession with slavery in rethinking race in its relation to our distinct national identities.

The insights offered in this book attend to the particular contributions of written language and would likely be enhanced if we were to explore the tremendous and immeasurable impact of West African rhythms on vast numbers of musical forms throughout the Americas and the reasons for their increased popularity in recent decades. From reggae to salsa to hip-hop to Afro-Brazilian funk, musical expression in the Americas continues to take revenge against slavery's legacies through the joy of fusion, facilitated more easily than in literature by music's "universal language" and, paradoxically, to some degree by the financial backing of multinational recording companies. Cuba and Brazil seem to have taken the lead in finding new sounds to express communal memory and poetry, particularly in live musical performance, when access to literary expression and to recorded music is limited for a variety of reasons. Other performing arts such as dance and drama have borne witness to the survival of forms of postslavery genealogical memory. I was recently privileged to see the extraordinary installation art of Maria Magdalena Campos Pons, from Cuba, who is among many contemporary visual artists revisiting the history of the Middle Passage and slavery's ruins in order to reproduce new aesthetic forms of memory and identity. Languages of the body—contained in dance, song, and poetry—have proven vital, subversive means of African cultural survival and adaptation under the violence of slavery and colonialism.

Literature moves us into a somewhat more problematic terrain, dominated as it is by the written word of Western culture, where African retention has been more challenging to identify. For this reason, literature is an ideal site to understand not slavery's history per se but where we as multiracial nations stand in relationship to it. Because stories have the power to remember the past, to shape the present, and move us toward the future, the stories we tell about slavery—in tales, poems, and narratives—more directly engage and combat the forces of historiography and official memory. They have the capacity of prophecy, since the way the past is remembered shapes how we live and identify ourselves now.

What accounts for this resurgent desire to return to slavery and to consider its genealogical, political, and cultural legacies, and how do we properly evaluate this phenomenon? As we have seen, one of slavery's legacies is the paradoxical need to continue to revisit it. It would be simplistic and dangerous to argue that national consolidation requires a moratorium on such vital discussion simply because it is deemed divisive, but it would be equally foolhardy, as most postslavery writers have discovered, to assume that there are no risks in returning to slavery. Chief among those risks is discovery of our own contemporary complicity with the structures of thought slavery has passed onto us, habits that perpetuate racial division and national egotism despite our intention to critique them. The writers I have examined treat such discoveries as tragic but implicitly argue that they are also healthy and necessary, since in the resultant disillusionment regarding our own racial innocence, we can hope to improve our ethical relationship to difference. Postslavery literature provides vital warnings that slavery is not fully behind us by demonstrating how slavery's legacies continue to inform the social, economic, and cultural lives of inhabitants of Plantation America. They also point to promising signs of more democratic and racially just possibilities for New World societies. I believe they have provided us with two key reminders that can help to balance our postslavery musings so that, ultimately, they are productive of more careful consideration of and respect for what unites us as well as of what distinguishes us in the Americas.

First, these writers have implicitly argued that racial difference exists as long as historical conditions contribute to different lived realities of individuals and groups according to the perception of racial difference and its imputed meanings. No matter how aggressively some may wish to dismiss race as a category of social and moral meaning so as to move on to societal organization beyond race, until the lived experience of those marked by signs of racial difference no longer differs in any significant way from those not so marked, racial difference will continue to require our measured judgment. Postslavery literature exposes persistent historical conditioning that has shaped racial identities and that therefore cautions us against contemporary haste to end dialogue about race. We cannot erase racial difference any more easily than we can erase history.

Despite complaints about too much "race" talk, true dialogue is, oddly, a rarity. These writers have implicitly and explicitly argued that the impact of historical and social conditions on racial difference can best be addressed by those who have experienced those forces. But I do not mean to suggest here that such witnessing needs to become another monologue; rather, like most recent postslavery literature demonstrates, it needs to take place in a totally open dialogue without the potentially inhibiting influence of intermediaries or the social equivalent of the narrative interventions we saw in several of the novels. Rhetorical claims to having completed the quest for racial justice, almost as common today as postslavery critiques of its failures, should be critically and carefully examined, especially when they come from white elites, since the legacies of slavery in the vast majority of postslavery societies have found new life even within the ideologies that supposedly are intended to bring those legacies down. Even when the official word seems to be that racism has indeed ended, we find that such rhetoric disguises more subtle and insidious forms of persistent racial oppression. That is not to ignore progress in many postslavery nations toward more democratic and just social organization, but to cease examining society for persistent forms of racial injustice gives dangerous liberty to those still with the upper hand in societies of unequal distribution of wealth and power.

Cuba is an interesting case in point. The revolution's rhetorical assumption in the early 1960s as the ultimate response to slavery's legacies, to the final and full liberation of the slave, all but blocked further investigation and eradication of racial discrimination. Racial questions have so insistently been taken up by the rhetoric of the revolution that little or no room remains to discuss racial difference or racism as persistent and independent problems. The parallels with the First Cuban Republic's refusal to discuss the racial question at the turn of the twentieth century are very apparent and, given the outcomes of Cuba's prior racial policies, are also very disturbing. The noticeable absence of postslavery literary themes in Cuba since the revolution, at least at the high level of intensity we have seen elsewhere in the Caribbean and in the United

States, could arguably be attributed to the significant and tangible improvements in race relations seen since 1959. But given the centralization of cultural and political power under the revolution, there are lingering doubts that the relative silence about race is also a result of some silencing that at least warrants an ideological diversification of the discussion. Postslavery literature bears witness to a need in all relevant societies for healthy and continual revisions to our historical imagination. Monomyths—where the riddles of the past find their ultimate ideological solution—inevitably become tools of oppression. That is not to say that racial discourse in the Untied States is not guilty of perhaps even more insidious racial monologues than Cuba, but one of the ironic byproducts of the long history of U.S. segregation is the development of persistent and diverse counterdiscourses rooted in local experience, even if they haven't always achieved their social goals.

The second reminder of postslavery writing is that comparative analyses of postslavery cultures can serve as a check against claims to unique or exceptional national status. We need critical apparatuses that can explore the transnational and diasporic dimensions of ethnic identity formation in order to understand how the United States and different areas of the Caribbean and Latin America have used each other as key backdrops or points of contrast by which to legitimate their own deficient claims to racial justice. Racial prejudice and institutional forms of racism of any kind can be effectively combated in a postnational context since the forging of national consciousness has so frequently avoided careful self-criticism. Access to a broader comparative context of lived experiences of blacks and whites who understand and articulate their experience in a diasporic context is imperative.

Comparative inroads have been made by critics in metalingual art forms such as performance, dance, and visual arts, but literary criticism lags behind in its appreciation of slavery's hemispheric impact. Of course, language barriers are partly to blame for this negligence, but one wonders what use the second and third language requirements for most English, Spanish, and Portuguese Ph.D.s are being put to, other than the obligatory translation exams? Conversely, in the age of such rapid and accessible translations of much (though certainly not all) literary production in the Americas, this neglect does not find explanation except perhaps in lingering national chauvinism.

Another factor, it appears, is that while U.S. politics and economics seem to mandate globalization of the book market internally (along with countless other markets), those same forces often limit access to more diverse reading lists in many Latin American and Caribbean nations. The U.S. embargo against Cuba, for example, holds Cuban universities hostage to short paper and computer supplies and often makes comparative readings an unreachable luxury. This seems to confirm Karl Marx's suspicion that notions of comparative literature or of world literature are a luxury facilitated by globalization and that they will therefore never succeed in escaping the logic of late capitalism. Indeed, comparative readings often enhance a false sense of empowerment, proving the adage that a little knowledge is dangerous. International conferences offer opportunities for increased dialogue, but they also can tend toward cultural imperialism. This is particularly true when in Caribbean and Latin American nations, North American scholars, holed up at the local resort–conference center are treated to feasts of regional cuisine, dance and song, shopping sprees, and bus trips through the local barrio, and thus the cultures of the folk are converted into exoticized parades of Africa, Native America, or the Poor in the eyes of academics-turned-tourists hoping to bring home the T-shirt.

There may be little hope that colonialism in the academy will be fully eradicated. However, unlike the Old World version of comparative literature that was, explicitly or not, dedicated to consolidating the Western European tradition, New World comparative studies (of which postslavery literature forms a crucial part) can begin by dedicating itself to delineating the various and overlapping diasporas that have followed in the wake of European colonization. I won't repeat my argument of the first chapter about how this works or why it is important theoretically, but it is worth restating that the impulse of the comparatism I advocate is precisely to deconstruct itself rigorously by following tenaciously the accidents of biology. And a crucial question is what this means pedagogically. In the context of American studies and American literature, we need to insist on identifying those moments in U.S. history where U.S. imperialist ambitions have been clouded by postcolonial rhetoric, including the Louisiana Purchase of 1803, the Mexican-American War of 1848, and the Spanish-American War of 1898, moments when the United States presented itself as the "post" to the colonialisms of the French and the Spanish while ignoring its own rather Anglo form of neocolonialism. The "Southwest," for example, should become no longer south nor west but part of a larger indigenous and Hispanic territory that includes Mexico. Other postnational configurations of "American" studies, in addition to that of the U.S. South and the Caribbean explored here, might include Asia and the U.S. Pacific Coast or the U.S. northern border and Canada.

Throughout the Americas, we need to look beyond the broad scope of the Western project of modernity. I am thinking specifically of those non-Western sites of resistance across national lines in the Americas, lines that have been forged largely to conform to that very project. These sites of resistance are found across the languages and geopolitical borders of the African Diaspora as well as across the similar borders of Amerindian societies. One could also examine other diasporas in the Americas: Asian, Middle Eastern, and so on. These multilingual, multiple geographies present us with a very different model of comparative practice. We can begin to see area studies that do not correspond to those created under the rubric of imperialist mappings of the globe. Although Latin American studies itself has always been a comparative field (how else can we adequately understand, say, Guatemala and Argentina in the same field?), such comparisons have not always aggressively worked against the grain of regional colonialisms but have often upheld them.

At the undergraduate level, this implies first the simple task of reading. Professors take risks every semester in adjusting their syllabi to include new material they want to learn about, so I am not being revolutionary by suggesting that Americanists or Latin Americanists read material from other areas of the Americas and begin to assign them in their courses. This might cause some disciplinary horror if we consider what forms of ignorance this could unleash, but clearly the best teaching (and the best literary criticism) never loses sight or seeks to hide what it doesn't know. More explicitly comparative courses are called for, but even when they are not possible or necessary, students can gain tremendous benefit from learning about the limitations inherent in the design of the very courses they are taking. This knowledge can come from some preliminary comparative reading. This also, I believe, helps to prepare the next generation of Americanists, in the broadest sense of the word.

Graduate programs in English, Spanish, Portuguese, and French need to reexamine their language requirements to find ways to make them more meaningful and integrated into the curriculum, so that we can move beyond more superficial readings of other national literatures. At both undergraduate and graduate levels, English departments tend to err on the side of excessive expansion into world literatures via translation and thereby ignore the importance of rigorous linguistic training (frequently offending their neighbors in departments of "foreign" languages), while programs in Romance languages tend to deprive their students of comparative readings in translation because of the pressures of language acquisition. Neither situation is ideal; they both contribute to cultural myopia.

I am not trying to blur entirely the distinction between comparative literature as a discipline and single-language doctorates, since as long as competing national traditions exist, both disciplines will be useful and necessary (comparative literature, as traditionally understood, has needed competing forms of nationalism for its own justification). Nevertheless, some muddying of the waters would be valuable. Otherwise, what are the implications of our current pedagogy? We imply that languages outside our primary focus are useful but only as an exercise in learning, not for their concrete applications. There may be limitations to those applications; no one will deny that comparative understanding is always only partial and usually insufficient, but the power of New World pedagogy is the power of its suggestion of our limitations and therefore of our mutual interdependence as students of culture in the Americas.

Notes

1. Narrative and Genealogy

1. Such historical studies include Nettleford, Foner and Genovese, Rubin and Tuden, and Blackburn.

2. Castronovo has similarly observed that in nineteenth-century novels of the United States, genealogy "registers both the continuities and the discontinuities that pervade inscriptions of the national past. . . . Genealogy is complicated by a tension that, on the one hand, seeks to delineate the nation with the order of patriarchy, and on the other, disorganizes any pretensions to transmit the nation via a singular, supposedly inclusive narrative that necessarily omits other lineages" (6–7).

3. In the postbellum American South, planters often argued that their daughters and wives were endangered by the black man's civil rights. For example, Blassingame observes that white men in New Orleans expected the authorities to protect "our persons from violence, our property from pillage, our houses from the torch, our homes from invasion, our wives and daughters from outrage and pollution" (204). Such fears of black intervention in the white family line acted, of course, as fronts for the planters' more pressing fear of the black man's threat to rise and compete economically.

4. It was imperative that the plantocracy control the definitions of racial and social status by means of what was known in many regions as the "Descent Rule" (M. Harris).

5. In *Home as Found*, Sundquist writes that the family and the genealogy of the writer, "by virtue of either their instability or their unwanted pressure act as surrogates for a more abstractly envisioned 'past,' and to this extent stimulate the writer's *desire* to find in the family a model for the social and political constructs still so much in question for a recently conceived nation" (xii). The couple in James Fenimore Cooper's *Home as Found,* Paul and Eve, are "natural pairs" for one another because they are "natural heirs" to the money and education in their backgrounds.

6. Two excellent sources on this subject are Martínez-Alier and Williamson's *New People*. Gelpí adds an important dimension to the discussion of the foundational aims of nineteenth-century fiction in Latin America by emphasizing the agency of a community to choose to read those texts as foundational, thus creating a tradition of reception that privileges paternal claims for the national heritage. This suggests that the discourse of criticism in many Latin American nations at the turn of the twentieth century was frequently created by intellectuals with more explicit projects of national consolidation than those of the fiction writers (*Literatura y paternalismo* 8).

7. Bhabha's theorization of national identity and narrative language follows similar lines even if he neglects to provide any historical specificity to explain why fiction can both found and resist a national identity in a postcolonial context. He contends that "history may be half-made because it is in the process of being made; and the image of cultural authority may be ambivalent because it is caught, uncertainly, in the act of 'composing' its powerful image" ("Dissemi-Nation" 3). Neither is the nation, then, ever wholly made within any given cultural expression: "[T]he scraps . . . of daily life must be repeatedly turned into the signs of a national culture, while the very act of the narrative performance interpellates a growing number of national subjects" (3).

8. Bennington explains that the wish to see narration at the nation's origin "should be enough to inspire suspicion; our own drive to find the centre and the origin has created its own myth of the origin—namely that at the origin is the myth. In this story, narration comes too easy, too soon; investigating the nation is here complicit with the nation's own story" (121).

9. I am indebted to Klein's *The Middle Passage* and Blackburn for these statistics and to Blackburn for pointing out this connection between the slave economy and modernity.

10. Solow explains that wherever the "slave-sugar complex went"—in her view, the greatest influence of slavery in the shaping of New World cultures—"a network of international trade flows followed: flows of labor, capital, manufactures, sugar, raw materials, shipping, banking and insurance" (731). See also Curtin.

11. A brief bibliography on these differences would include Ortiz, Stinchcombe, R. Guerra, Fraginals, *Patricios y plebeyos* by Quintero Rivera, and *African Slavery* and *Slavery in the Americas* by Klein.

12. This point is made by Williamson in *New People*.

13. Dash points out that Martí developed his ideas in the "shadow of North American imperialism" in contrast to the notion of Manifest Destiny (*Other America* 10). The irony is that Whitman's vision of democratic possibility would prove helpful in justifying aspects of that ideology. A recent publication edited by Belnap and Fernández does an excellent job of exploring the various ideological directions Martí's thinking has been taken. Sommer's essay on Whitman and Martí in that collection is particularly helpful on this point. L. Guerra also has

done a fascinating archaeology of the early uses and abuses of Martí and how interpretations of his political philosophies were polarized in the First Cuban Republic ("Marbling Martí").

14. E. Lewis insists that in studies of black communities, "few have discussed the process of 'othering' so critical to community-building . . . [or the] permeability of boundaries and the multipositional nature of most human actors" (786–87).

15. On this point as it relates to U.S. policy in Haiti, see Schmidt.

16. Zamora notes that "the very inadequacies of the terms 'North American' and 'South American' suggest the problems facing the critic or reader who is interested in evolving a comprehensive American critical context. Though 'American' does, after all, apply to the whole hemisphere, the term is rarely used in the U.S. to refer to anything beyond its own borders." The Spanish term, *estadounidense*, has no English equivalent ("Usable Past" 11).

17. Porter argues that "the point [of turning to Latin America], however, would not be simply to track a different story, making Cuba or Mexico the protagonist. Rather, the aim would be to see one story in relation to the other, to resituate both in a history of "unsettlement" that would lead well beyond the national borders produced by that history" ("What We Know" 519).

18. Porter and other Americanists have neglected not only the literature but the cultural and theoretical imagination of Latin America. Porter cites, for example, a variety of exemplary studies by Americanists but makes no mention of Pérez Firmat (ed.), Chevigny and Lagaurdia (eds.), MacAdam, Fitz, Pratt's important essay "Arts of the Contact Zone," theorists of the extended Caribbean such as Glissant, or the comparative work of such critics as Sommer and Zamora. The edited compilation of Kaplan and Pease draws on excellent scholarship but nevertheless, in its scope, largely ignores Latin American and Caribbean articulations on the subject. There are a few excellent, recent contributions to comparative literatures of the Americas, particularly Cohn and Belnap and Fernández's edited volume.

19. A 1996 conference sponsored by the California American Studies Association was entitled "Expanding Borders and Boundaries: Rethinking 'America.'" Dayan has observed that despite recent rhetoric, a "bounded practice" of nation-building continues: "[W]orking under the cover of the borderless, [this practice] excludes the differing conceptual possibilities originating outside our borders" (811–12). To avoid this trap, Mignolo has called for a comparatism that is not based on "epistemic homogeneity" or on a singular, "monotopic" disciplinary lens through which two national traditions are compared. Rather, he calls for a pluralization of epistemological tools by which comparison takes place and for multiplication of the sites of knowledge production ("Los límites de la literatura").

20. White has claimed that all narrative "presupposes the existence of a legal system against or on behalf of which the typical agents of a narrative account

militate. And this raises the suspicion that narrative in general, from the folktale to the novel, from the annals to the fully realized 'history,' has to do with the topics of law, legality, legitimacy, or, more generally, *authority*" (17).

21. White further explains that this is because "the more historically self-conscious the writer of any form of historiography [becomes], the more the question of the social system and the law which sustains it, the authority of this law and its justification, and threats to the law occupy his attention" (ibid.).

22. This book compiles a series of lectures Foucault gave in 1973 that form the basis of his *Discipline and Punish*. I have consulted the lectures directly, despite the awkward task of translating from the Spanish (which was translated from the Portuguese), because I do not find these ideas as concisely articulated in *Discipline and Punish*.

23. Tobin has additionally argued that "when in some such manner ontological priority is conferred upon mere temporal anteriority, the historical consciousness is born and time is understood as a linear manifestation of the genealogical destiny of events" (7).

24. The term is Louis Mink's. He argues that "as historical [narrative] claims to represent, through its form, part of the real complexity of the past, but as narrative it is a product of the imaginative construction which cannot defend its claim to truth by any procedure of argument or authentication" (qtd. in Carr 10).

25. Foucault agrees that "historians take unusual pains to erase the elements in their work which reveal their grounding in a particular place and time" (*Language* 54).

26. The discussion that follows appears in somewhat more detail in my article "'It's an unbelievable story.'"

27. Da Costa emphasizes that "the concern with production and profit and the need to protect his capital imposed a limit on the slave owner's violence that never existed in any concentration camp or prison" (300).

28. One such study is Guetti's *Limits of Metaphor*.

2. Reading in the Dark

1. Paquette observes that Cuban planters believed that "it was cheaper to work field slaves to death in five years or so and replace them by purchase than to see to their long-term maintenance and reproduction" (55).

2. I use the term *Afro-Cuban* to refer to both blacks and mulattoes.

3. For a very helpful overview of the various uses of transculturation in a variety of geopolitical settings, see Spitta's introduction to her book *Between Two Waters*.

4. The only other study I know of that has mentioned these two novelists together is E. González's, in which he traces an imaginary line of confluence from Villaverde's novel to other fictional works of various periods and nations that all wrestle with the problem of "mulatez." He creatively imagines that the New Or-

leans decor of Cable's novel would make a great setting for a film of *Cecilia Valdés*.

5. Pollard, *The First Year of the War* (Richmond: West, 1862). The translation is entitled *Historia del primer año de la guerra del sur*. The history assumes a critical position with respect to Jefferson Davis but is nevertheless clearly on the side of the South. Pollard was also the author of *The Lost Cause* (1866), in which he argued that the Civil War was essentially a legal debate over the interpretation of the Constitution. His *Black Diamonds Gathered in the Darkey Homes of the South* (1859) nostalgically propagated the ideology of the Sambo figure.

6. This story is a curious exploration of the threat of incest. The two unwitting lovers are saved at the last minute when they learn that their supposed kinship has been the result of a falsification of their birth documents. Their marriage quickly ensues after a legal clarification of their genealogy.

7. E. González has observed the oddity of Villaverde criticism that celebrates the novel's representations of local customs while ignoring the central issue of incest.

8. She further argues that Villaverde refuses to pander to the authority of a white reader's obsessive need to contain the significations of black testimony, but there seems little reason to believe that narrative ambivalence can always be reduced to signs of the author's conscious intentions.

9. On the influence of Domingo Del Monte's moral determinism on Villaverde and other antislavery writers in Cuba, see Schulman.

10. *Casket girl* refers to French women who were sent to the early sites of exploration and colonization as a supply of wives for the mostly male population in the New World. It was feared, and since held true in legend, that because of the shortage of women, the settlers turned to the Indian women, whose blood was then mixed into the Creole family tree.

3. Reading behind the Face

1. In the United States, there were, of course, many novels more in the genre of romance that explicitly defended the age of slavery by means of overt sentimentalism. Plantation fiction saw its heyday in the 1870s and the 1880s when the once critical depictions of slavery were transformed into a Camelot legend, a strategy that originated in the South in an attempt to heal its wounds after the war and to protect its damaged image. The writers discussed in this chapter not only respond to these overtly nostalgic depictions of slavery but to the perhaps more subtle longings found in much realist fiction as well.

2. Recent research into extralegal "traditions" of segregated public space in Cuba's Santa Clara province reveals how long-lasting and deeply rooted these segregationist practices were. L. Guerra has documented periodic blow-ups over segregation in the 1920s. On the basis of oral history, Guerra has concluded that in the cities of Cienfuegos, Santa Clara, and Trinidad, de facto segregation of

public parks continued until the 1959 Revolution (telephone interview, 16 June 1999).

3. Regarding this positioning in front of the cultural eyes of white society, Morrison has commented: "The interest in vision, in seeing, is a fact of black life. As slaves and ex-slaves, black people were manageable and findable, as no other slave society would be, because they were black. So there is an enormous impact from the simple division of color—more than sex, age, or anything else. The complaint is not being seen for what one is" (qtd. in Leclair 376).

4. For more on the racial conflicts of 1912 and the use of the myth of racial brotherhood to justify antiblack violence in Cuba, see Helg, Fernández Robaina, and Kutzinski.

5. Despite his anti-U.S. rhetoric here, he did vote in favor of the Platt Amendment, evidence of his deep ambivalence regarding the United States.

6. I am indebted to L. Guerra, who, in a telephone interview, pointed out these important details regarding the publication of the novel and their significance in understanding the character of Sofía.

7. Luis states that "Morúa questions the racial nature of slavery. The concept of destiny as a consequence of race becomes an important issue when Sofía, as a white, is subjected to the same conditions as blacks" (*Literary Bondage* 147). Given the date of the novel's completion, it seems more likely that he questions the persistent racial nature of postslavery colonial Cuba.

8. Kutzinski's analysis of tobacco labels demonstrates that their representations of plantation life similarly implied Cuban internalization of the foreigner's view of island customs.

9. It should be noted that by modern standards, his actions—caressing and fondling her in his arms after she fainted—would constitute an outright sexual assault. It appears, however, that Morúa does not intend us to read this as a violation of Ana María but as a humanization of Liberato. He even suggests that Ana María feels a mutual attraction that she must repress for the sake of maintaining the family name.

10. For an in-depth analysis of the relationship between these riots and Chesnutt's novel, see Sundquist, *To Wake the Nations* 406–45.

11. An example of this rhetoric is cited in Saks's study of miscegenation law. One court in Georgia in 1869 ruled that "the offspring of these unnatural connections are generally sickly and effeminate, and . . . they are inferior in physical development and strength to the full-blood of either race" (64).

12. Specifically, Chesnutt was apparently first motivated to be a writer after reading Albion Tourgee's novel *A Fool's Errand* (1880), which for him demonstrated the limitations of white representations of black culture despite his appreciation for the novel's political aims (H. Chesnutt 20).

13. *White slavery* is also invoked by Morúa in his novels, but in Cuba the term was understood to refer to the subordination of black slavery to the primary concern for liberation from Spain.

14. Harper was personally acquainted with the way in which her own identity as a "white Negro" posed challenges to the interpretative skills of those whites who saw her. She wrote to Colonel Hinton: "I don't know but that you would laugh if you were to hear some of the remarks which my lectures call forth: 'she is a man,' again 'She is not colored, she is painted'" (Foster 126–27). She had also been called a "red Mulatto" and "a Cuban belle." In their efforts to name her color and to give metaphorical meaning to her puzzling appearance, her white audiences revealed their own "American" anxieties concerning the instability of the racial signifier.

15. See McDowell for an example. McDowell faults Harper for giving in to the white stereotype of the white Negress in order to appeal to a white reading audience. What she fails to notice, however, is how Harper transforms the meaning of this stereotype in the very moment in which it serves to makes its appeal to that audience, thus moving her white readership in an ideological direction that favors racial integrity.

16. On this point, see Young. See also Ernest, "Mysteries to Histories," and Sale.

4. Between the Insular Self and the Exotic Other

1. For a discussion of the effect of American ideologies on Puerto Rico after 1898, see Picó. Although he explains that the fragmentation of family structure was already under way with the advances in the nineteenth century of sugar and coffee production, the U.S. presence contributed to the continued decline of the family into the twentieth century (196).

2. Williamson explains that these changes also affected race relations in the South, leading eventually to the height of lynchings in the 1920s: "In the decades after the Civil War, modernity began to invade the region with railway and industrial expansion, an influx of the very visible products of technological innovation, and a reorganization of money, banking, and credit. In the 1880s, in particular, Southern whites seemed concerned about their own loss of sexual civility. . . . In the same years, civil awareness of the evils of alcohol commenced a distinct rise. In the turn-of-the-century decades, great numbers of Southern whites combined them specially to black people" (*William Faulkner* 162).

3. Alonso argues that for this reason, modern Latin American cultural practices are undecided in terms of their own modernity; they are both modern and antimodern since they appeal for exemption from the demands of modernity while they simultaneously seek new (modern) origins for their cultures (23). He explains that Latin American writers have had to come to terms with the fact that "historical misfortune is not the outcome of Latin America's cultural errancy or self-ignorance, but the condition of its possibility" (35).

4. Miller explains that the realistic impulse of narration is "validated by the testimony of the individual witness or spectator," and therefore the vacillation that results is because "the truth of a realistic narrative is relative to the subjec-

tivity of that witness, and so liable to be distorted or partial" (150). His idea is presumably based on his performative reading of *Absalom, Absalom!*, but I would suggest that it is constative in that it provides a reflection of the historical conditions of postslavery societies.

5. For an excellent study of the structure of this tension in García Márquez's genealogical investigations of *One Hundred Years*, see Ludmer's *Cien años de soledad*.

6. As González Echevarría has argued, there may not be as much distance between his first novel and his later fiction as he would have us believe. See his chapter on *Ecue-Yamba-O* in *Alejo Carpentier* (34–96). The slippage between a cultural essence and the journey toward that essence represented perhaps more self-consciously and ironically in more recent literature may in fact have prevailed in earlier attempts at autochthonous literature as well. Latin American writers have always been plagued by the question of cultural essences, of identity and origins, and what Alonso calls the "affirmation of having lost or abandoned that essence" is not new but rather conditional of Latin American cultural practices. See Alonso's chapter "The Exoticism of the Autochthonous" in his *Spanish American Regional Novel* (1–37).

7. The words are those of Fuentes in his description of a conversation with Carpentier (23).

8. González Echevarría has argued most persuasively for Carpentier's spiral conception of historical development. He writes that "there are repetitions and returns in *Explosion in a Cathedral,* but not historical cycles that mirror each other. . . . The characters return to what appears to be a previous moment in their lives, as history appears to repeat itself in certain events. But the return is not [to] the same point; it is rather to one that is merely similar and creates the illusion of sameness but is really far removed from the previous one" (*Alejo Carpentier* 233).

9. I am indebted to Stinchcombe's brief but provocative comparisons between the two wars in his chapter "French Revolutions and the Transformation of the French Empire" (201–30).

10. Several critics have pointed out the hemispheric themes of Faulkner's novel, among them Ladd, Spillers, Godden, and Stanchich. Stanchich argues, for example, that "Faulkner extends the curse of Southern slavery outside the South, encompassing the entire American agenda in and out of its borders" (604). Spillers additionally reminds us that "the politics of the New World cannot always be so easily disentangled as locally discrete moments. Nowhere is the narrative of involvement more pointedly essayed than in Faulkner's *Absalom, Absalom!* that choreographs Canada, the Caribbean, Africa, Europe, and the United States as geographical and/or figurative points of contact in this fictive discourse" ("Who Cuts?" 9).

11. On the differences between Cable and Faulkner's texts, Ladd has observed that Faulkner pursues a "counternarrative of division and recalcitrance

and defeat by history . . . with as much diligence as Cable's texts pursue the reconcilationist dream of reunification and transcendence of tragic history" (29).

12. Certainly Sutpen's biography was something close to home for Faulkner, since his own great-great-grandfather, on whom he based various stories, made a similar rise from orphanhood to self-made success that included owning slaves. For discussions of this intriguing character in Faulkner's own genealogy, see Williamson's *William Faulkner.*

13. Stinchcombe observes that both plantations and the traditionally identified western frontier "created great waves of immigration, great increases in the capital value of land and farm or plantation installations, great rates of social mobility, and a strong tendency towards lawless 'adventure capitalism'" (50).

14. Godden constructs a provocative reading of the novel on the basis of this anachronism. He argues that the Haitian Revolution that Sutpen anachronistically witnesses represents the challenge to the planter's authority. But "Sutpen becomes a planter in Mississippi (1835) only because what happens in Haiti (1827) allows him to repress what he saw in western Virginia (1820). Put tersely, Sutpen can raise the Hundred because, having experienced slavery as the suppression of revolution, he can, in his own defense, displace his knowledge that the master's mastery depends upon the body and consciousness of the bound man" (699).

5. The Emancipation of/from History

1. This is a paradox common in much recent ethnic and women's writings because, as Kunow explains, they "return to historical narrative" and render "problematic the notion of history while insisting on it—keeping the frame while changing the canvas" (258).

2. Baker insists that "for place to be recognized by one as actually PLACE, as a personally valued locale, one must set and maintain boundaries. If one, however, is constituted and maintained by and within boundaries set by a dominating authority, then one is not a setter of place but a prisoner of another's desire. Under the displacing impress of authority, even what one calls and, perhaps, feels is one's own place is, from the perspective of human agency, placeless" (104).

3. Hulme adds that "attention to [the novel's] local circumstances suggests that it also needs reading as a reworking of the materials from *Jane Eyre* inflected by the received traditions of a planter 'family history.' In other words, literary production is viewed here less as a matter of individual creativity than as a transgenerational formation from 'event' to 'family memory' to 'literary text'" (75).

4. Essays that explore the anti-imperialism of the novel include those by Spivak and Oates and Friedman's "Breaking the Master Narrative."

5. On this point, Franco has strongly argued that "to found feminist theory on a general theory of colonialism [does not] work. It is definitely NOT the same struggle. The hierarchy that subordinates the feminine to the masculine not only

finds itself profoundly implicated in language, but it shapes the constitution of subjectivity. . . . Once we begin to understand that this hierarchy is fundamental to the literary institution, we open up space to begin investigation of how textual authority has been constituted not only in the present but at distinct historical junctures" (35).

6. This idea is an adaptation of what Howells calls "the limits of his imperialism" (108).

7. This is a theme that Walcott explores in his poetry in numerous ways, particularly in "Air," "The Sea Is History," and "Verandah," which was quoted in chapter 1. His point seems to be that New World history is one that contains too much death, pain, and suffering for history books to hold, and that because of the intentional forgettings of such episodes as the Middle Passage, the verdant and extreme growth of nature in the region, here noticed by Rochester, takes the place of an absent history. Consequently, Walcott argues that we must learn to read nature as a present record of an otherwise absent New World history. The difference with Rochester is that although he suspects the absence of a history, he does not exhibit patience with history's illegibility (*Collected Poems*).

8. The ironic distance between white Creole and Afro-Caribbean was apparent in Rhys's own racial ambivalence. On one occasion, she remarked: "I hate. I hate. Do they understand? . . . I hate them. We didn't treat them badly. We didn't. I hate them. And yet, I was kissed once by a Nigerian, in a café in Paris, and I understood, a little. I understood why they are attractive. It goes very deep. They danced . . . in the sunlight, and how I envied them" (qtd. in O'Connor 33). On another occasion, Rhys indicated that she was acutely aware that even her strongest convictions were maintained by ignoring the other side: "I became an ardent socialist and champion of the down-trodden, argued, insisted on giving my opinion, was generally insufferable. Yet all the time knowing that there was another side to it. Sometimes being proud of my great grandfather [a slave owner], the estate, the good old days, etc. . . . Sometimes I'd look at his picture and think . . . having absolute power needn't make a man a brute. Might make him noble in a way" (qtd. in O'Connor 36).

9. DuPlessis remarks that the paradigm of much nineteenth-century romance literature is either the marriage or death of the female protagonist. She explains that "death occurs because a female hero has no alternative community where the stain of energy (whether sexual or, in more general terms, passionate) will go unnoticed or even be welcomed" (16). Many twentieth-century women writers have attempted to revise these romantically framed options by "writing beyond the ending," which "means the transgressive invention of narrative strategies, strategies that express critical dissent from dominant narrative. These strategies, among them reparenting, woman-to-woman and brother-to-sister bonds, and forms of the communal protagonist, take issue with the mainstays of the social and ideological organization of gender" (5). Since the protagonist's death is already scripted by *Jane Eyre*, Rhys writes beyond that ending by exploring the

psychological and social history behind Bertha's mad and futile attempts to find community in horizontal affinities when vertical affiliation has left her socially dead.

10. Unless otherwise noted, I will refer in this chapter to Ferré's own 1991 translation of the novel, *Sweet Diamond Dust*.

11. The influence of the *hacendado* class on Puerto Rican identity has been amply noted by scholars. For examples, see Quintero Rivera's *Patricios y plebeyos*, Gelpí's *Literatura y paternalismo*, and Mintz.

12. In the 1930s, a period that saw the beginnings of movement for educational reform, the educational system in U.S.-controlled Puerto Rico was characterized by three objectives: to Americanize the populace, to teach English, and to extend education to greater numbers. The system was a tool for Americans to acculturate new colonial subjects, and that period saw a new wave of students from previous ineligible sectors of the small and medium-sized land owners (Rodriquez 88–91).

13. On populism in Puerto Rico and in the Caribbean, see Sommer's *One Master for Another;* Rodriguez Castro and Alvarez-Curbelo; and Carrión, García Ruiz, and Rodríguez Fraticelli.

14. Alonso contends that regionalism became a particularly important strategy for many Latin American writers in the wake of 1898 and more especially after U.S. Secretary of State James G. Blaine proposed a "Pan-American Conference" in 1889, which essentially served as a benign cover for U.S. imperialist ambitions. Sundquist has indicated that regionalism within U.S. literature was a response to similar expansionist tendencies within the U.S. economy: "[R]ealism from the 1870s through the early 1900s [was] a developing series of responses to the transformation of land into capital, of raw materials into products, of agrarian values into urban values, and of private experience into public property" ("Realism and Regionalism" 501).

15. I am indebted to Gelpí's argument about the perpetuation of paternalism in Puerto Rican literature: "If one of the foundational myths with which our literary history has armed itself is trauma . . . the wound, the fissure of colonialism . . . our critical discourse, then, is going to dedicate itself to sealing or healing this fissure; it will try to cure it" (*Literatura y paternalismo* 8). Cox similarly argues that U.S. regionalism depends on the fact that "regions are always ending. That is the fate of their imaginative space before the ever-encroaching Union" (783).

16. Acosta Cruz has similarly argued: "Using narrative techniques that question the very notion of authority, Ferré presents history not as objective "truth" but in relation to the social position and identity of the Puerto Rican woman" (23). Although I concur that women's status is a primary concern in this piece, I would argue that Ferré, by virtue of differences in the social positions of women and men who narrate this story, offers us representation of the interface among class, race, and gender in the construction of narrative discourse.

17. Considering my position regarding the discipline of American studies explicated in chapter 1, I am aware that there is certain irony in making this argument on her behalf. Following her lead can potentially undermine the very concerns I outlined regarding the tendency of American studies to neoimperialistically incorporate and integrate new signs of difference, since *independistas* would argue that Ferré's conception of Puerto Rican culture is not satisfactorily inclusive. She was apparently convinced that "Mr. Clinton's remark [that statehood for Puerto Rico should not have to mean abandoning its language] acknowledged that ethnic diversity has become a fundamental value in the United States" ("Puerto Rico, U.S.A."). It is as if Ferré has provided a self-fulfilling prophecy by insisting that the United States is now a safe harbor for Puerto Rican culture. If the academy's disciplinary structures were adequate to the task of assessing her career, then her faith in Clinton and in contemporary U.S. attitudes toward ethnic diversity might be justified, but an ideal U.S. tolerance for difference still remains an issue independent from considerations for Puerto Rican cultural and political autonomy. Curiously, the most recent plebiscite in Puerto Rico (13 Dec. 1998) advocated a continuation of Puerto Rico's commonwealth status, indicative of continued division regarding the island's identity, as Ferré's novel explores.

18. This makes Ferré's recent assumption of Laura's view of Puerto Rico, as a hybrid between Anglo and Hispanic cultures, all the more ironic. Ferré has written that "when I travel to the States I feel as Latina as Chita Rivera. But in Latin America, I feel more American than John Wayne. To be Puerto Rican is to be a hybrid" ("Puerto Rico, U.S.A."). Ferré appears to have generated her theory of Puerto Rican hybridity by relishing stereotypes that are related to her own whiteness and that ignore other stereotypes that black Puerto Ricans, for example, might be subject to both on the island and on the mainland.

19. Martínez Echazabal has argued that Ferré's novel belongs with the essays by J. L. González because of their shared interest in "breaking with, or attempting to break with traditional canons and debunking history" (494). She asserts, however, that Ferré's work and its profound reconceptualization of history have not received the same critical attention of González's essays because of the patriarchal bias toward male essayists in Puerto Rican culture.

20. This admission occurred during my interview of Ferré on 18 May 1994 in her residence in Santurce, Puerto Rico.

21. I have elaborated on this theory of testimonial language in Ferré's work as well as in the work of Rigoberta Menchú in "'It's an unbelievable story.'"

22. Batty has persuasively articulated this point. She writes: "In *Song of Solomon*, Morrison uses voice and music to disrupt the relentless specular impulses of white male characters such as Quentin Compson in *Absalom, Absalom!* and to resituate in the latter text the unvoiced but not locatable site of black desire. It is precisely through the musicality of her language and the language of music

that Morrison's repetition of Faulknerian refrains has the effect of exposing and unsettling our hegemonic readings of Faulkner's texts" (89).

23. This connection between Clytie and Circe has also been made by Dimino and Batty. Dimino stresses the fact that Circe is more outspoken than Clytie and is able to bear witness to history that is obscured by the story of Sutpen. Batty also notes that a similar scene with a house full of dogs takes place in the story "Evangeline," by Cable.

24. Weinstein explains that recourse to fixed, ahistorical categories of identity sets the stage for this oedipal cycle of repetition in Faulkner: "If action is coded white and male and reaction coded black and female, then . . . the result [would] be . . . the repeated outrages that constitute *Absalom, Absalom!*" (62). W. Handley also insists on the historical basis for the structures of language and allegory in Morrison's work: "[H]istorical loss can be encountered as the grounding for our structures of representation" and therefore "the history of slavery . . . suggests that the structure of allegory and mourning is neither universal nor inevitable as a human and linguistic predicament" (682, 685).

25. According to African tradition, "the name is the expression of the soul; because of this, the choosing and keeping of the name is a major ritual. To lose the name or, in Afro-American terms, to be 'called out of one's name' is an offense against the spirit" (Byerman 70).

26. Rushdy contends that "memory exists as a communal property of friends, of family, of a people. . . . In individual experience, memory is painful, as Milkman and Sethe discover. In shared experience, memory is healing" (159). Dixon has similarly asserted that "Morrison's novels require us to read the life of a community as the text and context of an individual's articulation of voice" (137).

27. C. A. Davis explores the comparisons between the flying African and the Daedalus story. She writes that in the case of the son who falls from Shalimar, "the son's 'fall' is the result of a situation beyond his control; [and] that the father's desire for freedom and his family ties are in conflict. . . . The conflict is not between *hubris* and common sense, but between 'absolute' freedom and social responsibility" (18).

Bibliography

Acosta Cruz, María I. "Historia, ser e identidad femenina en 'El collar de ca-
mandulas' y 'Maldito amor' de Rosario Ferre." *Chasqui: Revista de literatura
latinoamericana* 19.2 (Nov. 1990): 23–31.

Alonso, Carlos J. *The Spanish American Regional Novel: Modernity and Autochthony.* New York: Cambridge UP, 1990.

Alvarez-Curbelo, Silvia. "La patria desde la tierra: Pedro Albizu Campos y el na-
cionalism económico antillano." *La nación puertorriqueña: Ensayos en
torno a Pedro Albizu Campos.* Ed. Juan Manuel Carrión, Teresa C. García
Ruiz, and Carlos Rodríguez Fraticelli. Río Piedras: Editorial de la Universidad de Puerto Rico, 1993. 83–95.

Anderson, Benedict. *Imagined Communities: Reflections on the Origin and
Spread of Nationalism.* London: Verso, 1983.

Bacon, Margaret Hope. "'One Great Bundle of Humanity': Frances Ellen Watkins Harper (1825–1911)." *Pennsylvania Magazine of History and Biography* 113.1 (Jan. 1989): 21–43.

Baker, Houston A. *Workings of the Spirit: The Poetics of Afro-American
Women's Writing.* Chicago: U of Chicago P, 1991.

Barnes, Fiona R. "Dismantling the Master's Houses: Jean Rhys and West Indian
Identity." *International Women's Writing: New Landscapes of Identity.* Ed.
Anne E. Brown and Marjanne E. Goozé. Westport: Greenwood, 1995.
150–61.

Barthold, Bonnie J. *Black Time: Fiction of Africa, the Caribbean, and the United
States.* New Haven: Yale UP, 1981.

Batty, Nancy Ellen. "Riff, Refrain, Reframe: Morrison's *Song of Absalom.*" *Unflinching Gaze: Morrison and Faulkner Re-envisioned.* Ed. Carol A. Kolmerten, Stephen M. Ross, and Judith Bryant Wittenberg. Jackson: UP of Mississippi, 1997. 77–98.

Belnap, Jeffrey, and Raúl Fernández, eds. *José Martí's "Our America": From
National to Hemispheric Cultural Studies.* Durham: Duke UP, 1998.

Bendixen, Alfred. "Cable's *The Grandissimes*: A Literary Pioneer Confronts the

Southern Tradition." *The Grandissimes: Centennial Essays.* Ed. Thomas J. Richardson. Jackson: UP of Mississippi, 1981. 23–33.

Benítez-Rojo, Antonio. "Cirilo Villaverde, the Seeker of Origins." *Coded Encounters: Writing, Gender, and Ethnicity in Colonial Latin America.* Ed. Francisco Javier Cevallos-Candau et al. Amherst: U of Massachusetts P, 1994. 255–63.

——. "The Repeating Island." *Do the Americas Have a Common Literature?* Ed. Gustavo Pérez Firmat. Durham: Duke UP, 1990.

——. *The Repeating Island: The Caribbean and the Postmodern Perspective.* Trans. James Maraniss. 1992. 2d ed., Durham: Duke UP, 1996.

Bennington, Geoffrey. "Postal Politics and the Institution of the Nation." *Nation and Narration.* New York: Routledge, 1990. 121–37.

Benston, Kimberly W. "I Yam What I Am: The Topos of Un(naming) in Afro-American Literature." *Black Literature and Literary Theory.* Ed. Henry Louis Gates Jr. New York: Methuen, 1984. 151–72.

——. "Re-weaving the 'Ulysses Scene': Enchantment, Post-oedipal Identity, and the Buried Text of Blackness in Toni Morrison's *Song of Solomon.*" *Comparative American Identities: Race, Sex, and Nationality in the Modern Text.* Ed. Hortense J. Spillers. New York: Routledge, 1991. 87–109.

Bercovitch, Sacvan. *The Rites of Assent: Transformations in the Symbolic Construction of America.* New York: Routledge, 1993.

Berzon, Judith R. *Neither White nor Black: The Mulatto Character in American Fiction.* New York: New York UP, 1978.

Bhabha, Homi. "DissemiNation: Time, Narrative, and the Margins of the Modern Nation." *Nation and Narration.* Ed. Homi Bhabha. New York: Routledge, 1990. 291–322.

——. "The World and the Home." *Dangerous Liaisons: Gender, Nation and Postcolonial Perspectives.* Ed. Anne McClintock, Aamir Mufti, and Ella Shohat. Minneapolis: U of Minnesota P, 1997. 445–55.

Binder, Wolfgang. "Entrevista con Rosario Ferré." *La Torre: Revista de la Universidad de Puerto Rico* 8.30 (1994): 239–53.

Blackburn, Robin. *The Making of New World Slavery: From the Baroque to the Modern 1492–1800.* New York: Verso, 1997.

Blassingame, John W. *Black New Orleans 1860–1880.* Chicago: U of Chicago P, 1973.

Bloom, Harold. *The Anxiety of Influence: A Theory of Poetry.* New York: Oxford UP, 1973.

Boyd, Melba Joyce. *Discarded Legacy: Politics and Poetics in the Life of Frances E. W. Harper, 1825–1911.* Detroit: Wayne State UP, 1994.

Byerman, Keith. "Beyond Realism." *Toni Morrison: Critical Perspectives Past and Present.* Ed. Henry Louis Gates and K. A. Appiah. New York: Amistad, 1993. 100–125.

Cable, George Washington. *The Grandissimes.* 1880. New York: Penguin, 1988.

———. *The Negro Question.* New York: Scribner's, 1890.

Cairo Ballester, Ana, ed. *Letras: Cultura en Cuba.* Vol 4. La Habana, Cuba: Editorial Pueblo y Educación, 1987. 6 vols.

Campbell, Michael L. "The Negro in Cable's *The Grandissimes.*" *Mississippi Quarterly* 27.2 (spring 1974): 165–78.

Carby, Hazel. *Reconstructing Womanhood: The Emergence of the Afro-American Woman Novelist.* New York: Oxford UP, 1987.

Carpentier, Alejo. *Ecue-Yamba-O.* 1933. Barcelona, Sp.: Editorial Burguera, 1985.

———. *El reino de este mundo.* 1946. Trans. *The Kingdom of This World.* 1949. New York: Noonday, 1989.

———. *El siglo de las luces.* 1962. Barcelona, Sp.: Editorial Seix Barral, 1983.

———. *Explosion in a Cathedral.* New York: Noonday, 1963. Trans. of *El siglo de las luces.* 1962.

———. "On the Marvelous Real in America." *Magical Realism: Theory, History, Community.* Ed. Lois Parkinson Zamora and Wendy B. Faris. Durham: Duke UP, 1995. 75–88. Trans. of "De lo real maravilloso americano." 1958.

———. *Tientos y diferencias.* Montevideo, Ur.: Arca, 1967.

Carr, David. *Time, Narrative, and History.* Bloomington: Indiana UP, 1986.

Carrión, Juan Manuel, Teresa C. García Ruiz, and Carlos Rodríquez Fraticelli, eds. *La nación puertorriqueña: Ensayos en torno a Pedro Albizu Campos.* Río Piedras: Editorial de la Universidad de Puerto Rico, 1993.

Castronovo, Russ. *Fathering the Nation: American Genealogies of Slavery and Freedom.* Berkeley: U of California P, 1995.

Chesnutt, Charles W. *The Marrow of Tradition.* 1901. Ann Arbor: U of Michigan P, 1969.

———. "MELUS Forum: Charles W. Chesnutt's 'Future American.'" Ed. SallyAnn H. Ferguson. *MELUS* 15.3 (fall 1988): 98–107.

Chesnutt, Helen M. *Charles Waddell Chesnutt: Pioneer of the Color Line.* Chapel Hill: U of North Carolina P, 1952.

Chevigny, Gale Bell, and Gari Laguardia, eds. *Reinventing the Americas: Comparative Studies of Literature of the United States and Spanish America.* New York: Cambridge UP, 1986.

Cheyfitz, Eric. "What Work Is There for Us to Do? American Literary Studies or Americas Cultural Studies?" *American Literature.* 67.4 (Dec. 1995): 843–53.

Clarke, Deborah. "'What There Was before Language': Preliteracy in Toni Morrison's *Song of Solomon.*" *Anxious Power: Reading Writing, and Ambivalence in Narrative by Women.* Ed. Carol J. Singley and Susan Elizabeth Sweeney. State U of New York P, 1993. 265–78.

Cohn, Deborah N. *History and Memory in the Two Souths. Recent Southern and Spanish American Fiction.* Nashville: Vanderbilt UP, 1999.

Cox, James. "Regionalism: A Diminished Thing." *Columbia Literary History of the United States.* Ed. Emory Elliott. New York: Columbia UP, 1988. 761–84.

Curtin, Philip D. *The Rise and Fall of the Plantation Complex.* New York: Cambridge UP, 1990.

da Costa, Emilia Viotti. "Slave Images and Realities." *Comparative Perspectives on Slavery in New World Plantation Societies.* Ed. Vera Rubin and Arthur Tuden. Vol. 292. New York: New York Academy of Sciences, 1977. 293–310. 897 vols.

Dash, J. Michael. *Edouard Glissant.* Cambridge, Eng.: Cambridge UP, 1995.

———. *The Other America: Caribbean Literature in a New World Context.* Charlottesville: UP of Virginia, 1998.

Davies, Carol Boyce. *Black Women, Writing and Identity: Migrations of the Subject.* New York: Routledge, 1994.

Davis, Charles T., and Henry Louis Gates Jr., eds. *The Slave's Narrative.* New York: Oxford UP, 1985.

Davis, Cynthia A. "Self, Society, and Myth in Toni Morrison's Fiction." *Toni Morrison: Modern Critical Views.* Ed. Harold Bloom. New York: Chelsea, 1990. 7–26.

Davis, David Brion. "The Comparative Approach to American History: Slavery." *Slavery in the New World: A Reader in Comparative History.* Ed. Laura Foner and Eugene D. Genovese. Englewood Cliffs: Prentice, 1969. 60–68.

———. "A Comparison of British America and Latin America." *Slavery in the New World: A Reader in Comparative History.* Ed. Laura Foner and Eugene D. Genovese. Englewood Cliffs: Prentice, 1969. 69–83.

———. "Slavery and the American Mind." *Perspectives and Irony in American Slavery.* Ed. Harry Owens. Jackson: UP of Mississippi, 1976.

Dayan, Joan. "'A Receptacle for that Race of Men': Blood, Boundaries, and Mutations of Theory." *American Literature* 67.4 (Dec. 1995): 801–13.

de Certeau, Michel. "History: Ethics, Science, and Fiction." *Social Science as Moral Inquiry.* Ed. Norma Haan et al. New York: Columbia UP, 1983. 125–52.

Delany, Martin. *Blake; or, The Huts of America.* Boston: Beacon, 1970.

Dimino, Andrea. "Toni Morrison and William Faulkner: Remapping Culture." *Unflinching Gaze: Morrison and Faulkner Re-envisioned.* Ed. Carol A. Kolmerten, Stephen M. Ross, and Judith Bryant Wittenberg. Jackson: UP of Mississippi, 1997. 31–47.

Dixon, Melvin. "Like an Eagle in the Air: Toni Morrison." *Toni Morrison: Modern Critical Views.* Ed. Harold Bloom. New York: Chelsea, 1990. 115–42.

Drake, Sandra, "All That Foolishness/That All Foolishness: Race and Caribbean Culture as Thematics of Liberation in Jean Rhys' *Wide Sargasso Sea.*" *Critica* 2.2 (fall 1990): 97–112.

DuPlessis, Rachel Blau. *Writing beyond the Ending: Narrative Strategies of Twentieth-Century Women Writers*. Bloomington: Indiana UP, 1985.

Duvall, John N. "Morrison and the Anxiety of Faulknerian Influence." *Unflinching Gaze: Morrison and Faulkner Re-envisioned*. Ed. Carol A. Kolmerten et al. Jackson: UP of Mississippi, 1997. 3–16.

Elder, Arlene. "'The Future American Race': Charles W. Chesnutt's Utopian Illusion." *MELUS* 15.3 (fall 1988): 121–29.

Elfenbein, Anna Shannon. *Women on the Color Line: Evolving Stereotypes and the Writings of George Washington Cable, Grace King, and Kate Chopin*. Charlottesville: UP of Virginia, 1989.

Elkins, Marilyn. "Reading beyond the Conventions: A Look at Frances E. W. Harper's *Iola Leroy, or Shadows Uplifted*." *American Literary Realism* 22.2 (winter 1990): 44–53.

Emery, Mary Lou. *Jean Rhys at "World's End": Novels of Colonial and Sexual Exile*. Austin: U of Texas P, 1990.

Ernest, John. "From Mysteries to Histories: Cultural Pedagogy in Frances E. W. Harper's *Iola Leroy*." *American Literature* 64.3 (Sept. 1992): 497–518.

———. *Resistance and Reformation in Nineteenth-Century African-American Literature*. Jackson: UP of Mississippi, 1995.

Ette, Ottmar. "'El realismo, según lo entiendo': Sobre las apropriaciones de realidad en la obra de Cirilo Villaverde." *Apropriaciones de realidad en la novela hispanoamericana de los siglos XIX y XX*. Ed. Hans Otto Dill [et al.]. Frankfurt, Ger.: Vervuert, 1994. 75–89.

Fabre, Genevieve. "Genealogical Archeology or the Quest for Legacy in Toni Morrison's *Song of Solomon*." *Critical Essays on Toni Morrison*. Ed. Nellie Y. McKay. Boston: Hall, 1988. 105–14.

Faulkner, William. *Absalom, Absalom!*. 1936. New York: Vintage, 1986.

Felman, Shoshona, and Dori Laub. *Testimony*. New York: Routledge, 1992.

Fernández Retamar, Roberto. *Caliban and Other Essays*. Trans. Edward Baker. Minneapolis: U of Minnesota P, 1989.

Fernández Robaina, Tomás. *El negro en Cuba, 1902–1958: Apuntes para la historia de la lucha contra la discriminación racial*. La Habana, Cuba: Editorial de Ciencias Sociales, 1990.

Ferré, Rosario. "From Ire to Irony." *Callaloo: A Journal of African American and African Arts and Letters* 17.3 (summer 1994): 900–904.

———. *Maldito amor*. 1986. Río Piedras, PR: Ediciones Huracán, 1988.

———. Personal interview. 18 May 1994.

———. "Puerto Rico, U.S.A." Op-ed. *New York Times* 19 Mar. 1998, late ed.: A21.

———. *Sweet Diamond Dust*. Trans. Rosario Ferré. New York: Available, 1991. Trans. of *Maldito amor*.

Finke, Laurie A. *Feminist Theory, Women's Writing*. Ithaca: Cornell UP, 1992.

Fitz, Earl E. *Rediscovering the Americas: Inter-American Literature in a Comparative Context.* Iowa City: U of Iowa P, 1991.

Fleischner, Jennifer. *Mastering Slavery: Memory, Family, and Identity in Women's Slave Narratives.* New York: New York UP, 1996.

Foner, Laura, and Eugene D. Genovese, eds. *Slavery in the New World: A Reader in Comparative History.* Englewood Cliffs: Prentice, 1969.

Foreman, P. Gabrielle. "'Reading aright': White Slavery, Black Referents, and the Strategy of Histotextuality in *Iola Leroy.*" *Yale Journal of Criticism* 10.2 (fall 1997): 327–54.

Foster, Frances Smith. *A Brighter Coming Day: A Frances Ellen Watkins Harper Reader.* New York: Feminist, 1990.

Foucault, Michel. *Discipline and Punish: The Birth of the Prison.* New York: Vintage, 1979.

———. *Language, Countermemory, Practice.* Ed. D. Bouchard. Ithaca: Cornell UP, 1977. 139–64.

———. *La verdad y las formas jurídicas.* Barcelona, Sp.: Gedisa, 1980.

Fox-Genovese, Elizabeth. *Within the Plantation Household.* Chapel Hill: U of North Carolina P, 1988.

Fox-Genovese, Elizabeth, and Eugene D. Genovese. *Fruits of Merchant Capital: Slavery and Bourgeois Property in the Rise and Expansion of Capitalism.* New York: Oxford UP, 1983.

Franchot, Jenny. "Unseemly Commemoration: Religion, Fragments, and the Icon." *American Literary History* 9.3 (fall 1997): 502–21.

Franco, Jean. "Apuntes sobre la crítica feminista y la literatura hispanoamericana." *Hispamerica* 15.45 (Dec. 1986): 31–43.

Friedman, Ellen. "Breaking the Master Narrative: Jean Rhys's Wide Sargasso Sea." *Breaking the Sequence: Women's Experimental Fiction.* Ed. Ellen Friedman and Miriam Fuchs. Princeton: Princeton UP, 1989. 117–28.

———. "Where Are the Missing Contents? (Post)modernism, Gender, and the Canon." *PMLA* 108.2 (Mar. 1993): 240–52.

Friol, Roberto. "Introducción a Cirilo Villaverde: 'Diario del Rancheador.'" *Revista Biblioteca Nacional José Martí* 15 (1973): 49–61.

Fuentes, Carlos. "The Novel as Tragedy: William Faulkner." *The Faulkner Journal* 11.1–2 (fall 1995–spring 1996): 13–31.

García Márquez, Gabriel. "Latin America's Impossible Reality." *Harper's Magazine* 270.1616 (Jan. 1985): 13–16.

———. *One Hundred Years of Solitude.* Trans. Gregory Rabassa. New York: Avon, 1971.

———. "The Solitude of Latin America: Nobel Lecture, 1982." *Gabriel García Márquez and the Powers of Fiction.* Ed. Julio Ortega. Asst. ed. Claudia Elliot. Austin: U of Texas P, 1988. 87–91.

Gates, Henry Louis, Jr. *Figures in Black: Words, Signs, and the "Racial" Self.* New York: Oxford UP, 1987.

——. *The Signifying Monkey: A Theory of African-American Literary Criticism*. New York: Oxford, 1988.

Gelpí, Juan G. "El discurso jerárquico en *Cecilia Valdés*." *Revista de crítica literaria latinoamericana* 34.17 (fall 1991): 47–61.

——. *Literatura y paternalismo en Puerto Rico*. Río Piedras: Editorial de la Universidad de Puerto Rico, 1993.

Genovese, Eugene D. "Materialism and Idealism in the History of Negro Slavery in the Americas." *Slavery in the New World: A Reader in Comparative History*. Ed. Laura Foner and Eugene D. Genovese. Englewood Cliffs: Prentice, 1969. 238–55.

——. "Slavery—the World's Burden." *Perspectives and Irony in American Slavery*. Ed. Harry Owens. Jackson: UP of Mississippi, 1976. 27–50.

Gest, Sydney G., trans. *Cecilia Valdés; or, Angel's Hill: A Novel of Cuban Customs*. New York: Vantage, 1962.

Gilroy, Paul. *The Black Atlantic: Modernity and Double Consciousness*. Cambridge: Harvard UP, 1993.

Glissant, Edouard. *Caribbean Discourse: Selected Essays*. Charlottesville: UP of Virginia, 1989.

——. "Creolization in the Making of the Americas." *Race, Discourse and the Origin of the Americas: A New World View*. Ed. Vera Lawrence Hyatt and Rex Nettleford. Washington, D.C.: Smithsonian Institution P, 1995. 268–75.

Godden, Richard. "*Absalom, Absalom!*, Haiti, and Labor History: Reading Unreadable Revolutions." *ELH* 61 (1994): 685–720.

González, Eduardo. "American Theriomorphia: The Presence of *Mulatez* in Cirilo Villaverde and Beyond." *Do the Americas Have a Common Literature?* Ed. Gustavo Perez-Firmat. Durham: Duke UP, 1990. 177–97.

González, José Luis. *El país de cuatro pisos y otros ensayos*. Río Piedras, PR: Ediciones Huracán, 1989.

González, Reynaldo. *Contradanzas y latigazos*. La Habana, Cuba: Editorial Letras Cubanas, 1983.

González Echevarría, Roberto. *Alejo Carpentier: The Pilgrim at Home*. Ithaca: Cornell UP, 1977.

——. "Socrates among the Weeds: Blacks and History in Carpentier's *Explosion in a Cathedral*." *Voices from Under: Black Narrative in Latin America and the Caribbean*. Ed. William Luis. Westport: Greenwood, 1984. 35–53.

Guerra, Lillian. "Crucibles of Liberation in Cuba: Nationalisms, José Martí and the Search for Social Unity, 1895–1933." Diss. University of Wisconsin–Madison, in progress.

——. "Marbling Martí: The Meaning of Memories and Monuments in the First Cuban Republic." Unpublished essay, 1999.

——. Telephone interview. 16 June 1999.

Guerra, Ramiro. *Azucar y población en las antillas*. La Habana, Cuba: Editorial de Ciencias Sociales, 1944.

Guetti, James. *The Limits of Metaphor: A Study of Melville, Conrad, and Faulkner.* Ithaca: Cornell UP, 1967.

Gunew, Sneja. *Framing Marginality: Multicultural Literary Studies.* Melbourne, Austral.: Melbourne UP, 1994.

Gutiérrez Mouat, Ricardo. "La 'loca deldesván' y otros intertextos de *Maldito amor.*" *Modern Language Notes* 109.2 (Mar. 1994): 283–306.

Hall, Constance Hill. *Incest in Faulkner: A Metaphor for the Fall.* Ann Arbor: U of Michigan Research P, 1987.

Hall, Gwendolyn Midlo. "The Formation of Afro-Creole Culture." *Creole New Orleans: Race and Americanization.* Ed. Arnold R. Hirsch and Joseph Logsdon. Baton Rouge: Louisiana State UP, 1989. 58–87.

Hall, Stuart. "Cultural Identity and Cinematic Representation." *Black British Cultural Studies: A Reader.* Ed. Houston A. Baker et al. Chicago: U of Chicago P, 1996. 210–22.

Handley, George B. "'It's an unbelievable story': Testimony and Truth in the Work of Rigoberta Menchú and Rosario Ferré." *Violence, Silence and Anger: Women's Writing as Transgression.* Ed. Deirdre Lashgari. Charlottesville: UP of Virginia, 1995. 62–79.

———. "Rereading the Nation as Family: Corrective Revisions of Racial Discourse in Martín Morúa Delgado and Charles W. Chesnutt." *Publication of the Afro-Latin/American Research Association* 1 (fall 1997): 66–79.

Handley, William. "The House a Ghost Built: *Nommo,* Allegory, and the Ethics of Reading in Toni Morrison's *Beloved.*" *Contemporary Literature* 36.4 (1995): 676–701.

Harper, Frances E. W. *Iola Leroy; or, Shadows Uplifted.* 1891. New York: Oxford UP, 1988.

Harris, Marvin. "The Origin of the Descent Rule." *Slavery in the New World: A Reader in Comparative History.* Ed. Laura Foner and Eugene D. Genovese. Englewood Cliffs: Prentice, 1969. 48–59.

Harris, Wilson. "The Tree of Life." *Review of Contemporary Fiction* 5.2 (summer 1985): 118–21.

———. *The Womb of Space: The Cross-Cultural Imagination.* Westport: Greenwood, 1983.

Hathaway, Heather. "'Maybe Freedom Lies in Hating': Miscegenation and the Oedipal Conflict." *Refiguring the Father: New Feminist Readings of Patriarchy.* Ed. Patricia Yaeger and Beth Kowalski-Wallace. Carbondale: Southern Illinois UP, 1989. 153–67.

Helg, Aline. *Our Rightful Share: The Afro-Cuban Struggle for Equality, 1886–1912.* Chapel Hill: U of North Carolina P, 1995.

Herrera McElroy, Onyria. "Martín Morúa Delgado, precursor del afro-cubanismo." *Afro-Hispanic Review* 2.1 (Jan. 1983): 19–24.

Holland, Norman S. "Fashioning Cuba." *Nationalisms and Sexualities.* Ed. Andrew Parker et al. New York: Routledge, 1992. 147–56.

Howard, Philip A. *Changing History: Afro-Cuban Cabildos and Societies of Color in the Nineteenth Century.* Baton Rouge: Louisiana State UP, 1998.

Howells, Corall Ann. *Jean Rhys.* New York: St. Martin's, 1991.

Hulme, Peter. "The Locked Heart: The Creole Family Romance of *Wide Sargasso Sea.*" *Colonial Discourse/Postcolonial Theory.* Manchester, Eng.: Manchester UP, 1994. 72–88.

Hunt, Alfred N. *Haiti's Influence on Antebellum America: Slumbering Volcano in the Caribbean.* Baton Rouge: Louisiana State UP, 1988.

Irwin, John. *Doubling and Incest/Repetition and Revenge: A Speculative Reading of Faulkner.* Baltimore: Johns Hopkins UP, 1975.

Irwin, Lee. "'Like in a Looking Glass': History and Narrative in *Wide Sargasso Sea.*" *Novel* 22.2 (winter 1989): 143–58.

Jones, Gavin. "Signifying Songs: The Double Meaning of Black Dialect in the Work of George Washington Cable." *American Literary History* 9.2 (summer 1997): 244–67.

Kaplan, Amy, and Donald E. Pease, ed. *Cultures of United States Imperialism.* Durham: Duke UP, 1993.

Kawash, Samira. *Dislocating the Color Line: Identity, Hybridity, and Singularity in African-American Narrative.* Stanford: Stanford UP, 1997

Kaye, Jackelyne. "La esclavitud en América: *Cecilia Valdés* y *La cabaña del tío Tom.*" Trans. Ana Puñal. *Casa de las Américas* 22.129 (Nov.–Dec. 1981): 74–83.

Klein, Herbert S. *African Slavery in Latin America and the Caribbean.* New York: Oxford UP, 1986.

———. *Slavery in the Americas: A Comparative Study of Virginia and Cuba.* Chicago: U of Chicago P, 1967.

———. *The Middle Passage: Comparative Studies in the Atlantic Slave Trade.* Princeton: Princeton UP, 1978.

Knadler, Stephen P. "Untragic Mulatto: Charles Chesnutt and the Discourse of Whiteness." *American Literary History* 8.3 (fall 1996): 426–48.

Kreyling, Michael. "After the War: Romance and the Reconstruction of Southern Literature." *Southern Literature in Transition: Heritage and Promise.* Ed. Philip Castille and William Osborne. Memphis: Memphis State UP, 1983. 111–25.

Kunow, Rüdiger. "The Return of Historical Narrative in Contemporary American Culture." *Ethics and Aesthetics: The Moral Turn of Postmodernism.* Ed. Gerhard Hoffmann and Alfred Hornung. Heidelberg, Ger.: Universitatsverlag C. Winter, 1996. 255–73.

Kutzinski, Vera. *Sugar's Secrets: Race and the Erotics of Cuban Nationalism.* Charlottesville: UP of Virginia, 1993.

Ladd, Barbara. *Nationalism and the Color Line in George W. Cable, Mark Twain, and William Faulkner.* Baton Rouge: Louisiana State UP, 1996.

Leclair, Thomas. "'The Language Must Not Sweat.'" *Toni Morrison: Critical*

Perspectives Past and Present. Ed. Henry Louis Gates Jr. and K. A. Appiah. New York: Amistad, 1993. 369–77.

Lewis, Earl. "To Turn as on a Pivot: Writing African Americans into a History of Overlapping Diasporas." *American Historical Review* 100 (June 1995): 765–87.

Lewis, Gordon K. *The Contemporary Caribbean: A General Overview.* Washington, D.C.: Woodrow Wilson International Center for Scholars, 1985.

———. *Main Currents in Caribbean Thought: The Historical Evolution of Caribbean Society in Its Ideological Aspects, 1492–1900.* Baltimore: Johns Hopkins UP, 1983.

Long, Edward. *History of Jamaica.* 3 vols. London, Eng. 1774.

Ludmer, Josefina. *Cien años de soledad: Una interpretación.* 2d ed. Buenos Aires, Arg.: Editorial Tiempo Contemporáneo, 1974.

———. "Tretas del débil." *La sárten por el mango: Encuentro de escritoras latinoamericanas.* Ed. Patricia Elena González and Eliana Ortega. Río Piedras, PR: Ediciones Huracán, 1985. 47–54.

Luis, William. "History and Fiction: Black Narrative in Latin America and the Caribbean." *Voices from Under: Black Narrative in Latin American and the Caribbean.* Ed. William Luis. Westport: Greenwood, 1984. 3–32.

———. *Literary Bondage: Slavery in Cuban Narrative.* Austin: U of Texas P, 1990.

Lyotard, Jean-François. *The Differend: Phrases in Dispute.* Minneapolis: U of Minnesota P, 1988.

MacAdam, Alfred. *Textual Confrontations: Comparative Readings in Latin American Literature.* Chicago: U of Chicago P, 1987.

Magarey, Kevin. "The Sense of Place in Doris Lessing and Jean Rhys." *A Sense of Place in the New Literatures in English.* Ed. Peggy Nightingale. St. Lucia: U of Queensland P, 1986. 47–60.

Márquez, René. *El puertorriqueño dócil (literatura y realidad psicológica).* Barcelona, Sp.: Editorial Antillana, 1967.

Martí, José. *Nuestra América: Volumen 1.* La Habana, Cuba: Editorial Trópico, 1939.

———. *Obras completas: Volumen 1 (Segunda Parte).* Ed. Jorge Quintana. Caracas, Ven.: 1964.

Martínez-Alier, Verena. *Marriage, Class and Colour in Nineteenth Century Cuba: A Study of Racial Attitudes and Sexual Values in a Slave Society.* New York: Cambridge UP, 1974.

Martínez Echazabal, Lourdes. "Maldito amor: Hacia una nueva hermeneutica de la historia." *La Torre* 3.11 (July–Sept. 1989): 493–503.

Masiello, Francine. "'Gentlemen,' Damas, y Travestis: Cuidadanía e identidad cultural en la Argentina del fin de siglo." Paper delivered at the annual conference of the Modern Language Association, Toronto, Can., 1993.

Mason, Theodore O., Jr. "The Novelist as Conservator: Stories and Comprehension in Toni Morrison's *Song of Solomon." Toni Morrison: Modern Critical Views.* Ed. Harold Bloom. New York: Chelsea, 1990. 115–42.

McClintock, Anne, "The Angel of Progress: Pitfalls of the Term 'Post-colonialism,'" *Social Text* 10.2–3 (1992): 84–98.

McDowell, Deborah E. "'The Changing Same': Generational Connections and Black Women Novelists." *New Literary History* 18.2 (winter 1987): 281–302.

McElrath, Joseph R., Jr. "W. D. Howells and Race: Charles W. Chesnutt's Disappointment of the Dean." *Victorian Studies* 51.4 (Mar. 1997): 474–99.

Mignolo, Walter. "Los límites de la literatura, de la teoría y de la literatura comparada: El desafío de las prácticas semióticas en situaciones coloniales." *Insula: Revista de letras y ciencias humanas* 47.552 (Dec. 1992): 15–17.

———. "Occidentalización, imperialismo, globalización: Herencias coloniales y teorías postcoloniales." *Revista iberoamericana* 61.170–71 (Jan.–June 1995): 27–40.

Mikics, David. "Derek Walcott and Alejo Carpentier: Nature, History, and the Caribbean Writer." *Magical Realism: Theory, History, Community.* Ed. Lois Parkinson Zamora and Wendy B. Faris. Durham: Duke UP, 1995. 371–404.

Miller, J. Hillis. "The Two Relativisms: Point of View and Indeterminacy in the Novel *Absalom, Absalom!*" *Relativism in the Arts.* Athens: U of Georgia P, 1983. 148–70.

Mintz, Sydney. *Caribbean Transformations.* Chicago: Aldine, 1974.

Moreno Fraginals, Manuel. *El ingenio: Complejo económico social cubano del azúcar.* Vol. 1. La Habana, Cuba: Editorial de Ciencias Sociales, 1978.

Morrison, Toni. *Beloved.* New York: Plume, 1988.

———. "Nobel Lecture." *Georgia Review* 49.1 (spring 1995): 314–30.

———. *Playing in the Dark: Whiteness and the Literary Imagination.* New York: Vintage, 1992.

———. *Song of Solomon.* New York: Plume, 1977.

———. "Unspeakable Things Unspoken: The Afro-American Presence in American Literature." *Criticism and the Color Line: Desegregating American Literary Studies.* Ed. Henry B. Wonham. New Brunswick: Rutgers UP, 1996.

Morúa Delgado, Martín. *Integración cubana y otros ensayos.* La Habana, Cuba: Publicaciones de la Comisión Nacional del Centenario de Martín Morúa Delgado, 1957.

———. *La familia Unzúazu.* 1901. La Habana, Cuba: Editorial Arte y Literatura, 1975.

———. "Las novelas del sr. Villaverde: Publicado por el autor, un negro." La Habana, Cuba, 1892.

———. *Sofía.* 1891. La Habana, Cuba: Publicaciones de la Comisión Nacional del Centenario de Martín Morúa Delgado, 1957.

Mullin, Michael. "Slave Obeahmen and Slaveowning Patriarchs in an Era of War and Revolution (1776–1807)." *Comparative Perspectives on Slavery in*

New World Plantation Societies. Ed. Vera Rubin and Arthur Tuden. Vol. 292. New York: New York Academy of Sciences, 1977. 897 vols.

Nettleford, Rex. *Caribbean Cultural Identity.* Los Angeles: Center for Afro-American Studies and UCLA Latin American Center, 1978.

Nowatzki, Robert. "Miscegenation and the Rhetoric of 'Blood' in Three Turn-of-the-Century African American Novels." *Journal of Contemporary Thought* 6 (1996): 41–50.

Oates, Joyce Carol. "Romance and Anti-romance: From Brontë's *Jane Eyre* to Rhys's *Wide Sargasso Sea.*" *Virginia Quarterly Review* 63.1 (winter 1985): 44–58.

O'Connor, Theresa. *Jean Rhys: The West Indian Novels.* New York: New York UP, 1986.

Olaussen, Maria. "Jean Rhys's Construction of Blackness as Escape from White Femininity in *Wide Sargasso Sea.*" *Ariel: A Review of International English Literature* 24.2 (Apr. 1993): 65–82.

Ortiz, Fernando. *Contrapunteo cubano del tabaco y azúcar.* La Habana, Cuba: Editorial de Ciencias Sociales, 1991.

Otten, Thomas J. "Pauline Hopkins and the Hidden Self of Race." *ELH* 59.1 (spring 1992): 227–56.

Paquette, Robert L. *Sugar Is Made with Blood: The Conspiracy of La Esalera and the Conflict between Empires over Slavery in Cuba.* Middletown: Wesleyan UP, 1988.

Patterson, Orlando. *Slavery and Social Death: A Comparative Study.* Cambridge: Harvard UP, 1982.

Paz, Octavio. *The Labyrinth of Solitude: Life and Thought in Mexico.* Trans. Lysander Kemp, Yara Milos, and Rachel Philips Belash. New York: Grove, 1985.

———. *Puertas al campo.* Mexico City: Universidad Nacional Autónoma de Mexico, 1967.

Pedreira, Antonio, S. *Insularismo.* 1934. Río Piedras, PR: Ediciones Edil, 1992.

Pérez, Louis A. *Cuba and the United States: Ties of Singular Intimacy.* Athens: U of Georgia P, 1990.

Pérez Firmat, Gustavo, ed. *Do the Americas Have a Common Literature?* Durham: Duke UP, 1990.

Picó, Fernando. *Historia general de Puerto Rico.* Río Piedras, PR: Ediciones Huracán, 1988.

Pollard, Edward. *Black Diamonds Gathered in the Darkey Homes of the South.* New York: Pudney, 1859.

———. *Historia del primer año de la guerra del sur.* Trans. Cirilo Villaverde. New York: Hauser, 1863.

———. *The Lost Cause: A New Southern History of the War of the Confederates.* New York, 1866.

Porter, Carolyn. *Seeing and Being: The Plight of the Participant Observer in Emerson, James, Adams, and Faulkner.* Middletown: Wesleyan UP, 1981.

———. "What We Know that We Don't Know: Remapping American Literary Studies." *American Literary History* 6.3 (fall 1994): 467–526.

Pratt, Mary Louise. "Arts of the Contact Zone." *Profession.* New York: Modern Language Association, 1991. 33–40.

———. *Imperial Eyes: Travel Writing and Transculturation.* New York: Routledge, 1992.

Quintero Rivera, Angel G. *Conflictos de clase y política en Puerto Rico.* Río Piedras, PR: Ediciones Huracán, 1976.

———. *Patricios y plebeyos: Burgueses, hacendados, artesanos, y obreros.* Río Piedras, PR: Ediciones Huracán, 1988.

Railey, Kevin. "Paternalism and Liberalism: Contending Ideologies in *Absalom, Absalom!*" *Faulkner Journal* 7 (fall 1991–spring 1992): 115–32.

Rama, Angel. *Transculturación narrativa en América Latina.* Mexico City, Mex.: Siglo Veintiuno Editores, 1982.

Ramos, Julio. "Cuerpo, lengua, subjetividad." *Revista de crítica literaria latinoamericana* 19.38 (fall 1993): 225–37.

———. *Paradojas de la letra.* Caracas, Ven.: Ediciones excultura, 1996.

Renan, Ernest. "What Is a Nation?" *Nation and Narration.* Ed. Homi Bhabha. New York: Routledge, 1990.

Reyes, Angelita. "Christophine, Nanny, and Creole Difference: Reconsidering Jean Rhys's West Indian Landscape and *Wide Sargasso Sea.*" *On the Road to Guinea: Essays in Black Comparative Literature.* Ed. Edward O. Ako. London, Eng.: Heinemann, 1992.

Rhys, Jean. *Wide Sargasso Sea.* New York: Norton, 1975.

Richardson, Thomas J. "Introduction: Honoré Grandissime's Southern Dilemma." *The Grandissimes: Centennial Essays.* Ed. Thomas J. Richardson. Jackson: UP of Mississippi, 1981. 1–12.

Rodriguez Castro, María Elena, and Silvia Alvarez-Curbelo, eds. *Del nacionalismo al populismo: Cultura y política en Puerto Rico.* Río Piedras, PR: Ediciones Huracán, 1993.

Rubin, Louis D., Jr. *George W. Cable: The Life and Times of a Southern Heretic.* New York: Pegasus, 1969.

Rubin, Vera, and Arthur Tuden, eds. *Comparative Perspectives on Slavery in New World Plantation Societies.* New York: New York Academy of Sciences, 1977.

Ruppersburg, Hugh M. *Voice and Eye in Faulkner's Fiction.* Athens: U of Georgia P, 1983.

Rushdy, Ashraf H. A. "'Rememory': Primal Scenes and Constructions in Toni Morrison's Novels." *Toni Morrison's Fiction: Contemporary Criticism.* Ed. David L. Middleton. New York: Garland, 1997. 135–61.

Saco, José Antonio. *Acerca de la esclavitud y su historia.* La Habana, Cuba: Editorial de Ciencias Sociales, 1982.

Said, Edward W. *The World, the Text, the Critic.* Cambridge: Harvard UP, 1983.

Saks, Eva. "Representing Miscegenation Law." *Raritan* 8.2 (fall 1988): 39–69.

Saldívar, José David. *The Dialectics of Our America: Genealogy, Cultural Critique, and Literary History.* Durham: Duke UP, 1991.

Sale, Maggie. "Critiques from Within: Antebellum Projects of Resistance." *American Literature* 64.4 (Dec. 1992): 695–718.

Sánchez-Eppler, Benigno. "'Por causa mecánica': The Coupling of Bodies and Machines and the Production and Reproduction of Whiteness in *Cecilia Valdés* and Nineteenth-Century Cuba." *Thinking Bodies.* Ed. Juliet Flower MacCannell and Laura Zakarin. Stanford: Stanford UP, 1994. 78–86.

Scarry, Elaine. *The Body in Pain: The Making and Unmaking of the World.* New York: Oxford UP, 1985.

Schmidt, Hans. *The United States Occupation of Haiti 1915–1934.* New Brunswick: Rutgers UP, 1971.

Schulman, Ivan A. "Reflections on Cuba and Its Antislavery Literature." *Secolas Annals* 7 (Mar. 1976): 59–67.

Scott, Rebecca J. "La dinámica de la emancipación y formación de la sociedad pos-abolicionista: El caso cubano en perspectiva comparativa." *Anuario de estudios americanos* 42 (1986): 87–98.

———. *Slave Emancipation in Cuba: The Transition to Free Labor, 1860–1899.* Princeton: Princeton UP, 1985.

Silva-Caceres, Raúl. "Un desplazamiento metonimico como base de la teoría de la vision en *El siglo de las luces.*" *Revista iberoamericana* 123–24 (Apr.–Sept. 1983): 487–96.

Slemon, Stephen. "Magical Realism as Postcolonial Discourse." *Magical Realism: Theory, History, Community.* Ed. Lois Parkinson Zamora and Wendy B. Faris. Durham: Duke UP, 1995. 407–26.

Sollors, Werner. *Neither Black nor White yet Both: Thematic Explorations of Interracial Literature.* Oxford: Oxford UP, 1997.

———. "'Never Was Born': The Mulatto, an American Tragedy?" *Massachusetts Review* 27 (summer 1986): 293–316.

Solow, Barbara. "Capitalism and Slavery in the Exceedingly Long Run." *Journal of Interdisciplinary History* 17.4 (spring 1987): 711–37.

Sommer, Doris. *Foundational Fictions: The National Romances of Latin America.* Berkeley: U of California P, 1991.

———. "Irresistible Romance: The Foundational Fictions of Latin America." *Nation and Narration.* Ed. Homi Bhabha. New York: Routledge, 1990. 71–98.

———. "José Martí, Author of Walt Whitman." *José Martí's "Our America".* Ed. Jeffrey Belnap and Raúl Fernández. Durham: Duke UP, 1998. 77–90.

——. *One Master for Another: Populism as Patriarchal Rhetoric in Dominican Novels.* New York: UP of America, 1983.

——. "Sin secretos." *Revista de crítica literaria latinoamericana* 28.36 (1992): 135–54.

——. "Who Can Tell?: Filling in the Blanks for Villaverde." *American Literary History* 6.2 (summer 1994): 213–33.

Spillers, Hortense. "Mama's Baby, Papa's Maybe: An American Grammar Book." *Diacritics* 17 (summer 1987): 65–81.

——. "Who Cuts the Border? Some Readings on 'America.'" *Comparative American Identities: Race, Sex, and Nationality in the Modern Text.* Ed. Hortense Spillers. New York: Routledge, 1991. 1–25.

Spitta, Silvia. *Between Two Waters: Narratives of Transculturation in Latin America.* Houston: Rice UP, 1995.

Spivak, Gayatri Chakravorty. "Three Women's Texts and a Critique of Imperialism." *"Race," Writing, and Difference.* Ed. Henry Louis Gates Jr. Chicago: U of Chicago P , 1986. 262–80.

Stanchich, Maritza. "The Hidden Caribbean 'Other' in William Faulkner's *Absalom, Absalom!*" *Mississippi Quarterly: The Journal of Southern Culture* 49.3 (summer 1996): 603–17.

Stinchcombe, Arthur. *Sugar Island Slavery in the Age of Enlightenment: The Political Economy of the Caribbean World.* Princeton: Princeton UP, 1995.

Stowe, Harriet Beecher. *Uncle Tom's Cabin; or, Life among the Lowly.* 1852. New York: Penguin, 1981.

Sundquist, Eric J. *Home as Found: Authority and Genealogy in Nineteenth Century American Literature.* Baltimore: Johns Hopkins UP, 1979.

——. "Introduction." *American Literature* 67.4 (Dec. 1995): 793–94.

——. "Realism and Regionalism." *Columbia Literary History of the United States.* Ed. Emory Elliott. New York: Columbia UP, 1988. 501–24.

——. *To Wake the Nations: Race in the Making of American Literature.* Cambridge: Belknap P of Harvard UP, 1993.

Tate, Claudia. "Allegories of Black Female Desire; or, Rereading Nineteenth-Century Sentimental Narratives of Black Female Authority." *Changing Our Own Words: Essays on Criticism, Theory, and Writing by Black Women.* Ed. Cheryl A. Wall. New Brunswick: Rutgers UP, 1989. 98–126.

Tobin, Patricia Drechsel. *Time and the Novel: The Genealogical Imperative.* Princeton: Princeton UP, 1978.

Tourgee, Albion. *A Fool's Errand.* Fords. 1880.

Tregle, Joseph. "Creoles and Americans." *Creole New Orleans: Race and Americanization.* Ed. Arnold R. Hirsch and Joseph Logsdon. Baton Rouge: Louisiana State UP, 1989. 131–85.

Turner, Arlin, ed. *Mark Twain and George W. Cable: The Record of a Literary Friendship.* East Lansing: Michigan State UP, 1960.

Umpierre, Luz María. *Ideología y novela en Puerto Rico: Un estudio de la narativa de Zeno, Laguerre y Soto.* Madrid, Sp.: Editorial Playor, 1983.

Villaverde, Cirilo. *Cecilia Valdés; o, Loma del Angel: Novela cubana.* La Habana, Cuba: Imprenta Literaria, 1839.

———. *Cecilia Valdés; o, Loma del Angel: Novela de costumbres cubanas.* 1882. Mexico City, Mex.: Editorial Porrua, 1986.

———. *Comunidad de nombres y apellidos.* 1846.

Walcott, Derek. *Collected Poems 1948–1984.* New York: Farrar, 1992.

———. "The Muse of History." *Is Massa Day Dead? Black Moods in the Caribbean.* Ed. Orde Coombs. 1974. 1–27.

Warren, Kenneth W. *Black and White Strangers: Race and American Literary Criticism.* Chicago: U of Chicago P, 1993.

Weinstein, Philip M. "David and Solomon: Fathering in Faulkner and Morrison." *Unflinching Gaze: Morrison and Faulkner Re-envisioned.* Ed. Carol A. Kolmerten, Stephen M. Ross, and Judith Bryant Wittenberg. Jackson: UP of Mississippi, 1997. 48–74.

White, Hayden. *The Content of the Form.* Baltimore: Johns Hopkins UP, 1987.

Whitman, Walt. *Democratic Vistas.* New York: Little Library of Liberal Arts, 1971.

Williams, Lorna. "From Dusky Venus to Mater Dolorosa: The Female Protagonist in the Cuban Antislavery Novel." *Woman as Myth and Metaphor in Latin American Literature.* Ed. Carmelo Virgillo and Naomi Lindstrom. Columbia: U of Missouri P, 1985.

———. "Morúa Delgado and the Cuban Slave Narrative." *Modern Language Notes* 108.2 (Mar. 1993): 302–13.

———. "The Representation of the Female Slave in Villaverde's *Cecilia Valdés.*" *Hispanic Journal* 14 (spring 1993): 73–89.

———. *The Representation of Slavery in Cuban Fiction.* Columbia: U of Missouri P, 1994.

Williamson, Joel. *New People: Miscegenation and Mulattoes in the United States.* New York: Free, 1980.

———. *William Faulkner and Southern History.* Oxford, Eng.: Oxford UP, 1993.

Wonham, Henry B., ed. *Criticism and the Color Line: Desegregating American Literary Studies.* New Brunswick: Rutgers UP, 1996.

Woodward, C. Vann. *The Strange Career of Jim Crow.* New York: Oxford UP, 1966.

Young, Elizabeth. "Warring Fictions: *Iola Leroy* and the Color of Gender." *American Literature* 64.2 (June 1992): 273–97.

Zamora, Lois Parkinson. "The Usable Past: The Idea of History in Modern U.S. and Latin American Fiction." *Do the Americas Have a Common Literature?* Ed. Gustavo Pérez Firmat. Durham: Duke UP, 1990. 7–41.

———. *The Usable Past: The Imagination of History in Recent Fiction of the Americas.* New York: Cambridge UP, 1997.

———. *Writing the Apocalypse: Historical Vision in Contemporary U.S. and Latin American Fiction.* New York: Cambridge UP, 1989.

Index

Absalom, Absalom! (Faulkner), 4, 10,
130–43; and Explosion in a Cathedral; 114–19, 135–36, 139, 140–
42, 143; and The Grandissimes,
67, 72, 74, 133, 139; and The Marrow of Tradition, 97; and Song of
Solomon, 174–76, 204 n. 22, 205
nn. 23, 24. See also Faulkner,
William
Acosta Cruz, María I., 162, 203 n. 16
African diaspora, 8, 10, 27, 28, 39,
146, 191
Africanist presence, 49, 176
Africanization, 10, 20, 42, 44, 48, 63,
70, 76, 81, 83, 86, 90, 110, 132.
See also miscegenation, fear of; racial difference; segregation
Alonso, Carlos, 163, 165, 199 n. 3,
200 n. 6, 203 n. 14
Alvarez-Curbelo, Silvia, 203 n. 13
American studies, limitations of, 9, 21,
25, 28–29, 190–91, 195 nn. 18, 19.
See also colonialism; U.S. imperial-
ism
Anderson, Benedict, 28, 105
antislavery literature, 3
Antoni, Robert, 186

Baker, Houston, 103, 106, 201 n. 2

Ball, Edward, 186
Batty, Nancy Ellen, 204–5 n. 22, 205
n. 23
Belnap, Jeffrey, 194 n. 13, 195 n. 18
Benítez-Rojo, Antonio 2, 19, 46, 53,
74, 128
Bennington, Geoffrey, 194 n. 8
Bercovitch, Sacvan, 24, 25, 28
Bhabha, Homi, 47, 176
birthmark, as racial sign, 54, 58, 86,
107

Blackburn, Robin, 17, 20, 193 n. 1,
194 n. 9
Bosch, Juan, 185
Boyd, Melba Joyce, 103
Brau, Salvador, 162
Brazil, 2, 5, 8, 19, 185, 186
Cable, George Washington, 4, 9, 10,
149, 161, 166; and Charles Chesnutt, 92–94, 95, 97, 98; and William Faulkner, 132–33, 139, 141,
200–201 n. 11; and Frances
Harper, 104; and Toni Morrison,
205 n. 23; and Martín Morúa Delgado, 90; and Cirilo Villaverde,
45–50, 53, 61–75, 79, 80, 196–97
n. 4. See also Grandissimes, The
Campos Pons, Maria Magdalena, 186

New World Studies

New World Studies publishes interdisciplinary research that seeks to redefine the cultural map of the Americas and to propose particularly stimulating points of departure for an emerging field. Encompassing the Caribbean as well as continental North, Central, and South America, books in this series examine cultural processes within the hemisphere, taking into account the economic, demographic, and historical phenomena that shape them. Given the increasing diversity and richness of the linguistic and cultural traditions in the Americas, the need for research that privileges neither the English-speaking United States nor Spanish-speaking Latin America has never been greater. The series is designed to bring the best of this new research into an identifiable forum and to channel its results to the rapidly evolving audience for cultural studies.

New World Studies

Vera M. Kutzinski
Sugar's Secrets: Race and the Erotics of Cuban Nationalism

Richard D. E. Burton and Fred Reno, editors
French and West Indian: Martinique, Guadeloupe, and French Guiana Today

A. James Arnold, editor
Monsters, Tricksters, and Sacred Cows: Animal Tales and American Identities

J. Michael Dash
The Other America: Caribbean Literature in a New World Context

Isabel Alvarez Borland
Cuban-American Literature of Exile: From Person to Persona

Belinda J. Edmondson, editor
Caribbean Romances: The Politics of Regional Representation

Steven V. Hunsaker
Autobiography and National Identity in the Americas

Celia M. Britton
Edouard Glissant and Postcolonial Theory: Strategies of Language and Resistance

Mary Peabody Mann
Juanita: A Romance of Real Life in Cuba Fifty Years Ago
Edited and with an introduction by Patricia M. Ard

George B. Handley
Postslavery Literatures in the Americas: Family Portraits in Black and White